DISCARD

SCOTCH IRISH PIONEERS

LONDONDERRY, IRELAND

SCOTCH IRISH PIONEERS

IN ULSTER AND AMERICA

BY

CHARLES KNOWLES BOLTON

AUTHOR OF "THE PRIVATE SOLDIER UNDER WASHINGTON," ETC.

WITH MAPS AND ILLUSTRATIONS DRAWN BY
ETHEL STANWOOD BOLTON

Baltimore
GENEALOGICAL PUBLISHING CO., INC.
1986

Originally published: Boston, 1910
Reprinted: Genealogical Publishing Co., Inc.
Baltimore, 1967, 1972, 1977, 1981, 1986
Library of Congress Catalogue Card Number 67-29400
International Standard Book Number 0-8063-0046-9
Made in the United States of America

PREFACE

THE following pages attempt for the first time a systematic treatment of the beginning of a migration of settlers of Scotch and English descent from the north of Ireland to the New World. Parker, Perry, Green, Hanna and other writers have collected much of general history and tradition; and they have so pictured the Scotch traits developed under Irish skies, that Scotch Irish blood, once a reproach, is now cause for pride. But the conditions in Ireland before the migration, the voyage across the ocean, the emigrants as they appeared to early observers — these phases of the story have now for the first time been treated in detail, drawing upon hitherto unexplored sources. If a large part of our American population traces back to Ulster, the early religious, political and economic life of the valleys of the Foyle and the Bann should interest many, for many, whether they are aware of it or not, are descended from the Scotch Irish. Clergymen and statesmen have from generation to generation extolled the rugged virtues of these pioneers, and a closer study of their lives will, it is hoped, deepen the hold which they already have upon our affections.

There has been a constant temptation to include in this study some account of emigrants from the west of Scotland; they had very much in common with their Ulster friends and kinsmen. But however desirable a wide scope may be, it has been my purpose here to include only those who were influenced by the peculiar environment of a life upon Irish soil.

I am grateful to many for assistance: To the trustees
of the Boston Public Library for the use of many books
relating to Ireland, a few of them purchased at my suggestion; to the Hon. James Phinney Baxter for his personal helpfulness as well as for access to his unrivaled
manuscript material relating to Maine; to Mr. Julius H.
Tuttle of the Massachusetts Historical Society; to Mr.
Edmund M. Barton and Mr. Clarence S. Brigham of the
American Antiquarian Society; to Mr. William P. Greenlaw
of the New England Historic Genealogical Society; to Dr.
Bernard C. Steiner of the Maryland Historical Society,
and to Mr. Alexander S. Salley, Jr., Secretary of the Historical Commission of South Carolina. I am under great
obligation, also, to Dr. Hugh S. Morrison, coroner of
Coleraine and Aghadowey, Ireland; to the Rev. Crawford
Hillis of Tanvally Fort, County Down; to Mr. W. T.
Pike of Brighton, England, publisher of an elaborate work
on Belfast and the Province of Ulster; to the editor of
the "Ulster Journal of Archæology"; and to others who
are mentioned in connection with each chapter.

C. K. B.

Pound Hill Place,
  Shirley.

CONTENTS

APPENDICES

ILLUSTRATIONS

SCOTCH IRISH PIONEERS

SCOTCH IRISH PIONEERS

I

IRELAND AND NEW ENGLAND BEFORE 1714

On the map of Ireland the province of Ulster gathers into a circle nearly a quarter of the territory of the island. Its southerly bound runs from Donegal Bay on the west to Carlingford Bay on the east. In the centre of Ulster lies County Tyrone, with the counties of Donegal, Londonderry, and Antrim along its northern borders to fend the sea. This is the heart of the Scotch Irish country. South of County Tyrone are Fermanagh, Monaghan, and Armagh, counties not so closely associated with early Protestant migration. South of Monaghan, bordering the Roman Catholic province of Leinster, is Cavan, and to the east, touching Armagh, lies County Down whose shores are less than a dozen miles from Ayrshire in Scotland.

Donegal and Tyrone are drained by the Finn and the Mourne, two rivers which unite at Strabane to form the Foyle. The Foyle flows northward across Londonderry to the sea. From Lough Neagh on the eastern border of Tyrone the Bann flows north also to the sea, separating the counties of Londonderry and Antrim. The source-lands of the Foyle and the Bann had supported a Scotch population for several generations before the year 1718; of this population and its interest in America the following pages give some account.

The temperature of Ulster is milder than that of New England, and even warmer than will be found in northern England. Snow rarely lies on the ground over a month in the winter. The gaunt, gloomy mountains and the barren moorlands give some parts of the country a forbidding aspect. There are fine streams which leap down the steeps and gurgle through the rocky foot-hills, sweeping gracefully and sleepily across the moors and meadows toward the sea.

In the days of the early eighteenth century mills for lumber and grain were dotted over this country, and everywhere in Northern Ireland were the patches of green grass upon which the flax was spread to bleach in the sun.

The villages comprised usually little more than a few houses along a winding country road, with a lane here and there to tie a wayward hut to the mother flock. The better houses were built with thick walls of stone, sometimes with projecting buttresses and old-fashioned turrets. Their windows were leaded, and over the door a carved stone gave the birth-date of the house. Upon this stone was lavished all the art of which the dwelling could boast.[1]

Of the houses at Omagh an English traveller says: "A number of the houses were thatched; being repaired at different periods, as necessity required, the roofs often presented a grotesque appearance, and were decked in all the colours of the year; the fresh straw of autumn on the part lately done, and

RUINS OF THE FIRST PRESBYTERIAN CHURCH BUILT IN IRELAND
AT BALLYCARRY, COUNTY ANTRIM

the green verdure of spring in the plentiful crop of weeds which grew on the more ancient."[2]

Of the people themselves much will be said from time to time in these pages. The Irish or Celts were everywhere, although less numerous than in the Southern provinces. They were largely Roman Catholics and therefore at the time legally deprived of the powers and privileges that the humblest la-

---

[1] Gamble's Sketches of History, Politics and Manners in Dublin and the North of Ireland in 1810, New Edition, 1826, pp. 284-286.
[2] *Ibid*, p. 251.

borer today expects as a matter of right. In the more remote regions the Irish were scarcely above the condition of savages, living upon game and abandoning agriculture to the conquering race.

The Scotch, invited by the King to inhabit confiscated Irish lands, were in almost every village, as their Presbyterian chapels bore witness. But during the century of their occupation of Ulster their thrift and energy had battled with but moderate success against the ravages of war and the burden of hostile laws.

The third element in the population was the ruling class. This class was largely English, supplemented by Scotch and Irish landowners, nearly all of whom through self-interest or conviction upheld the Established Church, and by virtue of this allegiance had access to the magistracy and the army.

Such a population offered endless opportunity for friction and discontent. And yet had there been an eighteenth century Lord Cromer to do for Ireland what the present administrator has done for Egypt, one may feel certain that the Irish question of today would never have existed.

The Scotch Irish who came from Ireland to America are criticised for their personal habits as much as they are praised for their more vital good qualities. That these defects persisted in Ulster is confirmed by a generous and kindly English traveller, John Gamble, who in 1810 saw them in their homes.

Stopping at a roadside cottage one day for dinner he decided that he would ask for eggs, as safer than some other foods of unknown composition. The good woman who presided over the home, roasted an egg or two in ashes before her blazing fire. When he asked if they were done "she took a long pin with which she had been picking her teeth and thrusting it into the side of the egg:—'Ah! weel-a-wot, surr,' proceeded she, presenting it to him: 'it's as weel done an egg as ony in Christendom.' " Bread, with butter dexterously spread with the thumb, after the custom of the people, completed the meal. Mr. Gamble then continues:

"A few years ago the Presbyterians in the Country parts of this Kingdom were not much cleaner than their Scottish ancestors. The inside of a vessel was seldom washed and the outside still seldomer."[1]

Confirmation of this view comes from Arthur Lee, who visited Pittsburg in 1784. He describes the town as inhabited almost entirely by Scots and Irish, living "in paltry log-houses, and as dirty as in the north of Ireland, or even Scotland."[2]

But there were characteristics of these Scotch Irish husbandmen more racial and permanent than mere habits of cleanliness. Gamble was a shrewd

---

[1] Gamble, p. 262.

[2] Life of Arthur Lee, 1829, Vol. 2, p. 385. My attention has been called to Lee and other writers by Mrs. Ruth D. Coolidge.

observer of these: "It is astonishing," he says,
"how little idea Presbyterians have of pastoral
beauty; the Catholic has ten times more fancy—but
a Presbyterian minds only the main chance. If he
builds a cottage, it is a prison in miniature; if he
has a lawn, it is only grass; the fence of his grounds
is a stone wall, seldom a hedge. . . . A Presbyterian has a sluggish imagination: it may be awakened by the gloomy or terrific, but seldom revels in
the beautiful."[1]

These were the people whom we call Scotch Irish,
a term which was in use as early as the seventeenth
century. They came to America, not as discoverers,
but as the pioneers of their race; they defended the
frontiers against Indians, and their numbers in the
South so much augmented the forces in the Revolutionary army that they may fairly be said to have
saved Washington from defeat. To these people the
British Colonies in America were not unknown.
Intercourse between Ireland and New England has
gone on with little interruption from very early
days. During the first century after the settlement
of Boston, non-conformist ministers of Ireland and
New England were in close touch; members of the
Mather family were as familiar with the streets of
Dublin as they were with the three green hills in
the Bay colony's chief town; and more than one
early attempt was made to transplant Ulster set-

[1]Gamble, p. 348.

tlers. Another century witnessed a steady migration of the Protestant inhabitants of Ulster, until
by estimation a third of the population had crossed
the Atlantic. During the last fifty years central and
southern Ireland have sent so many Roman Catholic
emigrants that our American cities one and all feel
the power of their numbers. The Atlantic States are

BANGOR CASTLE, COUNTY DOWN
The Rev. Robert Blair preached at Bangor

today a New Ireland, influenced in the rural districts by those of Scotch Irish descent, and governed
in the cities by the Celtic Irish.

In 1636 a desire to emigrate took firm hold upon
the people in the towns near Belfast. Their leaders
were four able men: the Rev. Robert Blair of Bangor, county Down; the Rev. James Hamilton who

preached at Ballywalter, a little village a few miles east of Belfast; the Rev. John McLellan of the neighboring town of Newtownards; and the Rev. John Livingston who had been deposed from the church at Killinchy in the diocese of Down.

These earnest clergymen, living within the radius of a few miles of Bangor, became more and more dissatisfied with the Established Church and its order of service. Blair was their leader, a man of "majestic, awful, yet amiable countenance," who gradually drew into his circle the clergymen of eight or nine adjoining parishes. He was suspended from his charge, and by the varying authorities reinstated and twice deposed for non-conformity, and finally his followers suffered a like fate. They found it difficult to preach in Ireland, and asked Livingston, a very eloquent speaker, to visit Boston in company with William Wallace, to obtain favorable terms from the Governor living there for a settlement in New England.

Mr. Wallace delayed so long to bid farewell to his family that the two agents lost the desired ships then sailing from London. Meeting Mr. John Humphrey they agreed to go in his ship, and so were unable to accept Mr. Bellingham's later offer of passage in a larger ship. At Dorchester, England, they tarried to listen to the Rev. John White, a promoter of the colony of the Massachusetts Bay; at last setting sail they encountered head winds and

were forced to put in at Plymouth. There Wallace
fell ill, and they decided to abandon the voyage. Livingston never became an emigrant, but his son Robert settled later upon the Hudson, and the soil of
Livingston manor nurtured a race of American
statesmen and soldiers.

Persecution still continued in Ireland, and a kindly
invitation from the Governor and Council in New
England determined the leaders to order a ship to
be built for them near Belfast, of about one hundred
and fifty tons burden. Full of hope they named her
the "Eagle Wing," from that beautiful passage in
Exodus where the Lord said to Moses: "Ye have
seen what I did unto the Egyptians, and how I bare
you on eagles' wings, and brought you unto myself.
Now therefore, if ye will obey my voice indeed, and
keep my covenant, then ye shall be a peculiar treasure unto me above all people: for all the earth is
mine."

One cannot but wonder, recalling the little settlement at Boston, what would have been the effect of
the arrival of four or five very able Presbyterian
ministers at that time. Blair and Livingston,
McLellan and Hamilton were men of education,
property, and family. Hamilton's uncle, Lord
Clandeboye, had befriended them; McLellan and
Livingston were by ties of marriage or descent
closely allied with the Scottish aristocracy. Blair
was a prince among leaders, and rose to be mod-

erator of the General Assembly in Scotland; in 1648
he represented it in an endeavor to have Cromwell
impose Presbyterianism upon England.

The "Eagle Wing" set sail September 9, 1636,
from Lough Fergus, but was soon compelled to put
in at Lough Ryan in Scotland to stop dangerous
leaks; she then turned her prow westward. Tem-
pestuous weather during the three or four hundred
leagues which the ship covered weakened and at last
crushed the rudder, "brake much of our gallion-
head, our fore-cross-tree, and tare our fore-sail;
five or six of our chainplaitts made up; ane great
beam under the gunner-roome door brake; seas came
in over the round-house, and brake ane plank or two
in the deck, and wett all them that were between
decks." Thus Livingston tells of those trying days
when men worked incessantly at the pumps, and
repaired the damage from wave and wind as rapidly
as they could find opportunity. Meanwhile their
leader Blair lay ill in the cabin; some of the company of one hundred and forty passengers died, and
a baby came into that storm-tossed world of water.
When the captain, who did not dare to face another
hurricane off the New England coast, turned the little ship toward Ireland the courageous Blair fell in
a swoon, unable to think of failure after so much
distress. Through it all Blair's infant son, who had
been ill at departure, lived and even grew stronger,
so that, in the quaint language of the chronicle, "it

pleesed the only wise God to twist in this small ply in Mr. Blair's rod."[1]

The early appearance of Scotch names in America is due largely to the wars between England and Scotland. Many prisoners taken at the battles of Dunbar and Worcester were sold into service in the colonies. These men worked out their terms of servitude at the Lynn iron works and elsewhere, and founded honorable families whose Scotch names appear upon our early records. No account exists of the Scotch prisoners that were sent to New England in Cromwell's time; at York in 1650 were the Maxwells, McIntires, Junkinses and Grants. The Mackclothlans,[2] later known as the Claflins, gave a governor to Massachusetts and distinguished merchants to New York city. In Prendergast's "Cromwellian Settlement of Ireland" reference is made to attempts to strengthen the Protestant population of Catholic Ireland by offering inducements to New England families to migrate. These efforts of 1651, 1655 and 1656 led to the transplanting of many Yankee families to Limerick and Garristown, where their descendants perhaps still reside.

During Charles the Second's time the harshness of the laws in Scotland as well as in Ireland led to

---

[1] Autobiographies of Blair and Livingston, published by the Wodrow Society; also Dictionary of National Biography.

[2] New England Historical and Genealogical Register, Vol. 1, p. 377. See also the Claflin Genealogy.

many plans for removal to America. Hugh Campbell, a Boston merchant, obtained permission from the Bay colony in February, 1679–80, to transport settlers from Scotland and establish them in the Nepmug country[1] in the vicinity of Springfield. None of these Scotchmen, however, can properly be associated with Ulster, and their interest in America is not germain to our subject.

What object the captain of the ship George of Londonderry had in his voyage to Boston in 1675 we now have no means of knowing. The records of the Court of Assistants [2] show that the mariners of the ship appealed to the authorities for payment of wages. The names of the members of the crew were Philip Owen, Charles Frost, John Bell, Arthur Richards and William Maxfeild.

The next effort to establish a colony originated in Ireland. Wait Winthrop in Boston wrote to his brother Fitz-John of Connecticut December 29, 1684, that a gentleman had lately come over, "a man of some interest there," and was looking out for a plantation for about one hundred families. Winthrop talked with him of Quinnebaug [3] and was told that an abundance of people would come over if they could be assured that they could have liberty of con-

---

[1] Massachusetts Bay Colony Records, Vol. 5, p. 264.

[2] *Ibid*, Vol. 1, p. 41.

[3] Plainfield, about twenty-nine miles north east of New London, in Connecticut.

science, their views being "much of the same stamp" as those in New England. [1] We know that conditions in a large part of Ireland were distressing; this was especially true in the counties of Derry and Donegal, where many ministers of the presbytery of Lagan resolved to emigrate to America. But the fever for migration that was rising subsided upon the death of Charles II, February 6, 1685; no movement to New England took place, although a few settlements were made in Maryland, Pennsylvania and the Carolinas, where ships engaged in the tobacco trade found their ports of destination. [2]

With the coming of James II to power, Roman Catholic influence began to be felt, and the Protestant population of Ireland was sure to suffer. In 1686 and 1687 high offices in the church and army were given to Papists, and an effort was made to bring English universities under Catholic rule. The Earl of Tyrconnel, Lord Lieutenant of Ireland, and an influential member of the Roman Catholic party at Court, at once "purged" the army in Ireland of its Protestant officers. But perceiving an opportunity to show loyalty to King James by sending to England three thousand men to aid him in his encounter with William, Prince of Orange, "it pleased God to so Infatuate the Councils of my Lord

---

[1] Massachusetts Historical Society Collections, Series V, Vol. 8, p. 450.

[2] See the next chapter.

Tyrconnel,'' as Walker, historian of the siege, puts
it, that he sent out of Ireland the Catholic regiment
quartered at Derry. Tyrconnel soon saw his error
in withdrawing this force from Derry, and dis-
patched the Earl of Antrim to the north. When the
news of Antrim's approach reached the city there
was great indecision; but caution soon gave way
before hotter blood, the bridge was drawn up and
the gates were locked. Thus began the defence of
Derry, April 20, 1689. Incident at once crowded
upon incident; sally and assault, plot and treachery,
vacillation and courage gave to each day a new sen-
sation, until Colonel Lundy, commander of the besieged forces, having advocated a secret withdrawal
of officers and gentlemen, leaving the citizens of
Derry to the mercy of the enemy, was forced to flee
in disguise with a pack on his back. Then in truth
began the famous days of waiting and fighting, under the leadership of a militant clergyman, the Rev.
George Walker, rector of Donaghmore in County
Tyrone. To add to the distress of the besieged their
enemies drove thousands of women and children
from the neighboring towns under the walls of Derry
where they had to be rescued and fed by a garrison
already short of stores. Then came the days when
horse flesh was served to the soldiers, while dogs
"fatned by eating the bodies of the slain Irish"
sold by the quarter for five shillings and six pence,
and cats brought four shillings and six pence each.

On the 30th of July, in the time of their direst extremity, two ships ladened with provisions came up the Lough, broke the boom and reached the town amid hysterical tears and thanksgiving. They had but one pint of meal for each man and nine lean horses left for food.

King William relieved the Presbyterians of some of their burdens by obtaining through his influence the Toleration Act (May 24, 1689). The waste lands soon began to respond to the plow, and thrifty settlers from the Scottish lowlands and Lancashire came over the water to aid those that had survived the war.

Under Queen Anne (1702-1714) the Presbyterians in Ireland again lost almost every advantage that had been gained, and became by the Test Act of 1704 virtually outlaws. Their marriages were declared invalid, and their chapels were closed. They could not maintain schools nor hold office above that of a petty constable.

The commercial acts of 1698, restricting the Irish woolen industry and encouraging the manufacture of linen, brought ultimate improvement in Ireland because lands formerly devoted to grazing could now be devoted in part to tillage; but for some years immediately following the passage of the acts there was great industrial depression. Distress due to the lack of work, together with the want of religious freedom and political opportunity, excited the sympathy of non-conformists beyond the bounds of Ireland.

During these years the Rev. Cotton Mather was in

The Rev'd Dr. Cotton Mather.

f Sarah Moorhead

close touch with religious and political affairs in
Scotland and Ireland. His father was a Master of

Arts of Trinity College, Dublin, and his two uncles, Nathaniel and Samuel, were well known in Dublin as preachers. To the University of Glasgow the Rev. Cotton Mather sent books and pamphlets from time to time, and had received there the honorary degree of Doctor of Divinity in 1710. He was therefore interested both in Ireland and in Scotland. Moreover he was a far seeing patriot of broad views and sympathies, to whom New England owes much. He was the leading clergyman in a colony where his religion was the foremost force in education, in society, and in official life.

On the 20th of September, 1706, Mather records: "I write letters unto diverse persons of Honour both in *Scotland* and in *England;* to procure Settlements of Good *Scotch* Colonies, to the Northward of us. This may be a thing of great consequence."[1] It was Mather's plan to settle hardy families on the frontiers in Maine and New Hampshire to protect the towns and churches of Massachusetts from the French and Indians. In his *Memorial of the Present deplorable state of New England* he suggests that a Scotch colony might be of good service in getting possession of Nova Scotia.[2]

With the death of Queen Anne in 1714 and the accession of George I the period of ferment in Irish

---

[1] MS. in the Massachusetts Historical Society.

[2] Massachusetts Historical Society Collections, Series V, Vol. 6, p. 41*.

emigration may be said to begin. In that year two clergymen set out for New England, and their residence in America probably had more to do with the great migration of 1718 than we can as yet demonstrate. They were the Rev. William Homes of Strabane in County Tyrone who settled on Martha's Vineyard, and the Rev. Thomas Craighead, his brother-in-law, of the town of Donegal, who lived for some years in Freetown, a village about ten miles east of Fall River. There was, however, no immediate migration resulting from their arrival in New England. A few passengers had arrived in the year 1716 in the "Truth and Daylight," the "Mary Ann," and the "Globe"; but in 1717 when piracy was rife along the New England coast the records, as communicated by Governor Shute to the Lords of Trade, show that only fourteen male servants or apprentices arrived from Dublin, in August, 1717, and nine from Belfast in September of that year.[1] None arrived at Boston from January to June 29th of the year 1718, although Captain Gibbs brought a few persons from Dublin to Marblehead in May. In less than two years from the arrival of the Rev. William Boyd in July, 1718, five or six hundred men, women and children had come over to settle.[2]

But before considering the careers and influence

---

[1] See Appendix 1.

[2] Maine Historical Society Collections, Baxter Mss., Vol. X, p. 106.

of Homes and Craighead, the economic and religious condition of Ulster at this time should be made clear.   Dean Swift, in speaking of tyrannical land-lords, wrote in 1720,[1] "Whoever travels this coun-try [Ireland] and observes the face of nature, or the faces, and habits, and dwellings of the natives, will hardly think himself in a land where law, religion, or common humanity is professed." And he explains that the landlords by "screwing and racking" their tenants had reduced the people to a worse condition than the peasants in France or the vassals in Ger-many and Poland.   The property owners were pressed by debt incurred often in London or on the Continent.   They felt forced to exact the last penny from their tenants, and too often turned a thrifty Scotch Protestant farmer from the land he had by incessant toil brought into good condition so that the land might go to two or more Catholic families who, while living together in poverty, could by their united efforts pay a greater return.   The Irish were not fond of the plow and the land suffered under their hands.[2]   Sir Thomas Phillips told King Charles I that the native Irish would give increasing rents rather than move; therefore the landlord could hope to reap only half the profit from English and Scotch farmers that might come from the Irish.[3]

---

[1] Proposal for a Universal use of Manufactures.

[2] Hill's Plantation in Ulster, p. 590.

[3] Dublin University Magazine, 1833, p. 474.

As late as 1790 Lord Chancellor Clare again repeated the explanation: ''The great misfortune of Ireland, and particularly [of] the lower classes of its inhabitants is, that at the expiration of every lease, the farm is put up to auction, and without considering whether it is a Protestant or a Papist— whether he is industrious or indolent—whether he is solvent or a beggar, the highest bidder is declared the tenant by the law agent of the estate, I must say to the disgrace of the landlord, and most frequently much in his advantage.''[1]

These were the conditions in Ulster which turned the eyes of the intelligent Protestant farmer toward the American colonies. The desire to emigrate had deeper and more immediate sources than a century of intercourse and sympathy between Ireland and America.

---

[1] Dublin University Magazine, May, 1833, p. 480. A very interesting account of the confusion and friction resulting from the occupation of the land by several tenants, each sharing the good and the poor plots of land, will be found in Mr. and Mrs. S. C. Hall's Ireland, Vol. 3, p. 261.

II

IRELAND'S RELATION TO MARYLAND, PENNSYLVANIA AND SOUTH CAROLINA BEFORE THE YEAR 1718

The early annals of the Presbyterian church in the colonies south of New England are closely linked with the name of the Rev. Francis Makemie of Ramelton on Lough Swilly, County Donegal, who was licensed by the Presbytery of Lagan in 1681, and came to America soon after. Makemie covered the Atlantic coast colonies in his ministrations, devoting much of his time, however, to Maryland. Before 1690 there were three and perhaps four congregations in Somerset County, which then included Worcester County, Maryland, with their meeting-houses at Snow Hill (1684), Manokin, Wicomico, and Rehoboth.[1] These places lie south of the present southern boundary of Delaware. It may be said that although two ministers, Doughty and Hill, were early Presbyterian preachers on the western shore of Chesapeake Bay these settlements on the east

---

[1] The sheriff of Somerset reported that the dissenters "hath a house in Snow Hill, one on the road going up along the seaside, one at Manokin, about thirty feet long—plain country buildings all of them." See Mrs. Mary M. North's "An Historic Church" (1904).

side formed the first stronghold of their faith in the South.

Another member of the Lagan Presbytery in Ireland, and a friend of Makemie, was the Rev. William Traill, a Glasgow graduate, who suffered imprisonment for his convictions, and upon his release came to Maryland in 1682. He probably founded the church at or near Rehoboth in Somerset County, where he had influential friends, including Colonel William Stevens, John White, John Shipway and others.[1]

A few months earlier, perhaps in 1681, came the Rev. Thomas Wilson to found a church at Manokin, a settlement now called Princess Anne. It is supposed that Wilson was the minister of the same name who had been at Killybegs, County Donegal. Among his friends were John Galbraith, Archibald Erskine, and David Brown. Possibly also Abraham Gale of Somerset County in 1684 should be counted as a neighbor and friend. Gale's wife Sarah and their sons James and John, sailing from Dublin to Virginia, fell in with a designing rascal who sold their services for a term of years to pay the sum required for their passage, although Gale himself stood ready to pay it.[2]

---

[1] Rev. J. W. McIlvain in Johns Hopkins University Studies, notes supplementary, 1890, No. 3, p. 19.

[2] Maryland Archives, Vol. 17, p. 352.

RAMELTON, ON LOUGH SWILLY, IRELAND

Home of the Rev. Francis Makemie

Another of Wilson's neighbors was John Wallis, Senior, "of Ireland and Monokin River, Somerset County," who was living in 1685 with his wife Jane, his nephew John Wallis, Junior, and his kinsmen Matthew and James Wallis.[1] Other settlers from Ireland were there. Edward Randolph, writing to the Commissioners of Customs from James City, June 27, 1692, adds to our knowledge of the Scotch Irish in Somerset County in the following reference to the new governor of Maryland:

"I hear he has continued Maj^r King to bee ye Navall Officer in Somerset Co^{ty} on ye eastern shore, a place pestred wth Scotch & Irish. About 200 families have within ye 2 years arrived from Ireland & setled in y^t Co^{ty} besides some hundred of family's there before. They have set up a linnen Manufacture, Encouraged thereto by Co^{ll} Brown, a Scotchman, one of ye Councill & by Maj^r King & other principall persons upon ye place, who support ye Interlopers & buy up all their Loading upon their first arrivall, & govern ye whole trade on ye Eastern shore, so y^t whereas 7 or 8 good ships from Eng^{ld} did yearly trade & load ye Tobb^o of y^t Co^{ty} I find y^t in these 3 years last past there has not been above 5 ships trading legally in all those Rivers, & nigh 30 Sayle of Scotch Irish & New Eng^{ld} men."[2]

---

[1] Maryland Calendar of Wills, Jane Baldwin, editor, Vol. 1.

[2] In Edward Randolph (Prince Society), Vol. 7, p. 364, to which Mr. Albert Matthews directed my attention.

A third Presbyterian minister in this region was the Rev. Samuel Davis,[1] possibly also from Ireland, who is said to have been pastor of the "famous and

OLD HOUSE IN SNOW HILL, MARYLAND

venerable" church at Snow Hill from an early date until 1698. He afterward settled at Hoarkill, now Lewes, in Delaware. The Rev. Mr. Makemie married a lady of wealth in 1690 and settled in Accomac

---

[1] Rev. William Hill, in his History of American Presbyterianism (Washington City, 1839) pp. 162–163, doubts a Scotch origin for all of the seven members of the first presbytery.   Mackemie, Hampton and McNish, he agrees, were Irish.

County, Virginia, a few miles south of Snow Hill.
Whether he or Davis was regularly in charge at
Snow Hill cannot now be determined. The Makemie
Memorial Presbyterian Church perpetuates the
memory of his ministry.

Along the western shore of Chesapeake Bay Colonel Ninian Beall was the leading Presbyterian layman. Through his influence a church existed at
Patuxent in 1704, and the members included several
prominent Fifeshire families of the present Prince
George County.

Makemie's successor was the Rev. John Henry,
who came from Ireland in 1709, having been licensed
by Armagh Presbytery in 1708. Although Makemie
was the chief Presbyterian minister of the early
pioneers there were several others in the colonies
at about this period. They are little more than
names to us, but they did faithful service, going from
plantation to plantation along the rivers, preaching
in the open air or in houses, where no church existed,
and living as traders when bread could not be earned
by the work of the ministry. The Rev. Josias Mackie
came to Elizabeth River, Virginia—the lands about
Norfolk—from St. Johnstown, County Donegal, a
town destined to try the soul of New England's
Scotch Irish leader, Boyd, half a century later when
he had returned to Ulster. The Rev. John Hampton, probably "master John of Burt," whose school
days were brightened by money from the Presbytery

of Lagan, settled at Snow Hill, and the Rev. George McNish, Scotch or Irish, officiated at Manokin and Wicomico. Others were the Rev. Hugh Conn of our present Bladensburg, Maryland, the Rev. Robert Orr of Maidenhead, New Jersey, the Rev. John Thomson of Lewes, and the Rev. Samuel Gelston who went down after a sojourn in New England to preach at Opequon in Virginia.

A question arises in considering the history of these early churches of Maryland and Virginia;— Were the Scotch Irish a real factor here before the year 1718, the date of the great migration to New England? In Maryland Presbyterianism was of the mild English type, and we find Presbyterians joining with Episcopalians in an appeal for an Established Church as a protection against the spread of Roman Catholicism. The same type of Presbyterianism prevailed in Philadelphia during the ministry of the Rev. Jedediah Andrews, a Yankee in the Quaker city. It is probable therefore that very few communicants, aside from the ministers, had ever lived in Ireland.

While few Presbyterians came from Ireland before 1718, the Quaker migration certainly began as early as 1682. The failure of this Quaker migration to influence the coming of Scotch Irish settlers is curiously illustrated by a table in Mr. Myers's invaluable book on the Irish Quakers in Pennsylvania. We learn there that of the one hundred and sixty-five families that came during the thirty-five years from 1682 to 1717 only one left a home in County Antrim, and none came from Londonderry or Tyrone, the Scotch Irish counties;[1] whatever Scotch Irish migration from Ulster existed before 1718 was not influenced by the Quakers' example.

In the next thirty-two years, 1718 to 1750, a period covering the great Scotch Irish migration from Ulster, two hundred and sixty-five Quaker adults or families came to Pennsylvania. Of these there were one hundred and thirty-five from Ulster, or just one half. They came largely from the meetings at Antrim, Ballinderry, Ballinacree and Lisburn, in county Antrim, the heart of the Scotch Irish country, and from Ballyhagan, Grange, and Lurgan, county Armagh. This tide, however, did not really set in until after the Scotch Irish had begun their removal, or until 1729, when in one year twenty-nine left Ireland as against seventeen in the preceding nine years. Evidently the sudden increase in the Ulster Quaker migration was due to the economic disturbances of the years 1728 and 1729, discussed so fully in Archbishop Boulter's letters.[2] It follows, therefore, that the Scotch migration of 1718 from Ulster was in no manner influenced by the migration of Quakers. That Quakers and Presbyterians had family ties may be inferred, however, from the fact

[1] Twenty-seven came from Armagh and Cavan.
[2] See Chapter III.

that James Logan, the Quaker, William Penn's friend, and Secretary of Pennsylvania, was a cousin of the Rev. William Tennent, who came to America from Ireland and settled at East Chester, New York in 1718.[1] Tennent became one of the great leaders in the Presbyterian church.

The passengers who arrived at Philadelphia from Ireland earlier than 1718 were for the most part Quakers or Celtic Irish. We have few contemporary references to the arrival of Scotch Irish companies of settlers, until the *American Weekly Mercury* of October 27, 1720, mentions a brigantine from Londonderry with ninety passengers on board. These were probably Presbyterians. The Presbyterian influence in the colonies was never strong until the migration from Ulster began. Mr. J. S. Futhey in his history of Upper Octorara Church bears testimony to this, and Mr. W. D. Mackey in his history of the church at White Clay Creek is another witness. Moreover, the Scotch Irish type of Maryland Presbyterianism was just coming into prominence when the Rev. Thomas Craighead went from Freetown in Massachusetts to become the first pastor at White Clay Creek in 1724.[2]

The next port on the coast which is associated with Scotch Irish immigrants at an early date is Charles-

---

[1] Webster's Presbyterian Church, p. 365.

[2] See Alfred Nevin's Presbytery of Philadelphia, 1888, Chapter 2, for a good summary of the early history.

ton. About the year 1683, if we may rely upon tradition, several emigrants, influenced by Sir Richard Kyrle,[1] a Protestant Irishman of some note, and led by a man named Ferguson, landed there, although little is known of them.[2] One tangible fact, indeed, we have in the presence at Charleston in 1692 of Richard Newton whose brother Marmaduke Newton still remained at Carrickfergus in old Ireland.[3]

The first Presbyterian church in Charleston was organized about 1685, with communicants largely if not entirely from Scotland and New England. It enjoyed a prosperous history for half a century. The Rev. Archibald Stobo of the original or "White Meeting House" became a famous Charleston preacher. He and his wife had come ashore in 1699 from the ship "Rising Sun," which then lay off the bar under jury masts, he having received an invitation to preach. A hurricane approaching unexpectedly, the ship and all her company, except Mr. and Mrs. Stobo and the longboat's crew, were lost. The people were on their way to Scotland from the unfortunate colony at Darien.[4]

The Rev. Mr. Stobo was an ardent missionary, and his efforts to widen the borders of his church by the creation of new congregations and the erec-

---

[1] Governor of South Carolina in 1684.

[2] Charlestown Year Book, 1883, p. 380.

[3] South Carolina Historical and Genealogical Magazine, Vol. 8, p. 204.

[4] Charleston Year Book, 1882, p. 397.

tion of new places for worship were successful. A letter from South Carolina published in 1710 speaks of five "British Presbyterian" ministers then in the colony.[1] These preachers heralded the faith which was in another generation to make itself felt in South Carolina, when the real migration from Ireland should begin.

The following incident is worthy of record here. A certain Mr. John Jarvie had been ordained by the Presbytery of Belfast instead of by that of Down as had been decreed by the Synod. An explanation of the irregularity was given by Mr. Robert Wilson, merchant, of Belfast: "That there was a ship in the Logh of Belfast bound for South Carolina; that the seamen and passengers amount to the number of 70; that it was earnestly desir'd that they may have a Chaplain on board, and if ordain'd, so much the better for the voyage, and also for the person to be ordain'd and the country whither they are bound—therefor desir'd, seeing Mr. Jarvie inclines to sail in the ship, that he may be ordain'd before he go, and that it may be done as soon as possible, because the ship will soon be clear to sail."[2] It is possible that these passengers were from Glasgow, since nearly all ships from that port called at Belfast on the voyage to America. Whether Scotch or Scotch Irish we cannot decide, but they sailed

---

[1] Hodge's Presbyterian Church, Vol. 1, p. 85.

[2] Records General Synod at Belfast June 15, 1714, p. 336.

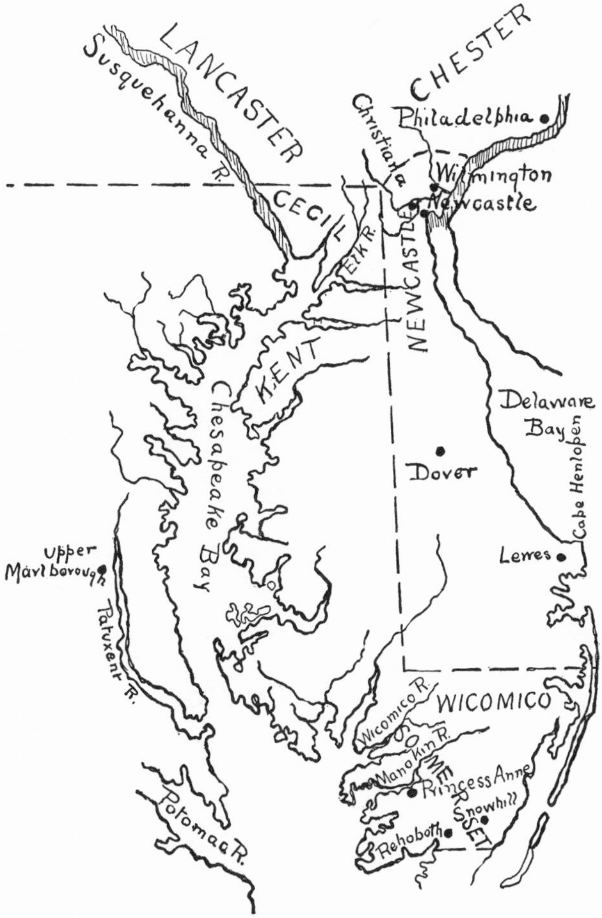

LANCASTER
CHESTER
Susquehanna R.
Christiana
Philadelphia
Wilmington
Newcastle
CECIL
Elk R.
NEWCASTLE
KENT
Chesapeake Bay
Delaware Bay
Cape Henlopen
Dover
Upper Marlborough
Lewes
Patuxent R.
Wicomico R.
WICOMICO
Manokin R.
SOMERSET
Princess Anne
Snowhill
Rehoboth
Potomac R.

from an Irish port with one of Ireland's Presbyterian ministers on board, and arrived at Charleston, probably in the summer of the year 1714.

Evidently there were a few Scotch Irish in and near Charleston, and on the rich lands between Philadelphia and Wilmington, at an early date. In New York also they held a place, and in the Presbyterian churches on Long Island. But in no case did the migrations before 1718 have great influence. They were, it is true, responses to a spirit of discontent and unrest in Ulster, but low rates of transportation on account of trade in tobacco had their force as well.

Such were the conditions at the opening of the year 1718. Yet we shall see that in less than a decade after Boyd and McGregor had set foot in New England, the ports of Philadelphia, Newcastle and Charleston were swarming with the Scotch Irish. James Logan of Pennsylvania reported in 1727 the arrival of eight or nine emigrant ships that autumn, and in 1729 six vessels in a single week came into port.

Before the year 1718 the growth of Scotch Irish influence and numbers cannot safely be measured by the spread of Presbyterianism, yet its early ecclesiastical history is of contributive value. In the year 1704 or 1705 the ministers who gathered in Philadelphia to ordain and install the Rev. Jedediah

Andrews of Boston agreed to form a General Presbytery. These men were:

Francis Makemie, Rehoboth.
Nathaniel Taylor, Upper Marlborough.
John Wilson, Newcastle.
George McNish, Manokin.
John Hampton, Snow Hill.
Samuel Davis, Lewes.
Jedediah Andrews, Philadelphia.

Although the Scotch Irish have their full share in this list of ministers, the people who listened to their sermons were very largely of Scotch and English ancestry; and in the next decade their growing families and the arrival of their friends from abroad so increased the number of Presbyterians that in 1717 the General Presbytery became a Synod with four presbyteries, Philadelphia, Newcastle, Snow Hill, and Long Island,[1] and twenty-nine ministers. Twenty years later the number of ministers had trebled,[2] for the great tide of migration which was identified with New England in 1718 soon turned toward Philadelphia.

---

[1] See Hodge's Presbyterian Church, 1839, pp. 93–97.
[2] Proceedings Presbytery of Baltimore, 1876.

III

ECONOMIC CONDITIONS IN ULSTER,
1714–1718

To understand the conditions in Ulster in 1718 it
will be necessary to know the Irish Society, or as it
was called legally The Society of the Governor and
Assistants of London, of the New Plantation in
Ulster, in the Kingdom of Ireland. This Society
held sway over the present county of Londonderry,
between the rivers Foyle and Bann, leasing or sub-
letting its valuable rights and privileges to local offi-
cials. The territory about Coleraine thus came by
lease into the hands of the Jackson family. Ambitious to acquire both property and power, they were
often at odds with the authorities in London, and
were driven by these conditions to hold their territory at excessive rates imposed by the none too
friendly London directors. In the year 1713 complaint was made that Mr. William Jackson had three
uncles who with himself and two tenants were aldermen, so that six out of the twelve aldermen of Coleraine obeyed his orders. Five of the twenty-four
burgesses, or members of the lower house, were his
tenants, and Mr. Jackson desired to fill a vacancy
with another tenant of his, living ten miles away at

Kilrea; this tenant was moreover brother of a bur-
gess, and both were sons of Alderman Adams. Thir-
teen members of the Common Council (which included Aldermen and Burgesses) called upon the mayor
for a judicial investigation of the matter, but the
mayor, who was a relative of Jackson's, refused to
accede to their request although it was made according to the law. This was but the beginning of discord in the Bann valley. In 1728 the Society
expressed dissatisfaction with the Jackson family,
which had opposed the political interest of the Society, and had through control of the Corporation of
Coleraine usurped the power to grant lands.

The long arm which reached out from London had
no sooner quieted Coleraine, than Derry (the early
name for Londonderry) was in trouble for disre-
garding its by-laws. These controversies probably
had little influence upon the lot of the humbler tenant except along the Bann where the Jackson sway
was felt. It was "commonly reported" that the
Hon. Richard Jackson was forced to raise the rents
of his tenants in order to meet his obligations; and
that these tenants, who lived upon lands within the
jurisdiction of the Clothworkers Company near
Coleraine, began agitation for the first great Scotch-
Irish emigration to America.[1]

The larger part of the lands in Ulster had es-

[1] Narrative of a Journey to the North of Ireland in the year
1802, by Robert Slade, Esq., Secretary to the Irish Society.

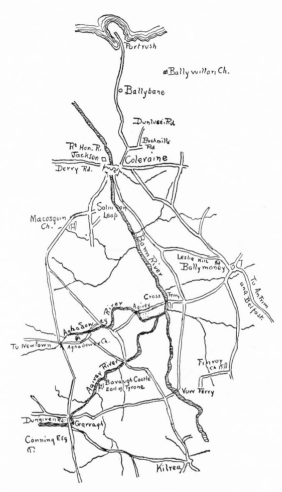

ROAD MAP OF THE BANN VALLEY

From Kilrea to Coleraine via Garvagh and Macosquin Twelve Miles

cheated to the crown early in the reign of James I, as confiscated property of Irish noblemen in rebellion. In order to plant a Protestant colony in Ulster the Lords of Council placed these lands in the hands of wealthy adventurers. That part now known as County Londonderry came under the jurisdiction of the Corporation of London, and by its officers it was divided between twelve of the chief London companies or guilds who came forward as ''undertakers'' or promoters of the project. The Irish Society was incorporated to have a general control of Derry and Coleraine, and of lands not granted to the twelve companies. It aided churches and schools, protected the settlers, and defended the rights of those who had invested in the enterprise. The twelve chief companies and their lands were noticed in the report of a journey of inspection made by Robert Slade in 1802.[1] They were:

Ironmongers, about Garvagh. Including more or less of the parishes of Aghadowey, Agivey, Macosquin, Desertoghill, Errigal.

Clothworkers, about Coleraine.

From the Atlantic S. E. along the Bann to Killowen; included Down Hill.

Drapers, about Moneymore.

Grocers, about Muff. Bounded N. by Lough Foyle; S. by Burntollet river.

---

[1] Early tenants are mentioned in the notes to Pynnar's Survey, reprinted in Hill's Plantation in Ulster.

Goldsmiths, near Londonderry. Bounded N. and W.
   by lough and river Foyle; S. by Tyrone.
Vintners, Ballaghy, west of Lough Beg.
Merchant Tailors, about Somerset, near Salmon
   Leap. Included most of Macosquin.
Mercers, near Kilrea.
Fishmongers, about Walworth, near Lough Foyle.
   "Alias Ballykelly."
Skinners, "Alias Dungiven."
Haberdashers, about Newtown Limavady, and Bally-
   castle.
Salters, about Magherafelt.

The charter granted by King James in 1615 was
in the reign of Charles I annulled in the Court of
Star Chamber, so that the Society and the twelve
companies and their subordinate companies, all lost
their powers. This decree was rescinded under
Cromwell; and a new charter was granted by
Charles II in 1662, whereby Derry became known
legally as Londonderry. It was at this time that
the control of Londonderry and Coleraine, with the
fisheries, woods, ferryage, and the right of patron-
age of the churches, was vested in the Governor and
Assistants of the Irish Society and not in the several
companies.[1]

This system went far toward established Protestant power in Ulster. Indeed if the Presbyterians in

---

[1] W. C. Hazlitt's Livery Companies of London, p. 28.

Ulster had been treated with consideration and wisdom by the leaders of the Irish Established Church, and with tact by the government in London, they would have had less inclination to brave the ocean to inhabit the frontiers of the colonies in America. It is evident that the economic changes in Mr. Jackson's territory along the Bann cannot alone explain the emigration fever which prevailed on the banks of the Foyle. The controlling influences were more wide spread and more vital in the lives of the people. They were to some extent economic, but they were still more political and religious. A Scot might starve in Ireland as peaceably as he was likely to do in a strange land beyond the sea, but to be thwarted in his views of right and of heaven stirred him to action.

The six years between 1714 and 1719 were notable in Ireland for their insufficient rainfall.[1] So long a period of injury to crops proved more and more discouraging, not only to those settlers who depended upon agriculture, but also to the weavers of flax who found the cost of food very high. In 1716 the sheep were stricken with a destructive disease known as rot, and severe frosts over Europe further crippled the supply of food. During the spring and summer of 1718 "a slow confluent small-pox" raged over Ulster in a malignant form; while the next three years brought fevers in the winter months.

---

[1] Rutty's "Weather and Seasons."

These misfortunes affected the Scotch farmer in Ulster just as they did the native Irish in Leinster or in Munster. The following note on Ireland in 1716 is from Archbishop King's papers, and it has the ring of Dean Swift. It shows, moreover, that in Ireland the farmer had to contend with difficulties that were less marked in England and Scotland.

"The common Irish[1] are laborious people, and if we set aside the holydays their religion injoins, they work as hard and as long as any in England. I confess not with the same success, for they have neither the assistance to labour nor the encouragement workmen have in England, their poverty will not furnish them with convenient tools, and so the same quantitie of work costs them p'haps twice the labour with which it is p'form'd in England; there are many accidental differences that increase their labour on them, as, for example, England is already enclos'd, and if a farmer have a mind to keep a field for medow, grazing, or plowing, it costs him no more but the shutting his gate, but the Irishman must fence his whole field every year or leave it in common, and the like saving of labour happens in the plow utensils in building houses and p'viding fireing. Neither hath the Irishman that encouragement

---

[1] "All persons born in Ireland are called and treated as Irishmen although their fathers and grandfathers were born in England."—Swift to Earl of Peterborough, 1726, quoted in A great archbishop of Dublin, William King (1906), p. 283.

to labour as there is in England, he has no markett
for his manufactories, if he build a good house or
inclose his grounds, to be sure he must raise his rent
or turn out at the end of a short lease. These and
many other considerations make the Irishman's case
very pitifull, and ought, as seems to me, to move
compassion rather than anger or a severe condemna-
tion. Upon the whole I do not see how Ireland can
on the p'sent foot pay greater taxes than it does
without starving the inhabitants and leaving them
entirely without meat or clothes. They have already
given their bread, their flesh, their butter, their
shoes, their stockings, their beds, their house fur-
niture and houses to pay their landlords and taxes.
I cannot see how any more can be got from them,
except we take away their potatoes and butter milk,
or flay them and sell their skins.'"[1]

The people suffered also from the devotion of the
great landlords to grazing, due to the profit to be
obtained from contraband trade in wool, and from
the sale of salted meat. Farm buildings gradually
disappeared or fell into decay and the herder with
his dog wandered over the desolate fields. Leases
forbade the use of the plow, and grain had to be
imported because Ireland did not supply enough to
satisfy the demand even at high prices. Archbishop
Boulter who, with King, and that other brilliant

---

[1] From (Great Britain) Royal Commission on Historical Manuscripts, second report, London, 1874, pp. 256–257.

churchman, Dean Swift, strove incessantly for legislation to make Ireland prosper, wrote to the Archbishop of Canterbury in 1727 that more tillage must be demanded of the landowner. The Irish House of Commons had tried in 1716 and again in 1719 to interest the England Parliament in a bill of this nature. Boulter writes to the Archbishop of Canterbury in February, 1727:—

"There is part of another bill which will go over, that is of great consequence to this kingdom; the title of the act is, I think, an act to prevent frauds, &c. in buying corn, &c. and to encourage tillage.

"It is the latter part of this bill about tillage that is of great moment here. The bill does not encourage tillage by allowing any premium to the exporters of corn, but barely obliges every person occupying 100 acres or more (meadows, parks, bogs, &c. excepted) to till five acres out of every 100; and so in proportion for every greater quantity of land they occupy. And to make the law have some force, it sets the tenant at liberty to do this, notwithstanding any clause in his lease to the contrary. We have taken care to provide in the bill, that the tenant shall not be able to burnbeat any ground in virtue of this act; and since he is tyed up from that, and from ploughing meadows, &c. the people skilled in husbandry say, he cannot hurt the land though he should go round the 100 acres in 20 years.

"I find my Lord *Trevor* objected to a bill we sent

from council that this was a breaking of private
contracts, and invading property: but I think that
nothing, since the lessor receives no damage by it,
and the publick is very much benefitted; and this
is no more than what is done every session in *England,* where rivers are made navigable or commons
inclosed; and in many road bills.

"I shall now acquaint your Grace with the great
want we are in of this bill: our present tillage falls
very short of answering the demands of this nation,
which occasions our importing corn from *England*
and other places; and whilst our poor have bread to
eat, we do not complain of this; but by tilling so
little, if our crop fails, or yields indifferently, our
poor have not money to buy bread. This was the
case in 1725 and last year, and without a prodigious
crop, will be more so this year. When I went my
visitation last year, barley in some inland places,
sold for 6 *s.* a bushel to make bread of; and oatmeal
(which is the bread of the north) sold for twice or
thrice the usual price; and we met all the roads full
of whole families that had left their homes to beg
abroad, since their neighbors had nothing to relieve
them with. And as the winter subsistance of the
poor is chiefly potatoes, this scarcity drove the poor
to begin with their potatoes before they were full
grown, so that they have lost half the benefit of them,
and have spent their stock about two months sooner
than usual; and oatmeal is at this distance from har-

vest, in many parts of this kingdom three times the customary price; so that this summer must be more fatal to us than the last; when I fear many hundreds perished by famine.

"Now the occasion of this evil is, that many persons have hired large tracts of land, on to 3 or 4000 acres, and have stocked them with cattle, and have no other inhabitants on their land than so many cottiers as are necessary to look after their sheep and black cattle; so that in some of the finest counties, in many places there is neither house nor corn field to be seen in 10 or 15 miles travelling: and daily in some counties, many gentlemen (as their leases fall into their hands) tye up their tenants from tillage: and this is one of the main causes why so many venture to go into foreign service at the hazard of their lives, if taken, because they can get no land to till at home. And if some stop be not put to this evil, we must daily decrease in the numbers of our people.

"But we hope if this tillage bill takes place, to keep our youth at home, to employ our poor, and not be in danger of a famine among the poor upon any little miscarriage in our harvest. And I hope these are things of greater consequence than the breaking through a lease, so far as concerns ploughing five acres in a hundred.'"[1]

After a potato famine from which many hun-

---

[1] Letters by Hugh Boulter to several Ministers of State, Oxford, 1769, Vol. 1, pp. 220–223.

dreds of the peasants died of starvation the English Council at last consented, avowedly for the benefit of the poor, to cancel the prohibitory clause in leases so that a small part of each farm should be plowed.[1]

Two industries in the counties of Antrim and Londonderry changed the character of the misfortunes of the settlers there, although it cannot be said that they warded off trouble. The Scotch in Ulster should have been prosperous even in years when other provinces of Ireland starved. But the industries of Ireland were crushed out at the behest of English merchants by laws favorable to home products.

The farms in Ulster were small, each having its field of potatoes. The soil was enriched by manure and lime, and after the crop of potatoes had been gathered the flax was sown, perhaps a bushel of seed by a family.[2] Each farm had also its bleaching green where the flax fibres were whitened in the sun, the drying season lasting for more than half the year.

All that has to do with the flax plant must be of interest to lovers of Ulster. When the seed had produced the graceful fields of flax, the women of the household kept down the weeds until the pretty blue petals had opened and had in turn given way to ripening seed-pods. The plants then were pulled or "plucked" in small handfuls and "bogged." "And

---

[1] I George II, Chapter 10.
[2] Arthur Young's Tour in Ireland, August, 1776.

why do you bog it, Larry?" asked Mrs. Hall, who was familiar with flax culture from childhood.

"Is it why we bog it, dear?—Why then, you see, we must all pass through the waters of tribulation to be purified, and so must the flax—the bad you see, and the good, in that small plant is glued together, and the water melts the glue, so that they divide— and that's the sense of it, dear!"

The plants were held in water by heavy stones— in running water if the fibres were to be good in color, although the processes of decay went on more rapidly in stagnant water. Sometimes they were laid out in the fields until a season's grass had grown up about and through them. In due time they were gathered and dried in the open air or over a fire. The coarse brown stalks were then slowly drawn over an upright post or chair-back and beaten inch by inch, this being the "scutching" process. The stalks in the next process were cleaned and split by rude combs of varying coarseness, and known as hackles. The task was tiresome and dirty, so that an itinerant workman usually did this part of the labor, going from cabin to cabin with his store of Dublin news and neighborhood gossip. The rough fibres were then subjected to many scaldings and dryings, until the bleaching greens began at last to appear white with the harvest of flax.

A century ago the hand loom produced finer linen yarn than any that came from the mill. In 1815 Cath-

erine Woods of Dunmore near Ballynahinch, a girl
of fifteen, spun yarn which gave 2,520,000 yards to
the avoirdupois pound of flax, requiring but 17
pounds, 6 ounces, 3½ drams of flax to go entirely
around the earth.[1]

This industry of spinning and weaving was carried to America by many thousands of emigrants
during half a century which preceded the Revolutionary war. It brought fame and comforts to the
Scotch Irish towns both north and south.[2] After
young Jerry Smith of Peterborough in New Hampshire, the future congressman, had acquired a little
book learning he chided his mother one day for her
unfamiliarity with the rudiments of grammar. Mrs.
Smith who had borne ten children in twelve years,
besides cooking and mending, digging sixteen bushels of potatoes in a day, and earning money by spinning to educate her boys, replied somewhat warmly:
"But wha taught you langage? It was my wheel;
and when ye'll hae spun as many lang threeds to
teach *me* grammar as I hae to teach *you*, I'll talk
better grammar!"[3]

The catching of salmon in the waters of the Bann

[1] Mr. and Mrs. S. C. Hall's Ireland, new edition, Vol. 3, pp.
85–91.

[2] Archibald Thompson of Abington and Bridgewater is said to
have made the first spinning foot-wheel of New England manufacture—a statement difficult of proof. He died in 1776 at the
age of eighty-five.

[3] Morison's Life of Judge Smith, p. 5.

and the Foyle was a great Ulster industry, and the
early settlers of Londonderry in New Hampshire
must have known its every detail, for many of them
had lived near the "Salmon Leap" on the Bann.
About the middle of August the salmon spawned in
all the streams that are tributary to the Bann and
the Foyle. As soon as they could swim they went
down to the sea. In January, when they began to
return to fresh water, their weight often exceeded
ten pounds. A year later their weight had doubled
and they were ready for the market. It was natural
that the Nutfield settlers should ask the American
Indians where they could go for the catching of fish.
This was an important occupation; but the linen
manufacture was more wide spread, and many of the
Scotch Irish who made their wills in America styled
themselves "weavers." The industry succeeded
the woolen manufacture which had been ruined in
1698 by an English law that forbade export of wool-
ens from Ireland except to England and Wales.[1]

The linen industry had one unfortunate circumstance peculiar to all manufacture. Depending to a
large extent upon foreign markets for its success, it
had years of great prosperity followed by others of
ruinous inactivity, and the causes of these fluctua-
tions, whether economic or political, lay wholly outside Ireland and beyond her control. When a period
of depression was concurrent with the expiration of

---

[1] 10 and 11 William III, Chapter 10 (English).

The Salmon Leap, Near Coleraine and Somerset, with Ruins of Mount Sandall Fort on the Bank

many leases, as once happened on Lord Donegal's Antrim estates, the people emigrated in great numbers to America. Arthur Young has an instructive paragraph on this point: "It is the misfortune of all manufacture worked for a foreign market to be upon an insecure footing; periods of declension will come, and when in consequence of them great numbers of people are out of employment, the best circumstance is their enlisting in the army or navy; and it is the common result; but unfortunately the manufacture in Ireland, is not confined, as it ought to be, to towns, but spreads into all cabins of the country. Being half farmers, half manufacturers, they have too much property in cattle, &c., to enlist when idle; if they convert it into cash it will enable them to pay their passage to America, an alternative always chosen in preference to the military life.'"[1]

It has often been said that the landlords in Ireland were always too much embarrassed financially to retain a Protestant tenantry. The highest bidder was usually an Irishman. Loving Ireland he did not wish to emigrate, and felt compelled to get the lease, even if the price was beyond his power to pay. He would share a single Scotch or English farmer's land with six or seven of his countrymen, all ekeing out a miserable existence; and when the unsuccessful Protestant bidder was far away clearing the New England field for planting, his Irish successors were

---

[1] Pinkerton's Voyages, London, 1809, Vol. 3, p. 869.

ready to abandon the land they had obtained at an impossible rental.[1] Never over a third and often not over a fifth of the profit went to the tiller of the soil,[2] and the slightest misfortune reduced the profit to the laborer below the point of subsistence. Archbishop King in a letter to Archbishop Wake, June 2, 1719, sums up the matter from the point of view of a churchman who loved Ireland.

"Some would insinuate that this is in some measure due to the uneasiness dissenters have in the matter of religion, but this is plainly a mistake; for dissenters were never more easy as to that matter than they have been since the Revolution, & are at present: & yet they never thought of leaving the kingdom, till oppressed by excessive [rents ?] & other temporal hardships: nor do only dissenters leave us, but proportionately of all sorts, except Papists. The truth of the case is this: after the Revolution, most of the kingdom was waste, & abundance of the people destroyed by the war: the landlords therefore were glad to get tenants at any rate, & set their lands at very easy rents; this invited abundance of people to come over here, especially from Scotland, & they have lived here very happily ever since; but now their leases are expired, & they obliged not only to give what was paid before the Revolution, but in most places double & in many

---

[1] Sir L. Parsons in 1793. Also Archbishop King's Life, p. 301.
[2] Boulter's Letters, Vol. 1, p. 292.

places treble, so that it is impossible for people to live or subsist on their farms."[1]

Add to these conditions a scarcity of small coin whereby the money required to pay the humble spinner for his yarn or the farmer for his produce cost the merchant over one and a half per cent;[2] and the attempts in England to cripple the linen industry,[3] and we are not surprised that the desire to emigrate passed over the land like a fever. Letters like the following show that Archbishop King, at the very outset of the great migration, was doing his best by eloquent appeal to awaken the English conscience. He wrote February 6, 1717–18 to the Archbishop of Canterbury: "I find likewise that your Parliament is destroying the little Trade that is left us. These & other Discouragements are driving away the few Protestants that are amongst us; insomuch that last year some Thousands of Families are gone to the West Indies. No Papists stir except young men that go abroad to be trained to arms, with Intention to return with the Pretender. The Papists being already five or six to one, & a breeding People, you may imagine in what conditions we are like to be. I may farther observe that the Papists being made incapable to purchase Lands, have turn'd themselves to Trade, & already engrossed almost all the Trade of the Kingdom."[4]

---

[1] King's Life, p. 301.

[2] Boulter to Newcastle, 1728; Letters, Vol. 1, p. 252.

[3] King to Archbishop of Canterbury, January 18, 1722–23.

[4] King's Life, p. 207.

Trade between the British Isles and the American colonies went very largely to the Delaware and Chesapeake Bay. Tobacco-laden ships sailed for Dublin, Liverpool, Belfast or Glasgow; returning to America with trifling cargoes of dress-goods, farm tools, and similar necessities, they gladly added to their revenues by transporting an occasional settler. There were few large parties of emigrants; if we except those who went to Williamsburg in South Carolina, few came to the South through concerted action until toward the middle of the eighteenth century. Few were led by ministers, but when they had settled along the banks of Christiana Creek, the Octorara, or the Neshaminy, they accepted ministers who had come to serve English Presbyterians, or they sent to Ireland for others.

The relations between New England and Ireland, on the other hand, were almost entirely intellectual and religious. There was no intercourse in trade to stimulate colonization. The migration of 1718 was so thoroughly a deliberate undertaking, clearly conceived and organized, that an agent was sent out to prepare the way. Ships were chartered for the voyage and their holds were filled with the household goods of the Bann Valley emigrants. It was this initiative in 1718 which led to an active but short-lived passenger trade between Irish ports and Boston. In this enterprise the Rev. William Homes's son, Captain Robert Homes, played a considerable part. The next year the more favorable conditions for settlement south and west of Philadelphia began to turn a large part of the traffic away from New England to Pennsylvania, and the Carolinas. This passenger traffic grew so rapidly that merchandise which had been of primary importance in Ulster's trade with the South ceased to be vital to the success of a voyage across the ocean.

IV

POLITICAL AND RELIGIOUS CONDITIONS IN ULSTER, 1714–1718

We now turn to the political oppression which was another cause for discontent in northern Ireland. In the early days of the London settlement and the succeeding Scotch migration when linen took the place of woolen, the new settlers felt that superiority which men who have a strong government behind them are wont to feel. They were independent, and even contemptuous of "the mere Irish." Under Cromwell they grew in strength until there were about eighty churches represented in the presbytery. With the return of Charles II, religious and political restrictions began to be felt. In Ulster sixty-one ministers were ejected from their churches, and curates were appointed to conduct Episcopal services; uniformity in church worship again became a dogma of the State.

It must not be assumed that the disabilities under which Presbyterians in Ireland labored were peculiar to the time or place. It was held by many to be for the best interest of the State that people should worship God in the accustomed way; and in Queen

Elizabeth's time[1] all persons had been commanded to attend church on Sundays and holy days where the Book of Common Prayer was used. This was no more tyrannical than the policy of the non-conforming assembly in Scotland, which was to induce Cromwell to make the Presbyterian religion paramount in England,[2] nor more exacting than the aim of the Presbyterians in Ireland who, as soon as they felt their strength, asked to have the army under Presbyterian influences only. The same strong spirit prevailed in early orthodox New England; and the present large but empty churches there, with ample but idle horsesheds, testify to a more effective and perhaps more wholesome spiritual and social life in country towns of old under the despotism of Cotton Mather and his immediate successors.

Roman Catholic supremacy in Ireland under James II came to an end with the arrival of William and Mary in 1688. In 1691 Parliament decreed[3] that the statute of Queen Elizabeth's time relating to uniformity of church services should not apply to Ireland, thus permitting attendance at non-conformist chapels. After January 1, 1691–2, all candidates for civil, military and ecclesiastical offices were to take oaths of allegiance to the royal family, and

---

[1] 2 Elizabeth 2, Section 3; also 35 Elizabeth 1.

[2] See life of the Rev. Robert Blair, in Dictionary of National Biography.

[3] 3 William and Mary, Chapter 2. (English Statutes.)

to make declarations against transubstantiation in the mass, and adoration of the Virgin Mary, provisions intended to bar Roman Catholics from office. Dissenters now had liberty to worship in their own chapels, and were not compelled to partake of the Lord's Supper according to the rites of the Established church in order to hold office. But they still had disabilities which could be made to bear heavily

PRESBYTERIAN MEETING HOUSE AT DUNGANNON, COUNTY TYRONE
Built Before the Year 1725

upon them; indeed if the magistrate chose, they suffered more than the Roman Catholics. The Synod which met at Antrim in 1698 declared its grievances to be an inability in many places to bury the dead until the Established service had been read, the requirement that school-masters partake of the Lord's Supper according to the customary rites, and the pressure to serve as church-wardens. In 1699 the Synod being asked for advice as to marriages decided that ministers had better continue to perform the ceremony "in an orderly way," as of old. In 1710 the Synod decided that it might be wise in some places to leave the performance of the cere- mony to the Episcopal clergy. In the second year of Queen Anne's reign (1703) a penal statute was carried by the help of the Bishops,[1] and they ob- tained in return for their support the introduction of a clause compelling in Ireland the sacramental test for office holders. This Irish Test Act seems to have been used unscrupulously as a weapon to place the Presbyterians on a level of disability with the Roman Catholics. Their ministers were almost everywhere turned out of their pulpits or threatened with legal proceedings. Dissenters were debarred from teach- ing schools and the legality of their marriages was denied. In 1716 Samuel Smith, Jr., and John Kyle of Belfast were called upon to defend their mar- riages in court. These were test cases, followed however by others. The Synod determined to stand by the defendants with the church's funds, but threats from prominent supporters of the denom- ination to withhold contributions in the future if the course were persisted in, caused the Synod to aban- don the attempt to uphold its claims in this way.

The Regium Donum, an annual government gift to non-conformist clergy in Ireland, in recognition of the Protestant defence of Ulster in 1688, was sus- pended. In short the hardships inflicted under this

---

[1] C. G. Walpole's History of the Knigdom of Ireland, p. 359,

law of Queen Anne from 1703 to 1719 had much to do with the migration to New England.

The Government found it impossible to pass a more moderate act to quiet discontent until vacancies in the ranks of the bishops could be filled by more tolerant men, and the Toleration Act[1] of 1719 was the first measure of relief that could be obtained. The oath still required loyalty to a King when excommunicated by the Pope; and the customary provisions to disfranchise Roman Catholics, namely: a declaration that in the Sacrament of the Lord's Supper there is no transubstantiation of the elements of bread and wine into the body and blood of Christ, and that the adoration of the Virgin Mary and other saints, and Sacrifice of the Mass are superstitious and idolatrous. There were exemptions for dissenters who did not favor baptism in infancy, and for Quakers, and there was no requirement to attend the Lord's Supper; but the thirteenth article of the act shut out all from its benefits who did not believe in the Trinity. This article struck a blow at Presbyterian Antrim which was just then divided over the doctrine of Christ's divinity, and weakened the nonconformist strength, although the act was considered by Archbishop King "such a wide Toleration as . . . is not precedented in the whole Earth." King George pressed the measure vigorously and the clergy which had been transplanted

---

[1] 6 George I, Chapter 5.

from England helped to pass it through the Irish parliament.

This concession did little to allay the fever for migration to America, which by 1728 aroused the fears of Archbishop Boulter of Armagh, and occasioned a series of letters, chiefly of defence against the charge that excessive tythes rather than rents caused the exodus. Extracts from these letters follow, but it should be recalled that their author was not so much in sympathy with Ireland as was Archbishop King of Dublin.[1]

Archbishop Boulter, writing to Lord Carteret from Dublin, March 8, 1728, says: "I do not doubt but some persons in the North may have been oppressed by the farmers of tythes. But I have at every visitation I have held had as great complaints from the clergy of the hardships put upon them by the people, in coming at their just dues, as the people can make of being any ways oppressed by the clergy or their tythe farmers, and I believe with as much reason.

"As to the expensiveness of the Spiritual courts which they complain of, that will be very much avoided by the act passed last sessions for the more easy recovery of the tythes of small value. And

---

[1] Relief from many of the penalties of Queen Anne's act came in 1737 (11 George II, Chapter 10), when Presbyterian marriages were declared legal, and in 1755, when dissenters were permitted to hold commissions in the militia.

indeed the gentlemen have, ever since I came hither, been putting it into the heads of their tenants, that it was not their rents, but the paying of the tythes that made them find it hard to live on their farms. And it is easy to see that this was a notion that would readily take with *Scotch* presbyterians.'' In a letter to the Bishop of London[1] the Archbishop contends that if the rent is doubled that implies that the value of the tythe is doubled; so the archbishop throws the responsibility on the landlord. The growth of the country after the wars of 1688 undoubtedly warranted somewhat higher rents. He continues: ''It is not the tythe but the increased rent that undoes the farmer. And indeed in this country, where I fear the tenant hardly ever has more than one third of the profits he makes of his farm for his share and too often but a fourth or perhaps a fifth part, as the tenant's share is charged with the tythe, his case is no doubt hard, but it is plain from what side the hardship arises. . . . When they find they have 7 or 8 £ to pay, they run away: for the greatest part of the occupiers of the land here are so poor, that an extraordinary stroke of 8 or 10 £ [judgment] falling on them, is certain ruin to them.''

In a letter to the Duke of Newcastle, written from Dublin March 13, 1728, Boulter shows what efforts were made to better the conditions of the moment,

---

[1] Boulter's Letters, Vol. 1, pp. 291–293, 297.

but he could scarcely have expected to upbuild the commercial well-being of Ireland, whatever influence he might have had, without the enactment of new laws relating to religious and political equality of dissenter and Episcopalian. He writes:

"The humour of going to *America* still continues, and the scarcity of provisions certainly makes many quit us: there are now seven ships at *Belfast* that are carrying off about 1000 passengers thither: and if we knew how to stop them, as most of them can neither get victuals nor work at home, it would be cruel to do it:

"We have sent for 2400 quarters of rye from *Coningsbery;* when they arrive which will probably be about the middle of *May,* we hope the price of things will fall considerably in the north, and we suppose they will mend pretty much when our supplies arrive from Munster."

The Established Church in Ireland was fortunate in having several leaders during this period who were able administrators, and conscious of their duty toward Ireland. Archbishops King and Boulter showed by their correspondence a lively sense of the deplorable condition of the people, both spiritually and as to their worldly estate. They also strove to bring the clergy to a higher plane. In 1714 King remonstrated with Dr. Ashe, Bishop of Clogher, for his long years of absence from Ireland, on the ground that his conduct justified the reproach of Mr. Boyse, the famous Presbyterian, that his bishopric was "only a pompous sinecure."[1] King himself gives some explanation of this unfortunate habit of the clergy when he says that there was little learning in Ireland and one could do no more than eat, drink and sleep.[2]

The archbishop felt handicapped in trying to rival the Presbyterian influence in the North by the practice of the rector who lived abroad, leaving his parish work to be done by a poorly paid curate. He writes:

"The people of the North have a peculiar aversion to curates, & call them hirelings; the difference in point of success amongst them is visible, between a grave resident minister that lives amongst his people, & spends part of what he receives from them in the place, & a poor curate that is not able to keep himself from contempt. . . . The people of the North do not grudge their tithes to the clergy, though they pay more than all the other provinces, because their landlords or the clergy must have them; the first must spend them in London or Dublin, whereas the clergy spend them on the place. . . . But if the clergy live in Dublin, 'tis as good for the people landlords had the tithes. . . . In short, the world begins to look on us as a parcel of men that have invented a trade for our easy and convenient living."[3]

---

[1] A great archbishop of Dublin, William King (1906), p. 249.
[2] King, p. 227.
[3] King to the Bishop of Clogher, 1704.

In behalf of the clergy it must be said that they were more devoted than the landlords, and a fourth or fifth of the resident justices were taken from the clerical ranks because no other men of education and standing were to be found in those communities, if we except the Presbyterian ministers who were barred by law from holding the office.

Archbishop King was so devoted to Ireland that Boulter was chosen with a view to counteracting his influence. King was no less devoted to his church. He went from town to town in his "parish visitation," exhorting his clergy to hold conferences with dissenters to bring them to conformity, making addresses to the public which "seemed to flow from the occasion, rather than by design," and obtaining results which seemed to him encouraging.[1]

King, in his struggle with the Scotch in Ulster, wrote a very able book which caused a bitter controversy for a generation, covering the period before the migration of 1718. The book bore the title "A discourse concerning the Inventions of Men in the Worship of God," and attempted to prove that the Presbyterians, who prided themselves on their devotion to Scripture, worshipped in direct opposition to its mandates, and rarely read it in their meetings. When the book appeared in print they were, as he said, "irate and excited almost to fury." The Rev. Joseph Boyse of Dublin, a grandson of Matthew

---

[1] King, p. 35.

Boyse who lived for a time at Rowley in New England, and the Rev. Robert Craighead, whose son migrated to New England and Pennsylvania, replied at great length. King had charged the Presbyterians with failure to attend public worship regularly, with neglect of the celebration of the Lord's Supper, and with being contented with scant instruction in Christian principles. Boyse, as the ablest of several defenders of the dissenters, made the best attempt to refute these charges. The dissenters felt the weakness of their Bible training, but so many ministers had been admitted to preach with insufficient education that it was difficult to raise the requirements. The proposition to have candidates for the ministry study the Psalter in Hebrew came before the Synod year after year and failed to pass. Finally Hebrew was deemed necessary, and in 1709 and 1710 the Synods voted that the Rev. Fulk White of Braid be paid £10 a year for teaching Hebrew. Candidates for the ministry were urged, also, to study the New Testament in the original Greek.

Archbishop King by the publication of his book started a discussion which undoubtedly awakened the minds of the people, and must have done good. He said, "Our people, who before almost in silence endured the scoffings and continual disputations of the dissenters, their ears deafened with frequent arguments, and scornful attacks; neither in meetings, drinking parties, nor feasts, could they any-

where rest, but conquered and helpless, remained
silent; now reviving as with new spirits, and in
their turn attacking the adversaries.'"[1]

It must be granted that the Established church,
even with its endowments, had a difficult field for its
labor. The Roman Catholics dominated the lower
provinces, and in Ulster the Scotch Presbyterians
outnumbered the English Episcopalians, while
together the Protestants scarcely exceeded the
Roman Catholic population. The "estated gentlemen" largely belonged to the Established church,
and it was feared that their dissenting tenants, if
granted privileges, would transfer their loyalty from
landlord to dissenting minister. While the dominant
class did not have the courage to be generous, it is
not unfair to assume also that the Presbyterians
were at times strangers to conciliation.

In an address which came before the House of
Lords at Dublin in 1711, relating to the "disturbance of the peace" at Drogheda by two Presbyterians who wished to gather a church, the following
charges are made:

1. Dissenters have refused to take apprentices
that will not covenant to go to their meetings.

2. When in a majority in Corporations they ex-
cluded all not of their persuasion.

3. They oblige those of their Communion married
by our Liturgy to do publick Penance.

---

[1] King, p. 38, Quædam.

4. Episcopal order hath been stiled *Anti-Scriptural;* our worship called *superstitious* & *idolatrous.*

5. Ministers openly and violently assaulted. Although Episcopalians have endeavored, by gentle Usage, to melt them down into a more soft and complying temper.

6. They seek to enlarge their borders by misapplying that Bounty of £1200 a year, extended to them for charitable purposes:—

to the propagation of schism,

to maintain agents,

to support lawsuits against the church,

to form seminaries to the poisoning of the principles of our youth,

to set up synods and judicatories.

The most unfortunate result, however, of a contentious spirit among Irish Presbyterians appeared when shades of belief became through violent debates among themselves the source of irreconcilable feuds, to be maintained with Scotch stubbornness.

Presbyterianism, which should have been strong in Ulster, was by virtue of its Scotch origin deprived of its united force through the great theological schism of the time: in other words, through the ascendancy of what we should now call Unitarianism, or the growing disinclination of ministers to subscribe to the Westminster Confession.

THE TOWN OF ANTRIM, ON THE RIVER BAIRD

Home of the Rev. John Abernethy

The master mind of this time in Scottish theology was Professor Simson, who began his instruction in Divinity at Glasgow a century after the death of the Dutch theologian Arminius, that is in 1708. His liberal views were espoused by Professor Hamilton at Edinburgh, and by a leader in Ulster thought, the Rev. John Abernethy of Antrim in Ireland. Abernethy, a friend of Simson, founded the Belfast Society which rapidly gained prominence as the supporter of ministers in Ireland who would not subscribe to the Westminster Confession. In 1707 a minister in the Synod of Aberdeen had been suspended for asserting that virtue was more natural to man than vice. The opposition of Arminius to the doctrine that God had selected his chosen few for the Kingdom of Heaven, leaving by predestination the unfortunate and sinful majority of mankind to an eternity in hell, became the basis of the liberal movement under Simson and the younger clergy of western Scotland and Ulster. In their platform were many beliefs that have since then influenced all creeds: that man is naturally able through his own powers to seek saving grace; that corruption which overcame the soul's purity was due to the body inherited from Adam; that the wish for happiness should inspire Christian living; that effective punishment for sin must be eternal, but that infants would be saved, and even the heathen would be judged according to their opportunity for light.

And, most important of all, the elect would, it was hoped, outnumber the damned.[1]

With these liberalizing theories went a change in preaching. Dogma became less important than conduct, and the younger ministers turned to ethics and morality for their themes, drifting away from the homely exhortation to worship and follow Christ. The "non-subscribers" to the Westminster Confession were joined to the Presbytery of Antrim, and then in 1726 were made independent. In 1736, after years of bitter discord, the Assembly ruled that ministers insist on supernatural revelation, that they base their sermons on Gospel subjects and "let their hearers know that they must first be grafted into Christ as their root before their fruit can be savoury unto God." County Antrim was a theological battle-ground during these opening years of the eighteenth century when the doctrinal articles were by many abandoned.

The theological disputes of the time left their impress upon the emigrants to America. To them religion was a vital subject, for constant thought and frequent discussion. In New England this earnest discussion grew into a spirit of discord which weakened the Presbyterian influence there. At the South the Presbyterians were of a milder temper, possibly because their greater numbers gave them less provocation to religious contention; possibly

---

[1] See Mathieson's Scotland and the Union, p. 224.

also because the milder English Presbyterianism had taken root early, and made itself felt even when the Scotch Irish had overrun the country.

Their devotion to self-government made them the pioneers in the movement for political independence. Referring to the Mecklenburg declaration a North Carolinian once said: "Och, aye, Tam Polk declared independence *lang* before anybody else!" This Colonel "Tam" or Thomas was the great uncle of President Polk. He was a leader among the Scotch Irish of North Carolina, and the opening paragraph of the "Declaration" which he read from the steps of the Court-house in Charlotte on a May afternoon in 1775 exhibits the courage of the race from Ireland. These are the opening words which he read:

"*Resolved,* That whosoever directly or indirectly abetted, or in any way, form, or manner, countenanced the unchartered and dangerous invasion of our rights, as claimed by Great Britain, is an enemy to this country—to America—and to the inherent and inalienable rights of man."

As the reading continued, and Colonel Polk's voice declared for a dissolution of the political bonds with the mother country, "that nation who have wantonly trampled on our rights and liberties, and inhumanly shed the blood of American patriots at Lexington," there was breathless silence followed by loud and long cheers. The Polks from Donegal were doing their part in America.

The Scotch Irish puzzled the traveller. Crèvecœur[1] speaks of the varying ability and thrift shown by the settlers. He adds: "One would think on so small an island an Irishman must be an Irishman, yet it is not so; they are different in their aptitude to, and in their love of labour."

If the Scotch Irish differed from the Irish they were not more like the Germans. The fundamental reason was a racial one, although the Scotch Irish selected slaty lands along the river banks where the soil is less productive than the lime-stone formations chosen by the Germans.[2] If we study the biographical dictionary, however, to compare Scotch Irish civic achievement with German participation in public life, we shall find the slaty field obstructed by stumps a more productive nursery of statesmen than the well-cleared field of loam that delighted the German heart.

[1] Letters from an American Farmer, N. Y. 1904, p. 83.
[2] Faust's German element, 1909, Vol. 1, p. 132. See also B. Rush's Essays, 1798, pp. 224, 228.

V

REV. WILLIAM HOMES AND REV. THOMAS CRAIGHEAD

The migration from the vicinity of Londonderry and from northern Tyrone to New England was much influenced by two Presbyterian ministers who had emigrated from Ireland a short time before, and were in sympathy with the Rev. Cotton Mather in his desire for the settlement of Protestant families from Ulster.

William Homes, the first of these ministers, was born in the north of Ireland in 1663, of a family which had been of consequence there for several generations. There was a Thomas Homes at Strabane, County Tyrone, in 1619; and at the time of which we write another Rev. William Homes, living at Urney, a few miles south of Strabane, was so well known that our William was called "the meek" to distinguish him.[1]

He had a happy combination of gentleness and ability which made his career in the ministry less eventful than that of the second minister referred to above, the Rev. Thomas Craighead. The boy

---

[1] William Homes, Junior, of Urney was ordained in 1696, and was probably a cousin.

Homes was carefully educated, and about 1686 he
came over to Martha's Vineyard where he obtained
a position to teach school. His teaching was acceptable, and he was urged to remain there, but a desire
to preach led him in July, 1691, to return to Ireland. He was reported from Lagan meeting in 1692
as "on trial in order to ordination," and having
gone through his second trials he was ordained December 21, 1692, as pastor of a church at Strabane

HOLY HILL HOUSE, STRABANE, COUNTY TYRONE
Standing when the Rev. William Homes preached at Strabane

in the Presbytery of Convoy. Strabane was at the
time a small village whose chief importance lay in
its situation at the point where the Mourne and the
Finn join to form the river Foyle. In the centre of
the town there was a neat but plain market house,
and farther down the road were two good gentle-

men's country houses, facing each other. In this town he was to begin his labors.

Mr. Homes received his degree of Master of Arts at the University of Edinburgh in 1693. Craighead had preceded him in 1691, and the names of several others of note later in America appeared on the college rolls soon after. From a copy of Mr. Homes's diary, preserved by the New England Historic Genealogical Society, many facts in regard to his family may be gleaned. William's father came from Donaghmore, county Donegal, a village a mile or more west of Castlefinn, and an hour's drive south west of Lifford on the road to Donegal and Ballyshannon. In the family lot there William's brother John, who was killed by lightning in 1692 in the parish of Raphoe, was buried; this John left five children, Margaret, John, Jolnot (?), Jane and Rebecca. Mary Ann, a sister of William, died in 1705. William married September 26, 1693, Katherine, daughter of the Rev. Robert Craighead, a venerable and distinguished minister of Londonderry.[1]

---

[1] Their children as far as known were:

ROBERT, born July 23, 1694, at Stragolan, County Fermanagh, several miles south of Omagh. He came to New England, and married Mary Franklin of Boston, April 3, 1716. She was a sister of Benjamin Franklin, the scientist and statesman. Robert was engaged for years as captain of a ship in transporting emigrants to America.

MARGARET, born February 28, 1695–96, at Strabane; married,

The Rev. William Homes and his brother-in-law the Rev. Thomas Craighead, with their families, arrived in Boston the first week in October, 1714, from Londonderry, on the ship "Thomas and Jane" of which Mr. William Wilson was then master. Homes brought four written testimonials, from the elders and overseers of his congregation at Strabane, from the Presbytery of Convoy, from the Synod, and from eight presbyterian ministers at Dublin, including the Rev. Joseph Boyse, a famous preacher and writer. The first testimonial was printed in the Boston Gazette for August 26, 1746; of this issue no copy is known to exist.

March 1, 1715–16, at Chilmark [Colonel] John Allen. She died April 26, 1778.

WILLIAM, born ——; died February 18, 1699–1700.

KATHERINE, born March 20, 1698–99; baptized by the Rev. Thomas Craighead at Strabane; married, May 30 (?), 1721, at Chilmark, Captain Samuel Smith.

JOHN, born July 30, 1700; baptized at Strabane by the Rev. Samuel Haliday of Ardstraw; died October 14, 1732, at Chilmark.

JANE, born August 30, 1701; baptized at Strabane by the Rev. William Homes of Urney; married, July 1, 1725, Sylvanus Allen of Chilmark; died December 17, 1763, at Chilmark.

AGNES, born May 31, 1704; baptized by the Rev. Mr. Homes of Urney; married, December 14, 1725, Joshua Allen.

ELIZABETH, born September 15, 1705; married by the Rev. Mr. Prince, February 5, 1729–30, to James Hutchinson.

HANNAH, born January 31, 1708–09.

MARGERY, born January 23, 1710–11; married, June 11, 1734, Benjamin Daggett.

See also a memoir of Mrs. Sarah Tappan.

The testimonial from Convoy was printed as part of the preface written by Joseph Sewall and Thomas Prince for Homes's "The Good Government of Christian Families Recommended," a memorial volume issued in 1747. It was signed by Francis Laird at Donaghmore[1] July 12, 1714.

It will be seen that Homes came well recommended. He was of gentle spirit, although something of a leader, having served in Ireland as moderator of the general Synod of 1708 which met at Belfast with fifty-four ministers and forty ruling elders present. He was a student of administration. His work, entitled "Proposals of Some Things to be done in our administring Ecclesiastical Government" (Boston, 1732) favored a council or presbytery of churches to check the friction which became evident on several occasions among New England ministers and people. The Rev. John White of Gloucester replied two years later in "New England's Lamentations," contending that, excepting ruling elders and the "third way of communion," the Congregationalists and Presbyterians stood on common ground. White held that no church in the whole consociation of churches would be so stubborn as to "sustain the dreadful sentence of non-communion." Nevertheless he felt secure in Congregational polity after reading the fifth chapter

---

[1] Laird was succeeded there in 1744 by the Rev. Benjamin Homes.

of first Corinthians, where "the Brethren" are admonished to come together and subject their sinning members to discipline.

Samuel Sewall welcomed Mr. Homes upon his arrival, and showed him many marks of respect. In his diary on October 5, 1714, Sewall wrote: "I wait on the Lieut. Govr, visit Mr. William Homes, Mr. Thomas Craighead, Ministers, in order to know what was best to be done as to the ship's coming up. Carried them a Bushel Turnips, cost me 5^s and a Cabbage cost half a Crown. Dined at the Castle, Lt Govr also invited Mr. Homes." On December 2d he records a gift of "an angel" (ten shillings) to Mr. Homes and Mr. Craighead, and in correspondence later he showed his good will.

The pulpit at Chilmark in Martha's Vineyard being vacant, Homes returned to the scene of his youthful labors. There he remained, faithful and honored, until his death June 27, 1746, in his eighty-fourth year. Mrs. Homes died April 10, 1754, in her eighty-second year. Thus were lost to the upbuilding of Ireland two worthy characters.

Parker says[1] that a young man named Homes, son of a Presbyterian clergyman, first brought reports to the people in Ireland of opportunities in New England. This was probably Captain Robert Homes, son of the Rev. William Homes; he had an unusual opportunity for intercourse with his

---

[1] History of Londonderry, p. 34.

father's former parishioners through his voyages to
Ireland. In 1717 two men with names later signifi-
cant in the Worcester and Falmouth settlements,
called to see the minister at Chilmark; they were
John McClellan and James Jameson. Three weeks
later (November 24th) Mr. Homes writes in his
diary: "This day I received several letters, one from
Doctor Cotton Mather, one from severall gentlemen
proprietors of lands at or near to Casco Bay, and
one from son Robert."

The above quotation points strongly to a conference held at Boston in November between Captain
Robert Homes, recently from Ireland and interested
in transporting Scotch Irish families, the Rev. Cotton Mather, eager to see the frontiers defended by a
God-fearing, hardy people, and the third party to
the conference, the men who were attempting to
plant settlements along the Kennebec. They must
have talked over the project for a great migration
(they all had written to the minister at Chilmark),
and undoubtedly Captain Robert Homes sent over
letters and plans to friends at Strabane, Donaghmore, Donegal and Londonderry. Perhaps no one
in Boston had so many relatives among the clergy
in Ulster, and as a sea-captain he had a still further interest in the migration. Robert himself sailed
for Ireland April 13, 1718, and returned "full of
passengers" about the middle of October.

The Rev. Mr. Homes in his diary describes his

journey to Boston on this great occasion. He lodged
with his son and preached twice, from Philemon i.
21, for the Rev. Cotton Mather at the North meeting house, and from Proverbs xii. 26 for the Rev.
John Webb at the New North; neither text seems
to have had any special significance.

The Rev. William Homes had two prominent

DONEGAL, COUNTY DONEGAL
Home of the Rev. Thomas Craighead

brothers-in-law, Robert and Thomas Craighead.
The Rev. Robert Craighead studied divinity at Edinburgh and Leyden and had a conspicuous career at
Dublin from 1709 until 1738, when he died. In 1719,
when the Presbyterian church in Ireland was in pro-
longed debate over the deity of Christ and subscrip-
tion to the Westminster Confession of Faith, he
served as moderator of the Ulster Synod. The Rev.

Thomas Craighead was educated in Scotland, but later entered upon his trials for the ministry as a probationer in the Presbytery of Strabane in 1698. He settled at Donegal. Here he remained until he removed with his brother-in-law Homes to America in 1714, being succeeded by the Rev. John Homes, who enjoyed a long pastorate at Donegal.[1]

The Rev. Thomas Craighead had the unhappy gift of discord and he led a somewhat stormy life, although he was a fearless and a useful minister. For some time all went well at Freetown. Mr. Craighead, when he settled there, had agreed to subsist on voluntary contributions from his flock. Probably his manner did not attract, and the support became gradually reduced until he was obliged to petition the General Court for a grant of money. They allowed ten pounds in June, 1718, for half a year's services. This was probably not the first grant of the kind to Mr. Craighead. In 1719 he brought his plight to the notice of the Justices of the Peace

---

[1] By his wife, Margaret, Mr. Craighead had:

THOMAS, born in 1702; married Margaret, daughter of George Brown, merchant of Londonderry, Ireland. A farmer at White Clay Creek, Delaware.

ANDREW, died unmarried.

ALEXANDER, died in March, 1766; an eloquent minister who lived in Pennsylvania, Virginia and North Carolina.

JOHN, of Cumberland County, Pennsylvania.

JANE, married, October 23, 1725, the Rev. Adam Boyd, pastor of a church at the forks of the Brandywine. Their son edited the *Cape Fear Mercury*.

for Bristol County, and at a Court of General Sessions of the Peace the town was ordered to lay a rate for his support. Many refused to comply and were thrown into jail. A petition to the General Court asking to have the men liberated, the rate declared annulled and Craighead's election as minister at Freetown void, was granted June 19, 1719. The unfortunate minister then petitioned for relief, having for four and a half years preached at Freetown, three of these years without pay, and being then deeply in debt. In December he was granted twenty pounds.[1] Among his enemies John Hathaway, a kinsman, was a conspicuous figure, and to him Cotton Mather addressed a stirring letter, as a last effort to restore peace. It was written July 21, 1719:

                                    "21 d V m 1719

"You cannot be insensable that the minister whom ye glorious Lord hath graciously sent among you is a man of Excellent Spirit, and a great Blessing to your plantation. Mr. *Craighead* is a man of Singular piety and Humility & meekness, & patience & self denial and industry in the work of God. All that are acquainted with him, have a precious esteem of him. And if he should be driven from you, it would be such a Damage [to] you, such a Ruine to your plantation, as ought not without Horror to be thought upon.

---

[1] Province Laws 1719–20, Chapters 43, 110.

"But, we are given to understand, from some who are the spectators of what is done among you, That Mr. Hathway's Coming unto a good, friendly & Christian Frame towards Mr. *Craighead* would much Contribute unto his Comfortable Countenance Among you. We do therefore, Exceedingly importune you, to put away Evil Differences towards that faithful Servant of God. and Come unto such a frame, as, if you now felt the last Pangs of Death upon you (which Cannot be put off) you would chuse to dy withal.

"It will be not a little for your own Reputation with Godly & Worthy Men, that your disaffection for that Valuable man were laid aside And if once you come to sit lovingly together, the more you know him the more will you Love him."

Craighead soon left Freetown, and in the spring of the year 1723 moved his family southward into "the Jerseys," as President Stiles of Yale makes record. He joined Newcastle presbytery January 28, 1724, and on the 22nd of the next month was installed minister of the church at White Clay Creek in Delaware. There Mr. Craighead preached eloquently for seven years, enjoying frequent revivals and building new churches through his zeal. In 1733 he moved to Lancaster County, Pennsylvania, and joined Donegal presbytery September 3rd. He was pastor of the church at Pequea from October 31, 1733, to September, 1736. Changing his residence once more he settled at Hopewell in 1738, and preached until he died while pronouncing a benediction, in April, 1739; his last church was within the bounds of the present town of Newville, a few miles west of Harrisburg, Pennsylvania. While serving in these pastorates he was known as "Father" Craighead, and attained a wide reputation, rising soon to be moderator of the Synod.

Craighead came of a distinguished family, and is the ancestor of many ministers in the southern states. Having relatives in Londonderry and Dublin he was able by correspondence to stir the spirit of migration. He stands as a link between New England and the colonies south of the Hudson. Many of the Scotch Irish went from the Kennebec settlements to happier surroundings in Pennsylvania. They left brothers and cousins throughout Massachusetts and New York. Their ties of sympathy, faith and blood, helped to bind the colonies together in 1775. Tidings of the fight at Lexington stirred North and South Carolina profoundly for there were kinships along the entire coast.

VI

ULSTER AND THE PRESBYTERIAN
MINISTRY IN 1718

In the early years of the Colonies, that is, before 1718, an occasional party of emigrants went out from Ireland in the ships which sailed to southern ports for tobacco and cotton. Through them the Carolinas became in a few years familiar to the people of Ulster. New England on the other hand received scarcely any immigration before 1718, and there was very little intercourse, unless we except that of a theological and literary nature which existed between leaders of thought in Dublin and Boston. This was perhaps the chief reason which led to the appointment of an agent by the Bann Valley colonists.

This agent, the Rev. William Boyd, was ordained at Macosquin in January, 1709–10. The Rev. Thomas Boyd, probably his father, was an Episcopal clergyman at the neighboring town of Aghadowey, and although deposed in 1661 for non-conformity, continued to preach there until his death in 1699, holding services also at Macosquin for the last ten years that he lived.

When the Rev. William Boyd had fulfilled his

mission in Boston and was ready to return to Macosquin, he preached a "return" sermon at the
weekly lecture on the 19th of March, 1718–19. It
was printed in 1719 with the title "God's way the
Best way" (Jeremiah vi. 16). The introduction by
the Rev. Increase Mather tells in rather quaint
language so much of interest relating to Mr. Boyd
and his mission to New England that it is given in
part just as he wrote it: "It was not before the last
Summer that he Arrived among us. He had his
Education in the University of Edinburgh in Scotland; and there commenc'd Master of Arts: and
afterwards Read Divinity in the Famous Colledge
and University in Glasgow[1] under the care of Mr.
Widrow, then Professor of Divinity there. Has
been Ordained a Minister of the Gospel, and Pastor
of a Church at Macasky in Ireland. Many in that
Kingdom having had thoughts of a remove to this
part of the World, have considered him as a Person
suitably qualify'd to take a Voyage hither, and to
make Enquiry what Encouragement or otherwise,
they might expect in case they should engage in so
weighty and hazardous an Undertaking, as that of
Transporting themselves & Families over so vast an
Ocean. The issue of this Affair has a great depend-
ence on the Conduct of this Worthy Author. The

---

[1]Among the Fasti are William Boyd, 1709, and Adam Boyd,
1711. References to the Boyds may be found in Miss Leavitt's
The Blair Family (1900).

Lord direct him in it. Since his being in New-England (as well as afore that) by the Exemplary holiness of his Conversation, and the Eminency of his Ministerial Gifts, he has obtained a good Report amongst all Good Men. . . .

"It is justly observed in the Sermon Emitted herewith, that Antiquity alone, is not a sufficient Justification of any Practice; Altho' Truth is more Ancient than Error."

Cotton Mather with his unfailing kindness sent Mr. Boyd away with a generous letter of commendation:

> "Boston, N. E.
> 20 d ii m 1719

"It is hereby Certified on Behalf of ye Reverend M^r. *William Boyd* That which he has Commenced among us, he has, as far as we Could know or learn Adorned Y^e Doctrines of God o^r Saviour, with unblemished Conversation, and improved ye Character given him in ye recommendations which he brought hither from *Ireland* with him. And that his public Labours in ye ministry of the Gospel, have been Desired and Accepted among the people of God in this Country: with whom he now leaves a very Good Name, & Reputation, At his Departure from us.

"Having furnished this O^r worthy Brother with Such a Testimony, we earnestly Commend him to ye Conduct & Blessing of o^r glorious Lord, in ye Voyage that is now before him.'"[1]

---

[1] American Antiquarian Society Manuscripts.

Before further reference is made to Mr. Boyd's subsequent career and the lives of his contemporaries, something must be said of the Presbyterian church in Ulster, its organization, its work and its ministry, for the ministers were closely allied with the first plan to form a Scotch Irish colony in America. The General Synod of the Presbyterian church in Ulster was held usually in June of each year. The Synod of 1717 is especially interesting for its long and important sessions, in which Boyd, McGregor, Cornwall and others who were interested in America took part. Nine presbyteries were represented, Down, Belfast, Antrim, Tyrone, Armagh, Coleraine, Derry, Convoy, and Monaghan; one hundred churches sent their ministers and in most. instances also a ruling elder. The aged David Cargill had come with the Rev. Mr. McGregor from Aghadowey; they were both appointed by the Synod members of the Committee "on funds." Matthew Clark and James Woodside were absent; Clark was excused, but Mr. Woodside did not have so good a reason for absence and was not excused.

The records of the Synod show among other activities an increasing interest in the Irish language, some ministers being able to read and others to preach in Irish. The Synod of Argyle also expressed a desire to aid Ulster in the conversion of the Irish, and there is mention of a Celtic catechism, ready to be printed. Of still greater importance, if Mr.

McGregor was already thinking and speaking of removal to America, was his appointment to travel about the counties of Londonderry, Antrim and Tyrone on a mission to convert the Celtic Irish.

The Synod declined after much discussion to transfer the Rev. Robert Craighead, brother of the minister soon to be in Massachusetts, from Dublin to Londonderry. Many other cases of ministerial transfers were discussed, including the Rev. Mr. Cornwall's request to be relieved of his work at Augher (near Clogher) on account of ill-health, the distance of his house from the church, and the inability of the congregation to meet expenses.[2]

A young man who wished to enter the ministry was examined by the Presbytery of Antrim which now reported to the Synod "that he hath neither a natural capacity nor learning any way equal to the work of the Ministry," and was advised to lay aside his purpose.

There are also in the records many discussions of charities, assignments to preach, admonitions to thoughtless or possibly sinful brothers. Taking them all in all, the records of the Ulster Synod are

---

[1] A second opportunity for the spread of the "fever" for emigration was offered by the appointment of the Rev. Mr. Cornwall to preach in August before the new Presbytery of Augher, erected from parts of the counties of Monaghan and Tyrone. The next year four young men were presented by this Presbytery for their "second trials," and it was announced that they were "designed for America."

orderly, concise, and sane—a monument to a century and more of religious work in Ireland. They convince the reader that a man privileged to take part in the meetings of his congregation, of his presbytery, or of the General Synod had an opportunity to fit himself for self-government. Indeed, the committee work and the exercise in speaking which these assemblies offered prepared the leading Presbyterian laymen in Ulster to participate in county and town affairs in America on equal terms with their neighbors. The Scotch Irish, from minister to laborer, were bred in an atmosphere of self-reliance, and they carried this force with them to the New World.

The emigrants of the year 1718 came largely from the Bann Valley. The Valley's chief town, Coleraine, still gloried in its buildings of the Elizabethan period, grouped along a good road leading to the square (now called the Diamond), and onward to the bridge across the Bann water. John Barrow, a traveller of a later date, writes:

"Standing on this bridge, the spectator has a fine view of the Bann on both sides of it; that to the northward embraces, among a number of decent-looking villas or farm-houses, a very pretty mansion and grounds on the left bank, close to the suburb, called, from the owner I imagine, Jackson Hall; and the view in the contrary direction, or up the river, exhibits many neat villas, well planted with

COLERAINE, FROM THE WEST SHORE OF THE RIVER BANN

Drawn by John Huybers

wood. Among them a parkish-looking place, on the left bank, caught my attention, and I walked along a good road, not merely to get a nearer view of it, but also to take a look at the salmon-leap, which I knew to be about the spot. This place is named Somerset. . . . The little cottages belonging to the weavers, are, like those of Antrim, built of stone, and have a neat appearance; but there is this distinctive character which makes them differ from an English cottage,—that they are all open to the road in front, and want that little paled-off garden enclosure, so common to our meanest cottages.'"[1]

The Presbyterian ministers of this region in 1718 were the Rev. William Boyd at Macosquin, a village three miles out of Coleraine on the road to Aghadowey; the Rev. James McGregor at Aghadowey; and a short distance south the Rev. James Woodside at Garvagh; all on the west side of the Bann.

---

[1] Barrow's Tour Round Ireland, p. 88. Thackeray in "The Irish Sketch Book" speaks of Coleraine "with a number of cabin suburbs belonging to it, lying picturesquely grouped on the Bann River." Farther on occurs his poem, "Peg of Limavaddy," beginning:

> Riding from Coleraine
> (Famed for lovely Kitty)
> Came a cockney bound
> Unto Derry City;
>
> Weary was his soul,
> Shivering and sad he
> Bumped along the road
> Leads to Limavaddy.

Farther south, near the Bann, the Rev. Matthew Clark, a survivor of the siege of Londonderry and a military man, preached at Kilrea; and the Rev. John Stirling was at Ballykelly, county Londonderry, a dozen miles west of Coleraine. At Coleraine was the Rev. Robert Higinbotham, famous in his day for his futile attempt to change his mind after having honored Mrs. Martha Woods with the offer of his hand; and about six miles south of Coleraine at Ballymoney, just across the river from Aghadowey, was the Rev. Robert McBride. Eight or ten miles north east of Coleraine at Billy or Bushmills was the Rev. John Porter, said by contemporaries to have been a "sprightly orator," and four miles to the south west of Bushmills the Rev. Henry Neill was at Ballyrashane.

At Londonderry no one at the moment held the pulpit of the Rev. Robert Craighead, who died August 22, 1711. At Donegal, a few miles west of Lifford and Strabane, was the Rev. John Homes, and at Donaghmore the Rev. Benjamin Homes. In County Tyrone the Rev. Samuel Haliday, father of the famous Dr. Haliday, was six miles south of Strabane at Ardstraw; the Rev. William Cornwall was twenty miles farther south at Clogher; he was thinking of America, and no doubt in communication with the Homes family. At Kilmore, county Down, was the Rev. Thomas Elder, and at Magherally the Rev. Samuel Young.

All these ministers are known to have had some interest in or sympathy with a proposal for migration to New England; but when Boyd was about to sail for Massachusetts Bay and a petition for lands for Scotch Irish settlers was prepared for him to present to Governor Shute, only four ministers, Higinbotham, Porter, Neill, and Elder, added their signatures, and not one who signed came over to New England to live.

The petition is headed by the Rev. James Teatte, probably the James Tate who served at Killeshandra, near the town of Cavan, from 1705 to 1729. If he had any ties with the Coleraine presbytery to which most of the clerical signers belonged we have now no means of discovering them.

Of the other clerical signers of this petition a few words only are necessary. Thomas Cobham was ordained at Clough, a village south of Ballymoney in county Antrim, in March, and only a few days before the petition was drawn up. Robert Neilson, an aged minister, whose trembling hand wrote a signature which Mr. Parker in his "Londonderry" very naturally printed "Houston," held no parish although long identified with Kilraughts in the Presbytery of Route (later the Presbytery of Coleraine). William Leech was the minister of Ballymena, county Antrim, 1698–1738, although the historians Killen and Hanna speak of the minister there as Thomas Leech. Robert Higinbotham of Coleraine,

John Porter of Bushmills and Henry Neill of Ballyrashane were all members of the Presbytery of Coleraine. The next signer, Thomas Elder, was from
County Down, although he may have lived at one
time in the Coleraine presbytery, since one of the
same name accompanied the Rev. Mr. Neill to the
Synod of 1716. James Thomson was to become minister at Ballywillan, near Coleraine, in a few weeks.
Alexander Dunlop, a signer, was not a minister in
Ulster, nor were two other clerical signers of the
petition to Shute, Archibald McCook and Samuel
Wilson, of whom nothing is known in the Presbyterian annals of Ulster. Dunlop, McCook and Wilson were Masters of Arts; all the others were Ministers of the Word of God, signing themselves
V[erbi] D[ei] M[inister]. The more one studies
the list the more one is puzzled by its composition.
It appears to have been prepared in some haste by
ministers in the Bann Valley, possibly at a presbytery gathering which Tate, Leech, and Elder had
attended.

The names of the other signers are also for the
most part well written and still easily to be read.
They have not as familiar a sound as one might expect, but if we recognize in one column Randall Alexander, in another Andrew McFadden, and in a third
Matthew Slarrow, we may assume that most of the
names were gathered in the Bann Valley towns. All
the names doubtless looked impressive to Governor

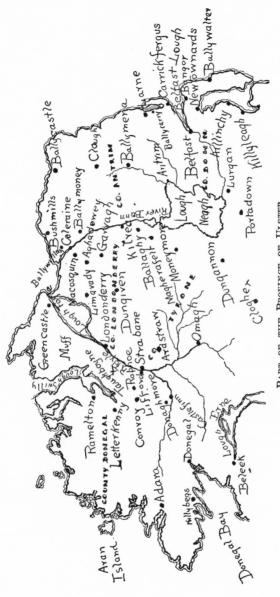

PART OF THE PROVINCE OF ULSTER

Shute, even if upon us the significance of many of them is lost. And perhaps both the Governor and Cotton Mather were no wiser than we are.

The petition to Governor Shute was engrossed on a sheet of parchment twenty-eight inches square, and is now deposited with the New Hampshire Historical Society, at Concord, where it may be seen.[1]

The ministers who accompanied the first colonists in 1718 were worthy men, but their departure from Ulster did not deprive the Presbyterian Church of any of its real leaders.

The Rev. William Boyd upon his return to Macosquin continued his work there until 1725, when Monreagh in County Donegal called him. This parish, on the west bank of the Foyle between Londonderry and Lifford, promised to build a meeting house and to secure to him £40 per annum. He was installed April 25, 1725, and died there in service May 2, 1772, leaving children. He last attended a synod in 1762, when he was probably in feeble health. His career was a troubled one, on account of a rival minister who built a church at St. Johnstown within his jurisdiction, and alienated many of his people. The General Synod took his part steadily, but was finally forced to recognize the new organization.

Monreagh was in Boyd's time also called Taboin or Taughboyne. The McClintocks were prominent Presbyterians in Taughboyne, and William McClin-

---

[1] See Appendix II.

tock, father of the Rev. Samuel of Portsmouth, New Hampshire, may have been of this race.

The Rev. James McGregor or McGregore followed the Rev. Thomas Boyd at Aghadowey, a small Londonderry village whose name means "Duffy's field." He was ordained there June 25, 1701, came to Boston August 4, 1718, and died at the American Londonderry of a fever after a short illness March 5, 1729.[1] A widow and seven, it is said, of their ten children survived him. The widow, Mary Ann McGregor, was married January 9, 1733, by the Rev. John Moorhead of Boston, to Mr. McGregor's Londonderry successor, the Rev. Matthew Clark, a vigorous and picturesque preacher.

Little is known of McGregor's education and early life; his name does not appear on the membership rolls of the universities, but he was a man of good abilities. He came possibly from the Scotch highlands, for his knowledge of Celtic enabled him to take a leading part in the movement to draw into the Presbyterian Church those of highland and Irish descent. It was found that both peoples could read

---

[1] *Boston News-Letter*, March 27, 1729. I have discovered very little about Mr. McGregor's children. Mr. Otis G. Hammond kindly searched the deeds and found mention of a daughter Jane, wife of Alexander Clark of Portsmouth, physician; a daughter Margaret, wife of Alexander Caldwell of Portsmouth, shopkeeper; and sons David of Londonderry, clerk or minister; James of Londonderry, yeoman; and Alexander of Rhode Island, schoolmaster. Parker's Londonderry, p. 280, mentions also Robert, Daniel, Mary, Elizabeth and John.

the Bible in Celtic, and Presbyterians vied with Churchmen in establishing missions. Two dissenting societies were organized in 1716 to study the language, and McGregor was appointed to preach to one of them at a meeting in Dungiven in August.[1] A few years earlier he had become associated in this work with the Rev. Archibald Boyd, and we find them both as followers of the Rev. William Boyd on New England soil in 1718. McGregor's coming was doubtless hastened by the poverty of his parish, which owed him eighty pounds at the time of his departure. The General Synod brought pressure to collect half the sum, but with what result we cannot tell, for Aghadowey was reported in 1728 to be religiously and financially in "a sinking state."

The rigid standards of the dissenters at this period bring the sins of the clergy into relief. In 1700 they were censured by the Synod because they, their wives and children, were "gaudy and vain" in their manner of dress. They were cautioned to avoid "powderings, vain cravats, half shirts, and the like," as well as "sumptuous, prodigal dinners" at ordinations. McGregor and Boyd, the apostles to the Irish, withstood the allurements of fashion, but were found wanting in other virtues. McGregor, having taken several cans of ale at Coleraine where, as he said, "less might have serv'd," was in 1704 after a vote of "not proven" severely admonished

---

[1] Records of the General Synod of Ulster.

before the whole Synod of Ulster. Curiously enough the chief of his accusers bore the surname of Love. McGregor's after life appears to have been exemplary. Archibald Boyd was deposed for sins against morality in 1716; he appeared in Boston in 1718, but no reference was made to his former ministerial position.

McGregor's son David became even better known than his father as a Presbyterian leader, while settled at Londonderry, New Hampshire. He was a controversialist and speaker whose influence was felt for many years in New England.

The weakness for excessive drinking affected men of all classes in Ireland. The archbishops admonished the clergy of the Established Church, and the Synod labored with the dissenters. John Gamble in his travels in the north of Ireland in 1810 refers to a certain Presbyterian clergyman who could lecture "on the seven churches, and on the seven candlesticks, as pat as if it was the Gospel o' St. Luke. Has but one fault in the world—he's *our* fond of the *wee drap.*" The Congregation were tolerant of this failing in their pastor, but a parishioner said: "*Ogh aye,* man, the Papists and the high kirk hold out their fingers at us, and gibe us, sore, on his account."[1]

The Rev. Mr. Clark, mentioned above, was at Kil-

---

[1] Gamble's Sketches of History, Politics and Manners in Dublin, and the North of Ireland in 1810, New Ed., London, 1826, p. 244.

rea; his connection with the congregation there was severed April 28, 1729. A few miles to the northwest the Rev. James Woodside had for many years preached at Garvagh. His arrival in New England will be describ'ed in an account of the Brunswick settlement. But a letter of encouragement from the Rev. Cotton Mather, written in February, 1718–19, has several interesting passages, and is given in full from the draft in the American Antiquarian Society:

[To the Rev. James Woodside]   "3ᵈ XIIᵐ 1718

"Tis more than Time that your Brethren here should bid you welcome to the western side of Ye *Atlantic* and make you a Tender of all the Brotherly Assistance that we are capable of giving you; especially under ye Difficulties which at your first Arrival you cannot but meet withal. The Glorious providence of God oʳ Saviour, which has been at work, in the Removal of so many people, who are of so Desirable a character as we see come & coming from ye North of *Ireland,* Unto ye North of *New England,* has doubtless very great Intentions in it; and, *what He does,* we *know* not *now, but we shall know hereafter.*

"He who Defeated ye purposes of such a removal attempted by some excellent persons of your Nation & Spirit, more than four score years ago, now seems to favor us.[1] Is it not because He has a work to do

---

[1] The "Eagle Wing" left Ireland in 1636.

which we are not yet aware of! Happy and Honoured, those of us Christians [?] by whom o^r glorious Lord comes to have these ends of ye earth for His possession!

"The people who are upon this Transportation, are of such principles, & so Laudable for their sobriety, their Honesty, their Industry, that we cannot but embrace you with a most fervent charity, and cherish hopes of noble settlements to be quickly made in a Region, which has hitherto been a Reputed Aceldama.[1].

"The people who were formerly taking Root there, carried not ye ministry of ye Gospel with y^m, and were once and again suddenly cursed of God. The Indians have never yett been permitted of Heaven to break up a Town that had a minister of ye gospel in it. It is a vast encouragement unto o^r expectations of a smile from God on the plantation now going forward, that we see a *Woodside* as well as a Cornwal, appearing there; and we have a prospect of more such ministers coming over, as will be ye Beauty & ye Safety of that Countrey, and be ye very life of y^r colonies that will be under their watchful & [illegible] Influences."

The Rev. William Cornwall, mentioned by Mather, belonged to a family not unknown in the ministry.

---

[1] Acts i, 19. The potter's field near Jerusalem, said to have been purchased by Judas with money received for the betrayal of Jesus.

Thomas Cornwall graduated at Edinburgh in 1694, and William "of Ireland" matriculated at Glasgow in 1687. They were possibly sons of Gabriel Cornwall who preached in 1656 at two villages a few miles northeast of Coleraine, Ballywillan and Bushmills. The Rev. William Cornwall returned to Ireland after a winter of hardship in Casco Bay, and settled at Taughboyne in 1722. He died March 13, 1734–5.

Two ministers whose names will always be associated with the early life of the Scotch Irish settlers in Worcester were the Rev. Edward FitzGerald and the Rev. William Johnston.

The Rev. Edward FitzGerald, leader of the company which settled in Worcester in 1718, deserves notice, but his history has not been found. An influential man of the same name was an original settler of Boscawen, New Hampshire, in 1734.[1] The last record of the Rev. Edward FitzGerald in Worcester is in 1725, when £2 were recorded in the Town Treasurer's report as due "to ye Revd Mr. Fits Gearld."[2] The town had called the Rev. Isaac Burr in February, 1725, and it would appear that, being in need of a temporary preacher, Mr. FitzGerald had been

---

[1] Another FitzGerald, Richard by name, married at Scituate in 1729, and was a Latin schoolmaster in Hanover, Massachusetts, from 1734 to 1746. The presence of two educated men of the name in New England at this time, both probably Protestants, suggests some kinship with the Rev. Edward FitzGerald of Worcester.

[2] Collections Worcester Society of Antiquity, Vol. 2, p. 41.

engaged until the ordination of Mr. Burr in October. This, however, is merely a conjecture.

The Rev. William Johnston, born at Mullagh-moyle, County Tyrone (?), in 1710, was the son of William and Elizabeth (Hoey) Johnston. After seven years at the University of Edinburgh, he came to Worcester. The Presbyterians there endeavored in March, 1736-7, to become exempt from taxation for the support of the town church that they might maintain Mr. Johnston in the ministry.[1]

Failing in this, he removed to Windham, New Hampshire, where he became the first minister of the town in July, 1742. In July, 1752, the parish had become so poor that he voluntarily withdrew and settled in New York State, dying at Florida, Montgomery county, May 10, 1782, after many years of service in various places.[2]

Of other Presbyterian ministers who came from Ireland in 1718 or possibly the year following, the most important in the Connecticut valley[3] were the Rev. John McKinstry[4] of Sutton, Massachusetts and Ellington, Connecticut, the Rev. James Hillhouse of New London, and the Rev. Samuel Dorrance of Vol-

---

[1] Collections Worcester Society of Antiquity, Vol. 2, p. 106.

[2] See a sketch of him in Morrison's Windham, p. 607.

[3] See an excellent paper on "The Irish Pioneers of the Connecticut Valley" in Connecticut Valley Historical Society Papers, Vol. 2, pp. 175-213.

[4] The genealogy of the McKinstrys has been published by the Hon. William Willis of Portland, Maine.

untown. McKinstry was born at Brode[1] on the eastern shore of Antrim, near Carrickfergus, in 1677, and took his Master of Arts degree at Edinburgh in 1712. Willis believes that he came in 1718, but I find no record of him so early. The town of Sutton voted December 25, 1719, to call him to be pastor at the meeting-house which the people had recently completed. Later he moved to Ellington, where he died January 20, 1754.

The Rev. James Hillhouse was born about 1688, the son of John and Rachel Hillhouse, owners of a large estate called Freehall, in County Londonderry. He studied at Glasgow under the famous Professor Simson, and was ordained by Derry presbytery October 15, 1718. Coming to America in 1720, he was called to a church in the second parish of New London in 1722, where he died December 15, 1740. His son William was a member of the Continental Congress, and William's son James was a Senator of the United States.[2] Mr. Hillhouse's widow Mary married the Rev. John Owen of Groton, Connecticut, who may have been of the Scotch Irish connection. Her third choice was also a minister, so that she was said to have spent her life "near the altar." This third husband, the Rev. Samuel Dorrance, was en-

---

[1] Brod appears in the Hibernian Atlas, but does not appear in the printed list of townlands.

[2] See Bacon's Sketch of the Hon. James Hillhouse, New Haven, 1860. James, uncle of the emigrant, was mayor of Londonderry in 1693. Abraham Hillhouse was at the siege.

tered as an Anglo-Hibernian at Glasgow University in 1709. He is said to have studied divinity at Edinburgh, although his name does not appear in the printed list of graduates; was licensed by Dunbarton presbytery in Scotland, and in 1719 was reported as received by the Presbytery of Coleraine, his testimonials having been read by the Synod of Derry. He settled in Voluntown, now Stirling, Connecticut, bringing with him several brothers and friends who became leaders in the community. Dorrance was ordained in 1723, not without opposition from those who opposed Presbyterian proclivities.

---

[1] Signers of the Westminster Confession at Voluntown:

Samuel Dorrance	George Dorrance
Robert Gordon	Samuel Church, Jun.
Thomas Cole	John Dorrance, Jun.
John Kasson	Nathaniel Deane
John Campbell	Vincent Patterson
Robert Campbell	Robert Miller
Samuel Campbell	Patrick Parke
John Gordon	Samuel Church
Alexander Gordon	Adam Kasson
Ebenezer Dow	William Kasson
John Keigwin	David Hopkins
William Hamilton	Charles Campbell
Robert Hopkin	Nath. French
John Smith	John Gibson
Daniel Dill	James Hopkins
Thomas Welch	John Parke
Jacob Bacon	Robert Parke
Daniel Cass	William Rogers
John Dorrance	John Gallup

—Larned's Windham County, Conn., Vol. 1, p. 250.

In 1750 this opposition became aroused, but again subsided, and their pastor was allowed to serve until March 5, 1771, when he was dismissed. Dorrance died November 12, 1775, at the age of ninety, leaving a large family. The first members of the church were asked to subscribe to the Westminster Confession of Faith. The English settlers held aloof, but the Scotch friends of Mr. Dorrance very generally signed. One might properly ask whether Dorrance had been long enough in Ireland to gather a following, or whether the Voluntown settlers came from Scotland. Since he was accepted by the Presbytery of Coleraine it seems probable that he came there to live, and finding many bent on migration joined in their well matured plans.[1]

Two of the earliest Scotch Irish ministers in western Massachusetts, where Presbyterian influences grew rapidly, were the Rev. John Harvey and the Rev. Robert Abercrombie. Harvey was ordained at Palmer, then known as "The Elbows," June 5, 1734, and resigned in 1747, when he removed to Blandford to be with his Scotch Irish friends in that settlement.

The Rev. Robert Abercrombie came to Boston late in 1740 with testimonials from the Presbytery of Kirkcaldy in Scotland, and from the Rev. Mr. Wilson of Perth. He settled in Pelham in 1744 and after a useful but somewhat troubled career died during the Revolutionary period.

Of the many ministers who served the Maine coast settlers several deserve notice. The Rev. William Cornwall who spent the winter of 1718–19 at Falmouth, and the Rev. James Woodside, an early minister at Brunswick, have both been mentioned. Little is known at present of the Rev. Hugh Campbell, Master of Arts at Edinburgh in 1714, who spent a year at Scarboro, Maine, in 1720, and was followed by the Rev. Hugh Henry in June, 1722. The Rev. Robert Rutherford, perhaps a student at Glasgow in 1708, was ordained at Ahma-Carte March 23, 1714, came over with the Dunbar migration in 1729, and preached at Bristol, Nobleboro, and Boothbay in Maine. He was minister at Brunswick from about 1735 to 1742, and died at Thomaston October 18, 1756, aged 68. The Rev. Robert Dunlap of Brunswick, Maine, was born in County Antrim, Ireland, in August, 1715. He studied at the University of Edinburgh, received his Master of Arts degree about 1734, and embarked for America in the spring of 1736. He was wrecked on the Isle of Sable and landed at the Isle of Canso. In December, 1746, Brunswick voted to invite Mr. Dunlap to preach on probation. He was ordained at the Protestant French Church in Boston the next year, and preached at Brunswick until October, 1760. He died June 26, 1776. The Rev. William McClanethan of Georgetown, Maine, was employed to preach for several years, beginning in 1734, but having no settlement. He moved to Blandford, Massachusetts, in 1744. The Rev. Alexander Boyd of New-Castle, Maine, labored there first in 1754. The presence of many Congregationalists raised dissention soon after, and he was removed in 1758. He had studied divinity at Glasgow, and being approved by the Boston presbytery in 1749 he preached at Georgetown, Maine, and elsewhere on the Kennebec for a year or two.[1]

In looking back over this rather cursory survey of the Ulster clergy we find that the migration of 1718–20 did not noticeably injure the Presbyterian ministry in Ireland where the Churches were well organized, and the leaders as a whole intelligent, prosperous and reasonably free from tyranny of law. If it had any effect it was upon the growing tide in later years. Men like McGregor and Homes represented a worthy standard, and their example must have influenced many in Ulster. A few, coming without proper credentials, or under a cloud, were less worthy of favor, but they had little effect upon public opinion. Other considerations often prejudiced the native clergymen and laymen.

The New England people after a century out of

---

[1] Jonathan Greenleaf's Ecclesiastical Sketches, pp. 77–79. The Rev. John Murray of Boothbay, Maine, first began a brilliant ministry there in 1763, a period rather too late to have influenced events described in these pages. His early life was less to his credit, and President Stiles of Yale devoted much space in his Diary to a review of Murray's sins.

England were still, as Professor Wendell has said, essentially Elizabethan; their speech and their habits, their polity and their ideals could not be in harmony with Scotch character developed on Irish soil, for the Scotch Irish were of the Hanoverian age. Where the early settlers were in a minority they tolerated a Presbyterian minister, or even came to love him; but Presbyterianism did not thrive in New England, where the English stock and the Congregational polity were all-powerful.

VII

AGHADOWEY AND THE SESSION BOOK

The Presbyterian records of Ulster will in good time yield a great store of information, of interest alike to the student of religion and genealogy. The official minutes of the Synod of Ulster are in print and have been invaluable in the preparation of these pages. But the records of the smaller organization, the presbytery, and the accounts of local congregations have never been published. These, when gathered together and made accessible to the student, will reveal, with a wealth of detail, the incidents of village life in Protestant Ireland at a period when out of almost every family group some member crossed the ocean to seek his fortune in America.

The records of the Presbytery of Coleraine, if they survive, will one day throw light on the migration to America. The most important town in certain respects of all those in the Presbytery was Aghadowey, the home of the Rev. James McGregor. In his day the people were, many of them, very poor. Today smoke curls from the same gable-end chimneys to tell of a more contented life within the ancient walls. The dark thatch of the cottages is in picturesque contrast to their white walls, and the white gates mark openings in the long, thrifty hedges. Sometimes bounds of field stone take the place of hedges; and there are fine trees arching over excellent roads. An American, looking at the eager

WALL AND IRON GATES ENCLOSING THE SITE OF THE
REV. JAMES MCGREGOR'S MEETING HOUSE

The present Presbyterian Church in the Distance

young faces that crowd the cabin doorway, might ask if a torrent of rain must not send its flood over the slightly raised threshold onto the stone floor within. But there each generation has kept a fire upon the hearth and broth in the kettle. And are not these the best answers to any doubting traveller?

The importance of Aghadowey and the Rev. James McGregor in the history of Scotch Irish emigration gives prominence to the Aghadowey Session Book, recently presented by the Misses Thompson of Cullycapple, Aghadowey, to the Presbyterian Historical Society of Ireland, and preserved at Belfast. This long ledger-like book preserves the records from the end of 1702 to the year 1733, covering the ministry of McGregor and the larger part of the troubled non-subscribing career of the Rev. John Elder. McGregor acted as clerk from 1704 to the time of his departure. He was quartered with one of the elders, and had a protracted struggle to obtain from his poor flock a separate roof for his increasing family and bread for their maintenance.

The twenty-first session, and the first to be noticed in this book of records, was held December 1, 1702, with these members: "Mr. James McGregore, David Miller, Hugh Reed, John Shirila [Shirley], Daniel McRelis, Robert Archbold, Mosses Dillape [Dunlap], Arthur Bapti, David Cargill, and Hugh Kennedy." Dunlap and Cargill were absent. The next entry reads:

"Directions from ⎰   A letter from the presbtry to
    ye Presbtry   ⎱ be comunicated concerning the
payment of steipends & a f[arm] & lodgings to our minister this session apoin[ts] the former colectors

to use there u[tmost] diligence to gett in the Re-
mainders of the steipends & Resolves upon another
Method for the Holintyde steipends & that this allso
to [be] mannaged wt all diligence. As to the farm
they promise to use there endeavours to pro[cure]
a farm as soone as possible & that they [are] agreed
that his Quarters be where formerly."

More members of the session were needed, and the
following who were "judged fitt for the work" were
warned to be present: "John Given, Thomas Willson, John Shirila, Juny^r, John Browstr [Brewster],
John Buy [Boyce?], John Thomson, John Gold [or
Gould], Thomas Nickel, and Hugh Hendry [or
Henry]."

At the twenty-second session, held January 26,
1702-3 "at the little house," the list of grants to the
poor seems to justify a remark in Mr. J. W. Kerno-
han's description of the manuscript, written for the
December number (1909) of the *Irish Presbyterian*.
"At one point," he says, "a wail is uttered by the
Session about the extraordinary number of poor, for
at every meeting there was a regular distribution of
charity." The records state that grants were made
to

	S. D.
James Boyd for burial of daughter	1-6
Grany OCahan	1-6
Jenet Brown	8

THE VILLAGE ROAD EAST OF MCGREGOR'S MEETING HOUSE

This part of Aghadowey is called Ardreagh

	S. D.
William Anderson	6
Robert Alison	3–0
John Gillmore	1–0
Nealy O Cahan	1–0
Jean Kearns	8
Margaret Miller	8
	10–6

To raise the money needed for these benefactions required collectors for each quarter, "North, South, East and West." Those appointed were Kennedy, Cargill, Miller, Archbold, Nickel, Dunlap, Henry, William Wallace and Robert Hunter.

At the Session held December 19, 1715, the following grants were recorded:

Silvanus Brooks	1–6
Marth McLevenny	1–0
Eliz Murch^n	1–0
George McFarland	1–0
Jen^t McElchiner	1–0
Will. Bouie	1–6
Jas. Gilmor	8
Hugh Millar	1–0
Isab. Porter	1–6
Alice Higins	8
Hellen Gilmor	1–0

The records which cover the period of Mr. McGregor's ministry throw many side lights on social life. Complaint was made that Captain Hugh Blair, who moved into town in 1703–4, did not present a certificate of his membership elsewhere. He came to occupy, perhaps, the famous Aghadowey or Blair's House which stood near the church. Dr. Hugh S. Morrison, in a letter dated December 25, 1909, speaks of a visit to this house the day before, of its modern stone finish with bow windows, and its walls in parts six feet thick, showing marks of port holes which have been filled up. In the garret are two large chests or "arks," lined with tin, and bound with primitive wrought iron bands and hinges. Here meal was stored, perhaps for the defenders of Derry.

Lapses from the standards imposed by social life are the source of many entries in the records. In 1702–3 Mary Clark was ordered to appear publicly before the Congregation to confess her too free conduct with James Cochran, a soldier in the year 1689.

At the twenty-fourth session, in 1704, the old adage "the better the day the better the deed" seems to have been disregarded: "It haveing been evident to this session that John Boyd did Joyn in company wt David Lawson to bring away Mr William Hustown's daughter unknown to her parrents upon the sabath day in order to be Maryed to the said Lawson & being very Active in this Affair upon the sabath day, this being a general offence to this

session and to all good people, this session apoints
Hugh Hendry to cite John Boyd to our next session,
the foresd Lawson not receeding in this congregation we cannot cite him.''

During the spring of the year 1715 Hugh Montgomery, the same Hugh who came to New England,
was paying his court to Miss Jane Cargill, whose sis-
ters, Mrs. McGregor of Aghadowey, Mrs. Gregg of
Macosquin, and Mrs. McKeen of Ballymoney (as-
suming that they all were married at this time)
formed an influential family circle. Perhaps Hugh
found some difficulty in getting within this circle. At
any rate, he and Miss Jane got beyond the circle's
outer bound and found themselves in far off Ballymena. There they were married on the 22d of May,
not by a minister but by the faith's arch enemy
Robert Donald, ''curate of Bellymenoch.'' All of
which is sworn to by John Freeland and William
Hodge, as if Mr. Donald's certificate was not evidence enough. The records state that Hugh ''ac-
knowledgth the disorder of his marriage & profess-
eth his sorrow for it,'' glad we may be sure that this
confession was permitted to be made before the Session instead of to the Congregation.

Others mentioned the same year were Thomas
Turner and Marion Hunter, and also Hugh Tor-
rence.

Mr. McGregor's last appearance at a Session was
on April 11, 1718. The next meeting was held April

RESIDENCE OF DR. HUGH S. MORRISON AT AGHADOWEY, IRELAND

29, 1719, when the business referred altogether to settlement of the accounts of the Congregation, showing a balance of 1s. 0d. remaining in David Millar's hands. "This is in his hand when all the Accounts are settled since our Minist. Left us

as wittnes

Mat Clerk."

The village street in Aghadowey is now called Ardreagh. Near it there is a tall chimney of a bleaching green. The thatched cottages along the road were built between 1690 and 1700, yet they are

tidy and comfortable, and are still occupied by the
heirs of the Scotch Irish who did not cross the Atlantic.   There are in Aghadowey several country
mansions, including the residence of Dr. Hugh S.

LIZARD MANOR, AGHADOWEY
Home of Charles E. S. Stronge, Esq., J. P., D. L.
(From a photograph by Miss Stronge)

Morrison, near Two Bridges, and the seat of Charles
E. S. Stronge, Esq., known as Lizard Manor, once
the Manor House of the Worshipful Company of
Ironmongers, of London.

VIII

THE ARRIVAL OF "FIVE SHIPS" IN AUGUST, 1718

It would not be difficult to picture to ourselves the excitement produced by the preparations of those who contemplated removing to America. Families were closely allied in Ulster, and the affairs of each one interested a wide circle. The itinerant weaver brought from Dublin tales of the New World, more or less accurate accounts of the life across the Atlantic, derived from ship captains, or even from American students at the University there. The frequent assignment of ministers for temporary service in other parishes than their own was a means of carrying the news. A few years after Boyd set forth Archbishop Boulter said that the desire for emigration had gone through Ulster like a fever; and we may well believe that letters from Cotton Mather, William Homes and Thomas Craighead had great influence.

There was much to be done by a family before removal. A supply of food, clothing and bedding was necessary; and the house-hold goods had to be packed for the long voyage. The land, the farm animals and the heavier tools must be sold. These were busy days, and the partings must have been hard for all, unless friends hoped to follow soon. In leaving their Churches the emigrants did not fail to procure testimonials of good standing to be used in forming fresh religious ties in New England. We find mention of these testimonials at Rutland, at Needham, Middleboro and elsewhere, but rarely the actual text. That brought over by William Caldwell, one of the defenders of Londonderry, was lost only a few years ago. It was written on parchment the size of a half sheet of note paper:[1]

"The bearer, William Caldwell, his wife Sarah Morrison, with his children, being designed to go to New England in America—These are therefore to testifie they leave us without scandal, lived with us soberly and inoffensively, and may be admitted to Church priviledges. Given at Dunboe Aprile 9, 1718, by   Jas. Woodside, Jr. *Minister*."[2]

Parker, in his History of Londonderry, says that the pioneers "embarked in five ships for Boston, and arrived there August 4, 1718." This statement has been repeated wherever the Scotch Irish have been mentioned, but with no added information since Parker's day. In one place only can the names of the ships be found, and it is not a little strange that no student of the subject up to this time has had the

---

[1] Mr. Edmund M. Barton obtained these facts from Mrs. Charles E. Stevens, daughter of Seth Caldwell of Barre.

[2] Barre Anniversary, 1874, p. 205. The "Jr." is omitted hereafter.

curiosity to bring these names to light. They are to many thousands of people as important as the Mayflower and the Speedwell are to those of pilgrim descent. Only one newspaper was being issued in North America in 1718, and of the files for July, August and September but one copy of each issue is known to exist. At the rooms of the Massachusetts Historical Society I examined these papers, and here print every known detail regarding arrivals from Ireland at the port of Boston for these three months.

It is our phenomenal good fortune that at this precise moment a gentleman in Boston was watching each ship as it discharged its passengers, and was writing his impressions to Governor Winthrop of Connecticut. The Scotch Irish had no William Bradford nor John Winthrop to chronicle their transplanting, but the *Boston News-Letter* and Thomas Lechmere's letters give us a not unworthy picture of the arrival nearly two centuries ago. To these sources let us add the diary of Cotton Mather, the patron of the "poor Scotch."

The *News-Letter* for July 21–28 mentions the arrival from Ireland of the ship "William and Mary," James Montgomery, master; the issue for August 25–September 1 states that she had cleared for Dublin.

The "William and Mary" brought over the Rev. William Boyd of Macosquin, the leader of the movement; and Cotton Mather writes July 25th: "A minister arrived from *Ireland,* wth Instructions to enquire after ye circumstances of this countrey[1] in order to ye coming of many more, gives me an opportunity for many services."

The next day Mather says:

"The many Families arriving from Ireland, will afford me many opportunities, for kindness to ye Indigent." Mather here uses "arriving" to mean "about to arrive," having found through conversation with Mr. Boyd that many settlers were on their way from Ireland.

The first of the Scotch-Irish emigrant ships is referred to in the *News-Letter* of July 28–August 4 as from Londonderry, John Wilson, master, but the ship's name is not given. She probably came in on the 28th, for Lechmere, having been instructed by his brother-in-law Winthrop to find a suitable miller among incoming passengers, wrote on the 28th at "Eleven of ye Clock at night": "Shipps are comeing in hourly, but no news; Irish familys enough; above 200 souls are come in allready, & many now hourly expected; so that I wish you were here; they are none to be sold, have all paid their passages sterl[s] in Ireland; they come upon some encouragement to settle upon some unimproved Lands, upon what other Towns I know not." . . .

---

[1] This seems to disprove the theory referred to by Professor Perry that Boyd "stayed the summer in Boston."

The next issue of the *News-Letter* seems to refer to this arrival in the following advertisement: "Sundry Boys times for Years by Indentures, young Women and Girls by the Year, portable Linnen, Woolen and Beef to be disposed of by Mr. *William Wilson* at his Warehouse in Merchants Row, Boston."

It may seem difficult to harmonize the varying views of Mather and Lechmere as to the standing of these emigrants, but Lechmere was interested in the better class, men with trades who had left remunerative occupations to come to New England, and they of course paid their passage-money before their arrival here. In the same ships came kinsmen who had no property and could cross the ocean only by agreeing to work out their passage-money. The passengers of this kind probably became the Worcester Colony. And with them were a few ignorant adventurers who came over as indentured servants to try their fortunes; in these Mather as a minister felt a kindly interest. But there is evidence that in several of the ships of July and August there were many prosperous, religious families from the counties of Londonderry and Antrim, influenced to migrate by Boyd, McGregor, McKeen, Gregg and other leaders.

The second emigrant ship reached Boston on the 4th of August, the traditional date of arrival among the descendants of the settlers of the New Hampshire Londonderry. The vessel is referred to in the *News-Letter* of August 4–11 as the brigantine "Robert," James Ferguson, master, "from Glasgow and Belfast in Ireland." The same day Lechmere, writing to Winthrop for himself and his wife Ann, says: "I have this day according [to] yor directions made Enquiry after a miller, & a Vessel comeing in this day from Scottland, I find there is a young fellow of about 24 years of age. . . . This day are likewise Severall Vessells come in from all Parts, but no News; I am of Opinion all the north of Irland will be over here in a little time, here being another Vessell y^t is a Third, with Irish familys come in, & 5 more, as they say, expected, & if their report be true, as I this day heard, if the Encouragem^{tt} given to these be liked at Irland; 20 ministers with their congregations in generall will come over in Spring; I wish their comeing so over do not prove fatall in the End." Lechmere's letter settles the point that the ship which arrived about the 25th with Mr. Boyd did not bring Scotch emigrants. We have then:

July 28th? ———, John Wilson, from Londonderry.

August 4th. *Robert,* James Ferguson, from Glasgow and Belfast.

August 4th. *William,* Archibald Hunter, from Coleraine.

The third Scotch Irish emigrant ship, the "William," set sail from Coleraine, the heart of the district from which most of the early settlers came. The *News-Letter* of August 4–11 mentions the ship "William," Archibald Hunter, from Coleraine; she cleared for Ireland the last week in August. Lechmere refers to her as the third ship with Irish families that had arrived, and states that she and the "Robert" entered on the same day.

Cotton Mather's dream of a great migration from Protestant Ireland was coming true. On the 7th of August he writes: "But what shall be done for the great Numbers of people, that are transporting themselves thither from ye North of Ireland:—Much may be done for ye Kingdom of God in these parts of ye world, by this Transportation." A month later, September 13th, he says: "Among ye Families arrived from Ireland, I find many & wondrous objects for my compassions. Among other methods of helping ym, I would enclose a sum of money wth a Nameless Letter, unto one of their ministers to be distributed among ym."

Although these emigrants were viewed with distrust by most New Englanders, the two chief figures in Boston at this time, Mather and Samuel Sewall, showed their ministers marked courtesy. On the 9th of August, Sewall writes in his diary that at seven "Mr. Macgregor and Mr. Boyd dine with me and my Son J. S. and James Clark. Gave the Scots Ministers each of them one of my Proposals."

Meanwhile Winthrop wrote from Connecticut that

THE WINTHROP MILL AT NEW LONDON

the miller whom Lechmere had selected was too expensive and hinted that his brother-in-law had been overreached. Lechmere was an improvident aristocrat, brother to Lord Lechmere, and Winthrop had reason at this time and later on to question the judgment of this husband of his sister. Lechmere replied rather hotly, and his estimate of the Scotch Irish, while not entirely reliable under these circumstances, is worthy of record. The letter is dated at Boston August 11, 1718, and reads: "As to ye Miller, the price is really as you are informed & whoever tells you that Servants are cheaper now then they were, it is a very gross mistake, & give me leave to tell you your Informer has given you a very wrong information about ye cheapness thereof, for never were they dearer then now, there being such demand for them, & likewise pray tell him he is much out of the way to think that these Irish are Servants, they are generally men of Estates, & are come over hither for no other reason but upon Encouragement sent from hence upon notice given y^m they should have so many acres of Land given them gratis to settle our ffrontiers as a barrier against ye Indians; therefore ye notion given you hereof is absolutely groundless; the price of the Miller as proposed was 20£ & did not think of selling his time under sd sum, but since I wrote you he tells me would not stand with me for 20 or 30 £—thinking I should pay him ready money for him. It is now too late to think any thing farther

of him. Many inquireing after him, & he was kept
for yor answer, which I think is somewhat darke, but
lett that be what it will, could I advance so much
bank stock, w^h is very low, I should still endeav^r to
gett him, & so it being out of my power I must wholly
desist from any such thought. I know yor necessity
is such I would willingly do anything for y^r interest
was I capable. . . .

Yo^r Very Affect^e Bro & Servt

Thos Lechmere

I should be glad you would send my Gunn down by
some body or other. These confounded Irish will
eat us all up provisions being most extravagantly
dear & scarce of all sorts."

The *News-Letter* which notices the arrival of the
ship "William" mentions also the ship "Mary
Anne," Andrew Watt, master, from Dublin; she
cleared about a fortnight later for Great Britain.[1]

It is doubtful if the "Mary Anne" brought any
Scotch Protestants from Dublin as part of the Bann
Valley company. But the emigrants on the other
ships beheld what must have been an unprecedented

---

[1] The same issue of the *News-Letter* has this advertisement:
"Newly Imported and to be disposed of at reasonable Rates by
Messieurs *Tho Steel* and *Geo Bethune*, at their Warehouse in
Merchants Row, Boston, sundry European Goods, *viz* Iron, Cord-
age, Broadcloths, Stuffs, Linnens and Madera Wines: Also
Servants bound by Indenture, some four and some for five Years
to be seen on board the 'Mary Anne' *Andrew Watt* Commander
now at Anchor near the end of the Long Wharff, Boston."

sight in Boston harbor, five ships from Ireland lying at anchor at the same time, the "William and Mary," the ship of the unknown name, the "Robert," the "William" and the "Mary Anne." This doubtless made a deep and lasting impression upon minds alert to every new sight and thought as the emigrants were borne slowly up the beautiful bay.

A month later a second ship from Dublin, the "Dolphin," John Mackay, master, came in. The *News-Letter* which notices her arrival has this to say of her cargo:

"Just arrived the Pink 'Dolphin' *John Mackay,* Master, with Servants, Boys, Tradesmen, Husbandmen, and Maids, to be disposed of by Mr *John Walker,* at his Warehouse at the lower end of Woodmansy Wharff in Merchants Row, or at Mr *Benjamin Walker's* House over against the Town House, Boston."

There were few if any Scotch Irish on the "Dolphin," but on the first of September a fourth emigrant ship arrived, the "Maccallum," James Law, master, from Londonderry. Lechmere states that she brought "20 odd familys," and among the passengers was probably a Scotch schoolmaster to whom Mather refers September 6th as here from Ireland and wanting employment. From Lechmere's letter it may be questioned whether the company on the "Maccallum" was closely allied with those on the ships from Belfast and Coleraine. He writes: "This day a Ship arrived from Irland wth 20 odd familys; they were first bound for N London but haveing a long Passage the M^{rs} perswaded y^{m} to putt in here, so the poor Creatures are left in ye Lurch." From the statement that their destination was not that of the other emigrants although they must have embarked at about the same time, it would seem that they had other plans in view, and had not come under the immediate influence of Boyd and McGregor. This company probably came with the Rev. James Woodside of Garvagh, in the Bann Valley.

The bargaining which went on for a week between Captain Law of the "Maccallum" and Captain Robert Temple, later a famous colonizer in Maine, came to naught. Temple could not persuade Law and his company to continue their voyage to Connecticut, and on the eighth of September the "Maccallum" sailed out of Boston harbor, for the territory owned by the Gentlemen Proprietors of Eastern Lands, at the mouth of the Kennebec River. Law then perhaps satisfied his desire to take on a load of staves at or near Kittery on the Piscataqua and returned to Boston by October 7th, when he appeared in court to give surety for several of his passengers. He cleared for Londonderry the first week in December, 1718.

Lechmere's letter describing the affair is so good an account of the trials of the bewildered and nearly helpless emigrants that I continue the quotation begun above: . . . "Pray if any thereof should still have any inclination to come yor way to settle in Connecticut, I should be glad. You would aggree to their Settling about Tantiusques, w^h in my Opinion is ye best place, & M^r. Temple is doeing what he can still to perswade ye M^r. to proceed for y^r place, he intends to load Bolts & Staves home for Ireland & when I saw him among other talke I assured him he might load cheaper wth you then at Piscataqua; how sd M^r. Temple will worke on him I know not. Y^e method they go in wth ye Irish is they sell y^m so many Acres of Land for 12^d ye acre & allow y^m time to pay y^t in. I know Land is more Valuable wth you, & therefore I am afraid 'twill be ye more difficult to aggree with y^m. Y^e only thing I can think off is y^r Quantity you allow y^m must be the less, you are the best judge so I leave it wholly to you, tho at same time should be glad of yr Thought thereof, & assure you y^{tt} in my opinion it would be greatly for yr Interest."

Lechmere's next letter shows Temple working to induce the company to settle at Merrymeeting Bay at the mouth of the Androscoggin. In this he was successful, and it is possible that the experience first turned his mind seriously to the transportation of Ulstermen to these Eastern lands. During the next two years several ships came over under his management with settlers for the Kennebec. The letter follows:

"Boston Sept[r] 8th 1718.

"As to y[e] Irish, I have acquainted Mr. Temple with what you write, he seem's not willing they should take up wth y[tt] proposall you mention; y[e] Gent. Propriet.[rs] of ye Eastern Lands hearing, I was talkeing with y[m] about Settling some of them have (as I hear) made new proposalls to them wherupon they have resolved with sd Mr Temple to visitt said Lands whither they are bound this afternoon; what they will conclude on I know not."

The deposition of David Dunning of Brunswick[1] in 1767 states that "on or about the year 1718 he came first to Boston in the same vessel with Andrew McFadden and wife (now a widow); soon after we came in the same vessel down together to the eastern country, and I have lived in Brunswick ever since 1718." Jane McFadden stated that they moved down to the Kennebec River and up Merrymeeting Bay to a place called Cathance (now Bowdoinham). Here we seem to trace the company which came over in the "Maccallum;" if the inference is correct this company left a record on Cyprian Southack's map of 1720 as "the Irish new settlement." McFadden came from Garvagh in the Bann Valley, and was probably of the Rev. James Woodside's company. We should expect all emigrants from the Bann to be followers of the Rev. William Boyd, who had

---

[1] New England Historical and Genealogical Register, Vol. 39, p. 184.

come out to Governor Shute as their accredited agent, but it is possible that Boyd and Woodside were not in sympathy, since Woodside's company intended to settle in New London — a town never mentioned by Boyd or McGregor.[1]

The *News-Letter* for September 22-29, 1718, prints a report that a vessel had arrived at Casco Bay from Ireland, with several passengers on board, and a minister. This report refers no doubt to this company which sailed out of Boston harbor on September 8th.

The followers of McGregor and James McKeen, also from the Bann Valley, must have sailed later in the season, for their ship upon arriving at Casco Bay was frozen in. Major Samuel Gregg in his reminiscences says that his grandfather James Gregg, a bleacher of linen cloth, in the Rev. Mr. Boyd's parish of Macosquin, near Coleraine, landed at Boston August 4th "with several other passengers that came in other ships. The ship that they [Gregg's immediate neighbors] came in as passengers went down East and spent the winter at Casco which is now called Portland."

This incident is so well established in the traditional history of the Londonderry Scotch-Irish— it accords so well with the known facts—that we may accept the statement that Gregg and his friends who

---

[1] It is just possible that Lechmere was misinformed and that the "Maccallum" never intended to go to New London.

went to Casco Bay sailed in the ship in which they
had crossed the ocean. These men under the immediate leadership of the Rev. James McGregor came
from Coleraine and neighboring towns in the Bann
Valley, and the next spring (1719) they founded
Nutfield, now Londonderry, New Hampshire. It
would seem to be a reasonable assumption that the
Nutfield colony, including the few who remained at
Casco Bay, had crossed the sea on the ship "William," which left Coleraine in April or May, or on
the brigantine "Robert" from Belfast, a more at-
tractive port of departure, or in both ships. The
"William" is reported as "cleared" in the *News-
Letter* for August 25–September 1 and as "outward
bound" September 15–22. She seems to have returned to Ireland.

Ferguson, captain of the "Robert," was in town
October 7th to attend court; and this suggests that
he may have lain in the outer harbor during the time
intervening between his clearing from Boston and
his attendance at court. With him on the voyage
from Ireland came John Armstrong, his wife and
five children, who were unable to convince the authorities in Boston that they were self-supporting.
Captain Ferguson was ordered before the Court of
General Sessions of the Peace to answer "for bringing in his vessell and landing in this Town John
Armstrong, his wife and five children who cannot
give Security to Indemnify the Town as the Law

BELFAST, ON THE LAGAN, 1793

requires." Ferguson's explanation that three of
the children were servants by indenture did not entirely satisfy the Court, and it was "Ordered that
the s^d fferguson carry the s^d Armstrong wife & two
youngest Children out of the Province or Indemnify
the Town." Finally the Captain and William Wilson, at whose wharf they probably landed, became
sureties in £100 each that the Armstrong family,
would not come back upon the town for support.[1] If
this is the same John Armstrong who later in the
year heads a petition from the Scotch Irish settlers at Falmouth, this is very good evidence that
he, who certainly came over from Belfast in the
brigantine "Robert," soon after went in her to
Casco Bay with the little company from the Bann
Valley. On the whole this seems probable, and it
would follow that the Rev. James McGregor and his
well-to-do connection, the Greggs, McKeens and
others who according to Major Gregg crossed the
ocean in the ship which afterward carried them to
Casco Bay, journeyed a few miles to Belfast to take
passage in the "Robert," while the families in more
moderate condition, with the heavier freight, came
down the Bann from Coleraine in the larger ship, the
"William."

We get some impression of the appearance of
these ships from the view of Boston drawn by Wil-

---

[1] Records Court of General Sessions of the Peace, Suffolk County,
October 7, 1718.

liam Burgis in 1722 and commonly called Price's
View. Lying off Boston are many forms of craft,
some at anchor and others bending to a good breeze.
In the foreground are two stately vessels, one like
the "William," a ship with full body, a blunt bow
and high stern, three masts and a wealth of rigging;

A BRIGANTINE OF 1718

another like the "Robert," with more rounding bow
and stern, a foremast square rigged like those of the
ship, but with the main mast fore-and-aft rigged like
a sloop. The "Robert" we think of as a herma-
phrodite brig, but the English sailor of old would
have called her a brigantine, as she was classed by
the *News-Letter*.

It requires some effort to realize that a great part

of our population owes its place on this side the
Atlantic to the slow, clumsy but rather impressive
ships of the types to be seen in the drawing by Burgis. Nor do we easily comprehend the weariness of
the voyage or even its hazard. The Pirate and the
God of Storms shared an annual harvest of lives
and fortunes. Let us take two incidents in a single
year. The ship "Friends Goodwill" left Larne on
the coast of Antrim about the first of May in the
year 1717. Meeting constant head winds the ship
made very poor progress, and food ran so low that
the fifty-two persons on board came to want. Captain Gooding or Goodwin fortunately fell in with
another vessel and obtained provisions. Continual
bad weather brought further delay, and hunger
again threatened. Short allowance of water, bread,
and meat brought only a temporary reprieve from
starvation, and the crew soon were set to catching
dolphins and sharks which a "good Providence"
placed in their path. Rains came and the water was
gathered from the decks to quench the thirst. When
May, June and July, months of constant anxiety, had
passed August brought so great a storm that the
ship lay like a thing deserted, her decks awash, her
sailors weak and exhausted. With September the
sun shone, but their hunger increased, and in des-
peration they began to speak of drawing lots to decide whom should be eaten first. The Captain however now held out hope of land and about the sec-

ond week of September the "Friends Goodwill"
crept up Boston harbor with only one of her company dead.[1]

A pirate could hardly do greater damage. Captain Codd who came into Philadelphia from Dublin
in October with one hundred and fifty passengers,
many of them servants, reported having been taken
off the Capes by Teach of "the Pirate sloop Revenge
of 12 Guns and 150 men." Teach took two snows;
from one he threw overboard a great load of staves
and crowded her with the passengers and crews of
subsequent captures; from the other he cast a load
of grain and turned her into a pirate ship. Out of a
sloop bound from Madeira Teach took twenty-seven
pipes of wine, cut down her masts, and left her to
drift. From another he took two casks and sank her.
Other captures were made before Codd was permitted to complete his voyage. During this enforced
delay the victims saw much of Captain Bennet who
had relinquished the command of the "Revenge" to
Teach on account of his slow recovery from wounds
received in a recent fight with a Spanish Man of
War. Bennet took a walk in his "morning gown"
after each day's breakfast, and then devoted his
time to study, surrounded by his books, of which he
had a good library on board. The pirate, with his

---

[1] *News-Letter*, September 9–16, 1717; November 25–December 2.
The *New England Weekly Journal*, November 10, 1729, describes
another voyage of even greater hardships.

guns and his books, was more than the average mer-
chantman could hope to resist. He added terror to
the long voyage of the emigrant from Ireland.[1]

---

[1] *News-Letter*, November 4–11, 1717. The researches made by
Mr. Edwin M. Bacon and Mr. John H. Edmonds have very gen-
erously been placed at my disposal in preparing this chapter.

IX

THE WINTER OF 1718–19 IN BOSTON

In July and August, 1718, from five to seven hundred Protestant immigrants from Ireland entered the port of Boston. Several followers of the Rev. Mr. McGregor set out early in the autumn for Andover where they spent the winter. Others as we have seen went to Casco Bay and the Kennebec River.

Family ties no doubt drew some into the neighboring towns, although all trace of these influences have been lost.

Among the early emigrants who came probably from the north of Ireland many were scattered through towns not known thereafter as distinctly Scotch Irish settlements. Where we find one family others are almost certainly to be found, disguised it may be by an English name. The following names are given as an indication of the wide distribution of the emigrants. Some families are merely known to be Scotch, others are Presbyterians who brought their babies to the Rev. Mr. Moorhead in Boston for baptism, while in still other instances the home town in Ireland has been or can be found by reference to

the local church records.[1] James Long was in
Charlestown, John Tom in Cambridge, Thomas
Karr or Carr, John Pike, James Lindsay, James
Taggart and John Brownlie in Roxbury, Robert
Burns and James Aull in Medford, James Moor in
Chelsea, Jeremiah Smith and John Longhead in
Milton, Archibald Thompson and Thomas Henry in
Bridgewater, and John Kennedy, with Abraham
Hunter, at Braintree. At Concord lived Samuel
Henderson; Robert Wilson was at Malden, Alex-
ander Smith at Billerica, Thomas Little, Charles
Richards, John Moor and James Gordon at Shirley,
Daniel Ritter and Thomas Harkness at Lunenburg,
Thomas Bogle at Sudbury, John McClure at Woburn
and James Wilson at Lexington. Dugall McCombs
was at Western, John McAllister at Westboro, Da-
vid McClure at Brookfield, Andrew McElwain at
Bolton, James Cargill at Mendon, Walter Beath at
Lunenburg and at Boothbay in Maine, William Le-
man at Wiscasset, and Mrs. James at Annapolis.
John Nichols lived at Freetown, John Wood and
James Henry at Providence, and Archibald Mac-
Kaye at Pomfret in Connecticut.

With James Glasford at Leicester was Matthew
Watson who came from Coleraine in Ireland. James
Smith of Needham brought a letter from the church

---

[1] I am indebted to my sons Stanwood and Geoffrey for many
references to Scotch Irish in country towns.

in Ballykelly. At Middleboro[1] was William Stro-
bridge or Strawbridge, from Donagh (also called
Cardonagh), Donegal, where the Rev. Thomas
Strawbridge was minister from 1721 to 1762. At
Lancaster there was a group of immigrants, Robert
and Elizabeth Bratten from the church at Termont
(or Clougherny), Tyrone, Robert Waite from Aghadowey, Jane Macmullin from Dawsonbridge (Castledawson), William and Ellinor White from Dunboe, Margaret Stuart from Bovedy, all in County
Derry, as well as Alexander Scott and his wife
"from Ireland." At Dracut was Thomas Holmes
from Coleraine, with a brother John at Boston.

On the other hand an occasional voyager drifted
back to Boston, perhaps forced from town to town
lest he become a charge upon the rates. Thomas
Crook came in the "Three Anns and Mary," Captain Richards, master, to Casco Bay, and from there
was carried in a fishing sloop to Salem "where he,
being sick, was turned out of Doors from House to
House, till at length he got so far as Lyn, being then
in a perishing condition & could proceed no further
by reason of his Legs being dropsical, that at Lyn
he was put under the Care & Direction of Dr. Brom-
stead."[2]

---

[1] In Middleboro there may have been several Scotch Irish settlers: James Nealson, John McCully, William McFall, Thomas
Pickens, John Montgomery, and an earlier Scotch or Scotch Irishman Alexander Canedy. (Weston's Middleboro, p. 434.)

[2] Massachusetts Resolves, 1719–20, Chapter 21.

The authorities in Boston could not very well warn from town so great a company as that which arrived in 1718, although they shared Mr. Surveyor-General Lechmere's anxiety lest the ''confounded Irish'' eat them out of house and home. The selectmen met August 13th and impowered Mr. John Marion to appear before the Court of General Sessions of the Peace for the county of Suffolk ''to move what he Shall think proper in order to Secure this Town from Charges wch may hapen to accrue or be imposed on them by reason of the Passengers Lately arived here from Ireland or elsewhere.''[1] During the winter many were warned to leave Boston, Thomas Walker, John Rogers, James Blare or Blair, with Elizabeth and Rachel, who had come over from Ireland in August;[2] Anne Hanson who came down from Casco Bay, and Mehitable Lewis, from Piscataqua; Robert Holmes and wife, William Holmes and child, also from Casco Bay; and Alexander McGregory, lately from Ireland with his family; they were all asked to leave or find sureties.

The selectmen could not hope to save the town from charges for the support of those who had brought with them their modest savings, if the price of grain continued to rise.

Before the Scotch Irish arrived the town had authorized the selectmen to expend for grain from time

---

[1] Selectmen's Records, Record Commission Reports, Vol. 13, p. 41.
[2] Suffolk Court Files, No. 12620,

to time as much as they thought best out of the sum of £1500 received from the sale of lands at Blue Hill. In October the following vote was passed by the selectmen to keep down the price of Indian corn: "Voted: that in case any considerable quantity of Indian Corn be imported into this Town before the Shutting in of yᵉ ensuing winter & exposed to Sale, In order to check an Exorbitant demand of yᵉ Sellers thereof:—

"Any four of the Sel. men agreeing may open the Townes Granary and order the Sale of corn at four Shillings & Six pence p. bushel."

On the 18th of December it was voted that "the Granaryes be opened for the Sale of Indian Corn on Fryday & Saterday next. vizᵗ the South granary on Fryday, and the North Granary on Satterday, and on the next week following on Tuesday at the South and on Fryday at the North, and Mr. Galpine is directed to Sell out to the Inhabitᵗˢ of this Town not exceeding one bushel to each buyer, at five Shillings p bushel, and he is directed to put up before hand one bushel in each of yᵉ Townes Baggs, and first receive each p'sons money and then Shift the Corn into their respective baggs, the hours appointed to attend the Same is from nine to twelve in the fore noon and from two to four in the after noon & he is to Imploy yᵉ Cryer to cry at that price each buyer to bring good bill ready changed & to cry thrᵒ the Town on thursday."

The need of wheat still pressing, the selectmen on December 19th agreed with the Hon. Jonathan Belcher for ten thousand pounds at forty shillings per hundred. The matter had become of so much importance that the Governor and Council advised the town to purchase grain in Connecticut if necessary in order to avoid distress. In January eight thousand pounds had been purchased. At the March town meeting, 1719, the inhabitants decided to lay out the entire sum of £1500 in grain to carry them through the spring months, and a committee of seven was appointed "to consult together for the Releife of This Town under their present distresses."

Through the kindness of Mr. Charles P. Greenough I have had access to the account kept by David Stoddard of his purchases in Boston during the years 1717, 1718 and 1719. Mr. Stoddard paid six shillings per bushel for wheat in the spring of 1717, and three shillings for Indian corn. In the spring of 1719, with the Scotch Irish in Boston, wheat had nearly doubled in price, selling for ten shillings per bushel, while corn which had brought three now brought five shillings. A study of the prices of small fruits and vegetables shows no material change due to the presence of the Scotch Irish.

PRICES.

BEFORE ARRIVAL.	AFTER ARRIVAL.
0-0-9 (May 31, 1718) 1 qt. gooseberries	0-0- 9 (May 31, 1719)
0-0-3 (June 25, 1718) 1 qt. currants	0-0- 3 (June 20, 1719)
0-1-0 (July 1, 1718) 1 qt. beans	0-0- 9 (June 27, 1719)
0-0-3 (June 28, 1718) 1 qt. cherries	0-0- 3 (July 13, 1719)

The prices after the arrival of the emigrants in the summer of 1718, and again twelve months later when presumably many had left Boston, were:

PRICES.

Summer of 1718.		Summer of 1719.
0-1-0 (Aug. 19, 1718)	1 cabbage	0-0-10 (Aug. 13, 1719)
0-0-2 (Aug. 27, 1718)	1 qt. Damsons [plums]	0-0- 3 (Aug. 31, 1719)
0-0-6 (Sept. 19, 1718)	1 cabbage	0-0- 4 (Sept. 14, 1719)
0-4-6 (Nov. 4, 1718)	1 bu. carrots	0-5- 0 (Nov. 16, 1719)

There were many taverns in Boston at this time, about half of them managed under the names of women. These became the resort of numbers of idle immigrants, and the members of the Council, Justices, selectmen, and overseers of the poor agreed among themselves in August that for the next eight weeks they would walk the streets by turns at night to suppress disorders, and by their presence show that the land of promise was not to be a land of license.

The winter of 1717–18 in Ireland had been very trying; small-pox, fevers and other afflictions prevailed there and especially in Ulster. We should expect to find further evidence of these conditions in the health of the passengers that left the ports of Ireland in the spring of 1718. As early as the year 1714 the ship "Elizabeth and Kathrin" from Ireland had landed sick persons on Spectacle Island[1] by order of the Government; and again in 1716 the

---

[1] Province Laws, 1714, Chapter 45.

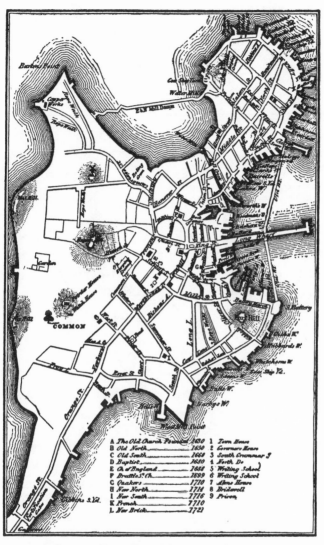

CAPTAIN JOHN BONNER'S MAP OF BOSTON

island was used for the same purpose. In 1717 a
pest house was built, but before its completion some
eighty persons from Ireland were put ashore. In
the year 1718 "seven several companies" were left
on Spectacle Island before June 17th,[1] a fact which
seems puzzling, since arrivals from abroad between
January 1st and June 17th of that year were few;
but the contemporary record is clear and beyond
controversy. Some of these infected companies
must have come from other American ports. A
large ship-load from Ireland was detained in November, 1719.[2] The inference from these facts seems
to be that if any of the immigrants of July and August, 1718, were detained with contagious diseases
they were inconsiderable in number and thus found
no place in the records.

These were busy days in Boston. The batteries
were repaired and the defences across the Neck were
finished. Streets were being paved, projects were on
foot for bringing in coal by sea, the weight and price
of loaves of bread were fixed, schoolmasters were
employed, and provision was made for the reading
of God's word, catechising, and the encouragement
of good spelling.

In so large a place it is not easy to discover the
names of those who arrived from Ireland in 1718
and 1719, and settled down to remain there. It is

---

[1] Province Laws, 1718–19, Chapter 19.
[2] *Ibid*, 1719–20, Chapter 68.

said that the Rev. John Moorhead, who was born
near Belfast, and came to Boston in 1727, was in-
duced to remain in town by the kindly welcome extended to him from resident families that he had
known some years before.[1]

We must remember, however, that Mr. Moorhead
did not arrive until the migration from Ireland had
been growing for several years. The records of
marriages performed in Boston after July, 1718,
show Scotch Irish names, as the following examples
indicate:—

William Blair and Mary Phillips, Oct. 29, 1718.

Cornelius Campbell and Eliza Short, September
17, 1718.

James Duncan and Eliza. Bason, December 16,
1718.

It will be found that the Campbells, Duncans,
Blacks, Bethunes and others came before 1718, and
most of them from Scotland. The following births,
however, may suggest the Scotch-Irish immigration:

Lydia, daughter of William Mackinley and Lydia,
born 12 March, 1718-19.

Lydia, daughter of William Forbish and Sarah,
born 12 March, 1718-19.

William, son of William Doke and Lydia, born 29
April, 1719.

But a careful study of Boston birth and marriage
records for 1718 and 1719 would seem to indicate

---

[1] A. Blaikie's Presbyterian Church in New England, p. 62.

that the immigrants of these years went very generally into the country.   The Boston Scotch Irish came later.

We know little of the feeling towards these Scotch emigrants from Ireland shown by Boston people, although elsewhere they were disliked.   An important incident of the next winter throws some light upon the subject, and for that reason it will be mentioned here.   Benjamin Gray, a bookseller and publisher, offered for sale books on religion, and from time to time published works by Scotch presbyterians.   Naturally then the Rev. William Boyd became a frequent visitor to Gray's shop.   Boyd, as a leader of men, as an able preacher, and as a writer, was for a few months a prominent figure in Boston. At this period he was living in Charlestown at Captain John Long's hotel, or "the great tavern," as it was called.

It happened that Mr. Boyd was in the shop on February 7, 1718-19, a Saturday, talking with friends when Edward Ellis, son of Robert Ellis, a surgeon, entered.   Ellis soon became abusive, and singling out the Rev. Mr. Boyd he said that the Scotch Irish clergyman was an immoral man, and as evidence asserted that Boyd had had improper relations with a maid-servant in Captain Long's employ.   Ellis was at once arrested and his case came before the Court of General Sessions of the Peace for Suffolk County on April 7th.   He was convicted, sentenced to pay twenty pounds, seven shillings, and to find sureties to be bound in twenty five pounds each that he would be of good behavior for six months, and he was ordered also to pay all the costs of the prosecution. The prominence of Ellis is made clear by the fact that the men who came to his assistance as sureties were both well known, Robert Auchmuty, Esquire, and Thomas Phillips, Innholder. Ellis was discharged November 10, 1719.

Over against this incident we may place the following sentence from the Rev. Increase Mather's Preface to Boyd's farewell sermon which was delivered March 19, 1719: "Since his being in New England (as well as before that) by the Exemplary holiness of his Conversation, and the Eminency of his Ministerial Gifts, he has obtained good Report amongst all Good Men."

At the close of the sermon, mentioned above, the Governor invited Mr. Boyd to dine, the company including the Rev. Cotton Mather, the Rev. James Woodside who had ordained Mr. Boyd in Ireland, Samuel Sewall, and a Mr. Stanton.

The Rev. John Moorhead, son of a respected farmer at Newton, near Belfast, county Down, was born there in 1703. He studied at the University of Edinburgh, and, upon his return to Newton, accounts that he heard of New England led him to emigrate to Boston. He arrived in 1727 and soon after undertook services, the people whom he gathered

THE REV. JOHN MOORHEAD,
"Minister of a Church of Presbyterian Strangers in Boston"
(Drawn by John Huybers)

about him calling themselves the "Church of Presbyterian strangers." He was ordained as their
pastor March 30, 1730. Among these people was
John Little, a prosperous gardener, who exhibited
much interest. He had a house on Milk Street, and
in May, 1729, purchased land for a garden at the corner of Long Lane and Bury Street. In Mr. Little's
barn which stood on this land services were held for
several years, the congregation making additions to
the barn and alterations from time to time. Elders
were first elected July 14, 1730, and John Young,
Robert Patton, Samuel McClure,[1] Richard McClure
and Thomas McMullen were chosen to fill this office.
They watched over those who had been baptized,
cared for the sick and needy, and reproved the err-
ing. Mr. Moorhead visited each family, whether in
town or country, once or twice a year to talk with
the parents and catechise children and servants. At
the close of each visit he knelt in prayer with the
family.

In June, 1735, Mr. Little conveyed the barn or
meeting house and land on the north east corner of
Long Lane to a Committee appointed by the Congregation to hold the property in trust. The members
of this Committee were George Glen, a tailor, who
had come from South Carolina in 1719, William

---

[1] Grandfather of the Rev. David McClure, D. D., whose Diary
has been published. David's son and grandson held the same
offices.

Hall a leather-dresser, William Shaw a tailor, and Andrew Knox a mariner, all of Boston.[1] Other members of the church interested in the negotiations which preceded the transfer were Edward Allen, tailor, George Sutherland, shopkeeper, Daniel Mac-Neal, laborer, Samuel Miller, gunsmith, and Abraham All or Aul, tailor. In 1744 a large and dignified building was erected, and in 1788 by a change of street name the place of worship became the Federal Street church. Mr. Moorhead married June 22, 1730, Sarah Parsons, an English lady of refinement and some artistic talent; they had several children, Alexander, Parsons, Mary, John, William, and Agnes or Ann Agnes. At least one of these, Agnes, who married Alexander Willson of Boston, left issue.[2]

His health began to fail a few years before his death; on the last Sunday in November, 1773, he preached twice, but upon returning home he became very ill and died on Thursday, December 2d.[3] The Rev. David McGregor of Londonderry preached the funeral sermon, which was printed in 1774. Moorhead was a tall man, and rather corpulent. His character is described in a notice printed soon after his death:

---

[1] Suffolk Deeds, Vol. 51, p. 14.

[2] Mary Moorhead, perhaps a relative, married in Boston, April 3, 1732, Andrew Menford.

[3] *Massachusetts Gazette* and *Boston Weekly News-Letter*, No. 3662, December 9, 1773.

"Very few men have left behind them a fairer or better character,—charitable and liberal to the poor, with a hearty disposition to render them every service in his power,—industrious and faithful in the dispensation of the word, and a most earnest desire for the good of souls which was the actuating and ruling principle of his life. His mind was deeply impressed with the importance of the truth of the atonement of Jesus Christ as the only well grounded hope of salvation and happiness in a future state; this made him anxiously desirous to communicate that impression to others. With this view his labors were incessant. In all his discourses from the sacred desk he held up this grand truth as the only principle upon which depended the very existence of Christianity; also frequently visiting the families of his flock, and endeavoring to inspire them to practice as well as believe the Gospel. His honesty of heart, open and frank manner of address, rendered him at all times an able and faithful adviser."[1]

The administrators of Mr. Moorhead's estate, William McNeil and the unmarried daughter Mary Moorhead, reported £ 223 – 3 – 11 to be divided between the son Alexander and the daughters Mary Moorhead and Agnes or Ann Agnes Willson.[2]

John Little, the early benefactor of the Scotch

---

[1] *Massachusetts Gazette* and *Boston Weekly News-Letter*, December 9, 1773.

[2] Suffolk Wills, Vol. 74, p. 356.

Irish in Boston, was a son of Archibald Little with whom he came to Boston. John Little at his death in 1741 left two minor sons John and Moses, a daughter Mary having died in infancy. His will provided for his family, but in case the sons were to die before marriage and before reaching the age of twenty one, he instructed his executors Henry Dering and Andrew Cunningham to transfer his property to the Overseers of the Poor to be invested by them as a trust. The annual income was to be used for the employment of a schoolmaster to teach reading, writing and arithmetic to the "poor Protestant children whose Parents are of the Kingdom of Ireland and Inhabitants of Boston." Their books and materials, with psalter, testament and Bible, were to be furnished free. Children between the ages of seven and fourteen were eligible.[1] Had his sons died in childhood Mr. Little's charity would have aided the Scotch Irish to this day and his name would have been known in our annals.

Among those who came to Boston in or about 1727 Peter Pelham, schoolmaster, painter and engraver, became the most eminent. He had close and kindly association with the Scotch Irish, and in 1751 he engraved a portrait of the Rev. Mr. Moorhead, one of the earliest of those of the Boston clergy made by him. John Little owed many favors to the Pelhams, and in 1741 he remembered Peter's son Charles in

---

[1] Suffolk Wills, Vol. 35, p. 476.

his will "as a token of my love for the Friendship receiv'd from his Father and Family."

William Shaw, a Boston tailor and a member of the committee to which John Little deeded the Presbyterian meeting house in 1735, died soon after, leaving a very interesting will. His bequest of land in Kingsfield to a sister Jane, wife of "William McClenenghen" of Kingsfield, suggests that Shaw was closely allied with these settlers, many of whom came from the Rutland company. The Shaws of Kingsfield, an early name for Palmer, Massachusetts, were Joshua, David, Samuel and Seth. The last three were deacons and men of influence. If Deacon Samuel is the "brother Samuel" Shaw of our William's will we have a numerous progeny for William's father Samuel Shaw of Boston. Captain John McClanathan married Martha Shaw, perhaps a sister of Jane mentioned above, who married William McClanathan. It is evident that William Shaw of Mr. Moorhead's church was closely allied with Palmer; he was a "petitioner" there in 1732 and owner of a fifty acre home lot. Tradition says that the Shaws came from Queenstown in 1720, but their alliance with Rutland families may mean that they had lived in County Tyrone and merely took ship from Queenstown.

Mr. Shaw left five pounds to the Presbyterian congregation in Long Lane, and his books to his friends. The titles of these volumes show what the Scotch

Irish pioneer read: The Practical Sabbatarian, by
John Wells, minister of St. Olave, Jewry; Lectures
upon the Fourth of John, by Arthur Hildersam, a
puritan divine at Ashby de la Zouch; A Sacramental
Directory, by John Willison, minister at Dundee;
Heaven upon Earth, by James Janeway, a minister
at Rotherhithe; and The Great Concern of Salvation, by Professor Thomas Halliburton of St. Andrews. The last volume Shaw left to Alexander
Thien. This book was published in 1721, so that the
owner must have purchased it in Boston if he came
in 1720. His great Bible and the work by Janeway
he gave to Mrs. "Eupham" Johnson, and to her husband George his case of bottles—discriminating
gifts, we may suppose! To their daughter Mary he
left his oval table and pocket Bible with silver
clasps, as well as the books by Willison and Hildersam, and his candlesticks and fire-tongs.

The clothing which he wore is described at some
length: To his brother-in-law McClanathan his
Camblet coat lined with green, and his black and
white jacket; to his brother Samuel Shaw a Duroy
coat, brown holland coat, and dimmity jacket; to
Alexander Thien his coat with metal buttons. The
father was to have the grey suit of clothes trimmed
with black, his "Rocquelo" or roquelaure, a loose
coat to be thrown over the shoulders, his silver shoe
buckles, his linen, and Burkitt's Expository notes
on the New Testament. To David Hoston or Huston

and wife he gave four pounds. The executors were
his father and George Glen, tailor, his fellow member on the Church committee. The witnesses were
William Hall, another member of the above mentioned committee, James Johnson, and James Bradford.[1]

Robert Patten became an elder in Mr. Moorhead's
church. But his father showed an interest in Trinity church and in his will remembered both faiths;
he left a gold ring and gloves to Mr. Moorhead, and
£ 40 to the minister, wardens and vestry of Trinity.[2]

The Charitable Irish Society of Boston, instituted
in 1737, was to be composed of persons ''of the Irish
Nation or extraction''; and since the managers were
to be Protestants (article viii) it is probable that the
earliest members also were of that faith. Those who
became members before the year 1742, when Roman
Catholics are first supposed to have been eligible to
membership, number one hundred and sixteen.[3]
Many of them had been in Boston for several years,
and had become prosperous merchants or mariners.

The Scotch Irish began to arrive in Boston in
considerable numbers as early as 1718. If we assume that most of these emigrants moved into the
country towns their whereabouts is made clear. If,
however, any great number remained in Boston we

---

[1] Suffolk Wills, Vol. 32, p. 179.
[2] *Ibid*, Vol. 69, p. 268.
[3] See Appendix IV.

may wonder that they made no impress on affairs before 1730, when the Presbyterian Church records begin. The surnames mentioned in these records give some idea of Boston Scotch Irish families, although parents came fifty miles for the rites of baptism, and in some cases there is no indication on the records that a family lived out-of-town.

X

THE WINTER OF 1718–19 IN WORCESTER

Cotton Mather had in mind very early that the emigrants from Ulster would be useful settlers on the frontier. In 1718 the village of Worcester could claim a position on the Massachusetts frontier, although it lay only forty miles from Boston. First settled in 1674, it was deserted in King Philip's war, 1675, and again in Queen Anne's war, 1702. In 1713 Jonas Rice courageously built a cabin at the northern end of Sagatabscot Hill, south east of the centre of Worcester and near the Grafton line. Two years later his brother Gershom settled at Pakachoag Hill in the south western part of the township, near a corner of the present Auburn. These English settlers and others built a fort or garrison house of logs in 1717 on the west side of the present Main Street, near Chatham Street. The same year Obadiah Ward built his mill a little south east of the garrison house, and a year later Joshua Rice finished a garrison house on the Jo Bill road, north of the Main Street garrison house. At the north east corner of Main and Exchange streets already stood Daniel Heywood's fortified tavern, a landmark even in those days on the great highway into the wilderness.[1]

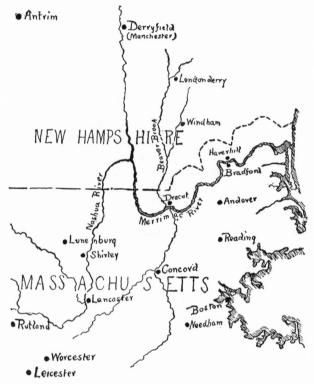

The little company of Scotch Irish settlers, poor, weary, laden with blankets and tools, flax-wheels and

---

[1] Wall's Worcester, 1877, Chapter 2. I am indebted to Mr. Lawrence Park of Groton for aid in preparing this chapter. Mr. Benjamin Thomas Hill of Worcester has read the manuscript and has placed his views of old houses at my disposal.

cradles, watched this sandy path as it ran on through woodland and meadow, and dotted at intervals with garrison houses, which must have reminded them of danger. They came to act as a buffer against the Indians, and instead of welcome they received surly conversation from the few inhabitants who turned out to meet them. At the head of the party of emigrants was the Rev. Edward FitzGerald from Londonderry, of whom less is known than of the other ministers of the migration. James McClellan was one of the leaders, and he may even have been in Worcester when the band of emigrants came slowly out from Boston, if he landed on July 28th, as seems possible. It was on Saturday, August 9th, of the week after the ships entered the harbor, that McClellan made terms with Gershom Rice of Worcester for a farm of seventy five acres.[1] The price was forty one pounds. The land was bounded partly westerly by land in the possession of Captain Prentice, easterly by land of Mr. John Smith, and every where else by common land, a country road six rods wide running through the farm. April 23d of the next year McClellan purchased from Nathaniel Jones

---

[1] Middlesex Deeds, Vol. 19, p. 328. In the publications of the Worcester Society of Antiquity, Vol. 3, p. 144, the early Proprietors' Records are given. A plot made November 21, 1718, shows land laid out on the right of Captain Thomas Prentice, deceased, and "Macklelans land" is shown to be on "the Comon road," west of the Captain's land. In 1720 William McClellan's land is shown (page 157).

another large tract of land bounded on the south by the town line and on the east by Gershom Rice's land and common land. These and later purchases formed a large farm between Pakachoag Hill and the Leicester line.

McClellan at once became a factor in the Worcester of 1718, with its fifty-eight dwellings and its two hundred souls. Log cabins were built rapidly on the common land. Mr. Wall in his Reminiscences of Worcester indicates on his map the probable sites in 1718 of the homes of the settlers, most of them Scotch Irish men who came with their families and so had to provide houses for them. Professor Perry thinks that at least fifty families of the old fashioned size settled in Worcester that autumn, doubling the population of the town.[1]

Religious services under the Rev. Mr. FitzGerald began in a garrison house near the intersection of the Boston and Lancaster roads,[2] at the north end of the town.

In the autumn of 1718 or the summer of 1719 the Presbyterians began to erect a church of their own, on the west side of Lincoln street, ''near the top of the hill, a little north of the Paine house.'' Through ignorance as to the religious views of the Scotch Irish, or more probably from a desire to force all the inhabitants of the town to attend and support

---

[1] Proceedings Scotch Irish Society, 2d Congress, p. 111.
[2] Lincoln's Worcester, p. 163.

one church, the rougher element came together one night and destroyed the frame before much progress had been made. It is said that Deacon Daniel Heywood of the orthodox church lent his influence to this movement[1] and that the "best people in town" were present. The destruction proved a crushing blow to those who clung tenaciously to their own form of worship. Many moved north onto a tract of land known as the settlers' part of the town. When, in 1722, forty or fifty families had gathered there this territory, six miles square, was incorporated as Rutland.

Many also went elsewhere, some gathering at Sutton to be under the Rev. John McKinstry, who began his ministry there about 1720; others moving to Londonderry in New Hampshire. The Scotch Irish did not entirely desert Worcester, although so few remained that they had no control of affairs in the annual town meetings, nor could they bear the burden of a minister of their own faith. The Rev. Mr. FitzGerald left them, but returned occasionally to preach, being referred to as late as 1729.[2] A few years later the Presbyterians again attempted to form a church, and they called the Rev. William Johnston who is said to have come from Mullowmale, or Mullaghmoyle, county Tyrone.

In 1737 John Clark and nine others, finding it

---

[1] Carl's tour in Main Street, pp. 8, 146.
[2] Lincoln's Worcester, pp. 166, 191.

burdensome to support Mr. Johnston and at the
same time aid the town's minister, asked the town
to free them from taxation for the support of religious services, but "ye Irish petition" was voted
down by "a grate majority." Evidently the desig-
nation "Irish" still clung to these Scotch and English settlers from Ulster. Through adversity and
isolation of old they had grown clannish and they
did not assimilate well with the older New England
blood.

If we could go back to these early years we should
probably find that after FitzGerald's departure the
Presbyterians attended the Congregational or town
services, except when an itinerant or a passing minister of their own communion gathered the loyal
band in a cabin to unite them in prayer or to baptize
their children.

The orthodox church was built in 1719 in front of
the site of the present handsome city hall. At this
period it was plain, without steeple, and at first
filled with benches. The committee on seating in
1724 had no Scotch Irish members, nor did they
grant any places for private pews to these new settlers. In the fore seat or bench was John Gray; in
the third seat were Matthew Gray, John Duncan;
in the fourth seat was William Gray; in the fifth
seat were James Hamilton, William McNal, Robert
Peables, J. McClellan, Andrew Farrend, Alexander
McConkey, John Killough and Robert Lothridge or

Lortridge; and in the sixth seat William McClellan, David Young, J. Bety or Batty, W. Mahan, James McClellan and [Thomas] Beard, or Baird, all or nearly all of them Scotch Irish.[1]

In 1733 there were in the "fore seet" John Gray with five English sitters; in the second seat William Gray, James Hambleton, Andrew McFarland, John Clerk, Robert Peables; in the third seat, Matthew Gray, Alexander McConkey, William Caldwell, John Duncan, William Gray, Jr., Matthew Gray, Jr., Andrew. McFarland, Jr., and John Gray, Jr.; in the fourth seat Moses Harper, James Thornington or Thornton, John Batty, Oliver Wallis, and Robert Blair; in the fifth seat James Furbush, Robert Lortridge, John Alexander, William Mahan, John Stinson, Duncan Graham, John McFarland, and Joseph Clerk; in the sixth seat John Patrick, James Glasford, John Sterling, and Hugh Kelso. In the fore seat in the long gallery were William and James McClellan,[2] and Robert Barber; in the second seat were Patrick Peables, John McConkey, John Peables; and in the second seat of the "frunt galiry" were Samuel Gray, Thomas Hambleton, and Matthew Clark. In most of the seats were other sitters who were probably not of the Scotch Irish stock.[3]

It will be seen that in 1733 there was a consider-

---

[1] Worcester Society of Antiquity, Vol. 2, p. 28.
[2] Perry adds John Cishiel.
[3] Worcester Society of Antiquity, Vol. 2, pp. 85–86.

able Scotch Irish colony within a church-going radius of the Worcester church.

In 1737 the Irish petition had been voted down. The lands now included in the town of Pelham were being opened for settlement, and on the 21st of January, 1738–39, John Stoddard arranged to settle a number of families "such as were inhabitants of the Kingdom of Ireland or their descendants, being Protestants." Their names were:[1] James and John Alexander; Adam Clark; Ephraim and George Cowan, the latter being of Concord; John and Thomas Dick; John Ferguson of Grafton; James Gilmore of Boston; John Gray, Jr., Samuel, and William Gray, Jr.; James Hood; Adam Johnson; John Johnson of Shrewsbury; Robert Lotheridge; Thomas Lowden of Leicester; Alexander and John McConkey; James McAllach; Abraham Patterson of Leicester; Patrick and Robert Peibols; John Stinson; James Thornton; James Taylor; Samuel Thomes; Alexander Turner. The proprietors registered in 1739 included also Andrew McFarland, James Breakenridge, Robert Barbour, William Johnson and Matthew Gray. John Gray, Jr., had 3–60 of the rights, Robert Peibols 5–60 and James Thornton had 14–60. All the others had one or two rights. As the place was to be called Lisburn after the town in County Antrim a natural inference would be that Thornton came from that "mother town."

---

[1] Parmenter's Pelham, pp. 17, 24.

He was a man of ability and his son was a signer of the Declaration of Indepedence.

Exact information may be had in regard to a few of the Worcester settlers. James McClellan, whose early purchase of land has already been mentioned, was a very religious, industrious and thrifty man. His will, on file at the Middlesex Probate office, was signed September 29, 1729, when he made his mark. It was probated October 31st. The will was written apparently by Samuel Jenison, who with Moses and Jane Harper were witnesses. McClellan mentions "Margaret my dearly beloved wife"; the son William to have lands at Boggerhoage,[1] 104 acres with buildings, and to give his mother yearly 100 weight of beef and 100 weight of pork; the son James to have 95 acres and one half the buildings, the other half to be Margaret's for life; James to haul and cut her fire wood, and to provide yearly ten bushels of Indian corn, three of English corn, two of malt, one barrel of cider, fodder for two cows, and a horse in the winter season, and also to fit (?) him in order whenever she wants to ride. To Margaret he gave the use of the orchard for life. To William's children William, Samuel and Ann he gave three pounds each, and to James's children James and Rebecca like sums. James he made executor. It is an excellent will, clear, simple,

---

[1] "The south part of the town, then known as Bogachoag (now Auburn)."—Carl's tour in Main Street, p. 119.

and thoughtful through all its details, worthy of the Worcester colony, and of the emigrant's distinguished descendants General Samuel McClellan, General George B. McClellan, and the mayor of Greater New York.

The Young family[1] have left on their grave stones valuable evidence of their Irish home. John and David both came from the Londonderry neighborhood, and this suggests that the Worcester company was from the valley of the Foyle; while the New Hampshire and Falmouth people were from the Bann Valley. John Young was born in the Isle of Bert or Burt near Londonderry, and died at Worcester June 30, 1730, aged 107. David was born in the parish of Taughboyne, Donegal, between Londonderry and Lifford on the west bank of the Foyle, and died December 26, 1776, aged 94.[2]

The will of Daniel McFarland, who died in Worcester in 1738, states that he had a daughter Margaret Campbell living in County Tyrone, Ireland. Daniel may have been a brother of John McFarland, mentioned in a paper in the Suffolk County Files, number 163,586, which shows that three emigrants of the name, probably those of Boothbay a

---

[1] Professor Perry says that the Youngs were of Celtic origin. See his article, p. 110.

[2] Worcester Society of Antiquity, Vol. 1. In the first cemetery in Worcester, where about seventeen were buried between 1713 and 1727, there are no stones. The earliest stone on the Common bears the date 1727.

little later, appear to have come from Ardstraw, County Tyrone, in 1720.

The paper reads:

> "This Bill bindeth us
> John McFarland, Sr.
> John McFarland, Jr.
> Andrew McFarland

in the sum of £ 13. 16. 0 for the payment of £ 6. 18. 0 unto Rev. Mr. Isaac Taylor or order within 30 days after arrival at New England for value recd. Dated 10 August 1720. In presence of Robert Temple, Alexander Hamilton.''

Taylor was assistant to the Rev. Mr. Haliday, minister at Ardstraw, Ireland. He may, however, have been at Brunswick for a few months in 1719 and 1720.[1]

Matthew Gray who came over as a child in 1718 and Robert who came as a youth of twenty-one are both referred to as "of the Company of immigrants who settled here in 1718." John Gray had land laid out to him by the town's committee November 26, 1718, and these were his children: Robert (born 1697, ancestor of Asa Gray the botanist), Samuel,

---

[1] James, son of Daniel McFarland of Worcester, was at Brunswick in 1738. Duncan McFarland of Rutland was probably a son of Duncan who died in Boston in 1696, although perhaps closely related to the Worcester family. An Andrew McFarland married at Billerica in 1725.

William, Matthew (ancestor of Professor Bliss Perry), John, Mary (called wife of William Blair of Aghadowey, and later wife of Matthew Barbour), and Sarah (wife of Robert Barbour, who was born at "Koppra," County Tyrone).[1]

It is evident that those with families were obliged to build log cabins and clear spaces for planting; but two families no doubt often lived together under the same roof. There were also many young men and girls who went from place to place in search of employment. Some of these in the course of ten years returned to Worcester to buy land. Others married and settled elsewhere. The chief Worcester Scotch Irish settlers bore the following names, but many others were transient dwellers in Worcester and will be referred to under Rutland, Pelham and Palmer.

Thomas Baird	Rev. Edward Fitz Gerald
Robert Barbour	Samuel Fleming
John Batley [Betty?]	James Forbush
Abraham Blair	Mrs. Isabel Gilmore
Robert Blair	John Gray
William Caldwell	James Hamilton
Robert Crawford	James Heart
John Duncan	Hugh Kelso
William Dunlap (1731)	Archibald Lamond (1731)

[1] No place name in Ireland begins with Ko. Perhaps Cappagh on the northern side of the Mourne, between Newtown Stewart and Omagh, is referred to. Clogher was not far away.

The McConkey–Goddard House in Worcester

The land, now on Grove Street, north west of North Pond, was bought by Alexander McConkey January 25, 1731

Robert Lollard
Robert Lortridge
James McClellan
John McClintock
Alexander McConkey
John McConkey
Daniel McFarland
William McHan

John McKachan
Robert Peables
David Thomas
James Thornton
William Walker
Matthias Wallis
David Young
John Young

Many men bearing these names will be found mentioned in the excellent history of Pelham. Most of the Rutland settlers came with the Worcester colony, and the names of the chief Scotch Irish families there belong almost as certainly with the Worcester as with the Rutland list. Some of these Rutland settlers brought letters of dismissal from their church in Ireland. That of Malkem Hendery was from the Rev. Mr. Haliday at Ardstraw in County Tyrone, the home of the McFarlands. The Stinsons, Hamiltons and Savages were closely allied, and it is possible that a large number of the Rutland colony came over from Ardstraw together. Of the following those with an asterisk prefixed probably represent Ardstraw colonists.

*Alexander Bothwell
James Browning
*John Browning
James Clark
John Clark

*Aaron Crawford
*John Crawford
*William Fenton
Robert Ferrell
Robert Forbush

Duncan Graham
Patrick Gregory
*John   Hamilton   (of
    Brookfield 1726)
*Malkem Hendery
John Lecore
William McCarter
Thomas McClanathan
John McClanathan
[Duncan McFarland]
John McIntire
*Robert McLem
Daniel McMains

James McPherson
*John Moor
John Murray
*Robert Patrick
Edward Savage
Matthew Slarrow
William Sloan
James Smith
William Spear
Robert Sterling
John Stinson
William Watson

Edward Savage mentioned above was the grandfather of the Philadelphia painter and engraver of portraits of Washington.

The chief Palmer settlers, who came largely from Worcester, were:

James Breakenridge
Andrew Farrand
Thomas Farrand, Jr.
Robert Ferrell
Joseph Fleming
John Glasford
James Lamont
Thomas McClanathan
William McClanathan
John McMaster

William McMitchel
Alexander McNitt
James Moore
John Moore
John Patterson
William Patterson
John Peables
Duncan Quinton
Robert Rogers
Samuel Shaw

Seth Shaw
James Shearer
Robert Smith
John Spence

Alexander Tackels
John Thomson
Robert Thomson

At Palmer and on lands across the Ware River in the present town of Ware the population grew rapidly. Sons and daughters from Worcester and Rutland did the first rough work of the pioneer. To their numbers were added those of the later immigrants who withstood the allurements of a warmer climate. There was Alexander McNitt from County Donegal whose son Barnard served as clerk and treasurer of the Proprietors of Common Lands. Several miles east of Palmer William Sinclair, born in the parish of Drumbo, County Down, in 1676, lived at this period in Leicester and Spencer.[1] His daughter Agnes became the wife of the chief man in this Scotch Irish neighborhood, William Breakenridge, the first representative to the Provincial Congress, and town clerk of Ware for eighteen years. He came to America from Ireland in 1727 when four years of age, with his father, James, a native of Scotland. Mr. Hyde in his address at Ware, says: "There is in the Brakenridge family an ancient manuscript music-book upon the fly-leaf of which is written, 'Mr. Jacobus Breakenridge, His Music Book, made and taught per me, Robt. Cairnes, at

---

[1] History of Spencer, 1841, pp. 114, 132; 1860, 204, 255.

Glenreavoll,[1] Sept. 1715.' Besides the scale and rudiments of music, it contains the date of his marriage, 1720, and the births of his children, giving the day, the hour and the time in the moon, with other memoranda. On one page is written, 'We departed from Ireland, July 16, 1727, and my child died on the 19th of Aug.' "

The newer towns drew from almost every county in Ulster.

The evidence relating to the origin of the Worcester-Rutland colony, however, seems to point to the valley of the Foyle as the home of its pioneer members. If McClellan had not come in the ship from Londonderry, John Wilson, master, which arrived July 28th he would have come on August 4th. In those days the space of time between August 4th and the 9th, Monday to Saturday, would have been short for the labors of bringing his family goods ashore, journeying out to Worcester, selecting a farm and looking it over, waiting for a deed to be drawn, and attaching his signature. All this could have been done in six days, but a careful, provident man would have felt hurried in so important a task in a strange land. If, however, McClellan arrived on the ship from Londonderry he had from July 28th to August 9th to reach Worcester and buy his farm. With him in Worcester were settlers from three counties, Londonderry, Donegal and Tyrone, but

---

[1] Perhaps Glenravil, barony of Antrim, County Antrim.

most of them came from County Tyrone. The Foyle, made broad by the union of two streams, flows by Lifford on the Donegal side, and Strabane on the Tyrone side, northward between the counties until it approaches the city of Londonderry. There the county of Londonderry seems to throw itself across the Foyle to encompass the city. These twenty miles of the Foyle from Strabane to the city drain a territory which has been a nursery of strong men "who fought naked for King William, our liberties, our religion, and all that was dear to us."

These men from the valley of the Foyle proved themselves sturdy of body and brain. They were, however, if we may judge from minor evidences, less prosperous and possibly less well educated at the time of arrival than those of the Bann companies. In this opinion I am supported by Professor Perry, who writes: "I entertain the opinion, gathered from scattered and uncertain data, that it was the poorer, the more illiterate, the more helpless, part of the five ship-loads who were conducted to Worcester."[1] Under these circumstances their success in the New World was remarkable.

---

[1] Page 110 of his article.

XI

THE WINTER OF 1718–19 IN DRACUT, ANDOVER, AND CASCO BAY

We have seen that many Scotch Irish immigrants passed the winter of 1718–19 in Boston, much to the discomfort of the town officers and citizens there. These immigrants were possibly from the territory around Belfast, comprising southern Antrim and the northern part of the County of Down. They must have treasured some memories of the sailing of the Eagle Wing nearly a century before, for many of their towns had sent out inhabitants on that fated expedition.

The Worcester company left Boston early in August, 1718. Other families and groups of immigrants struck out for themselves. James Smith, who had come from Ballykelly, a town between the Foyle and the Bann, near Newton Limavady, wandered about for a few months and settled down in Needham, where his third son Matthew was born in April, 1720. The Rev. Jonathan Townsend, writing there in February, 1723–4, states that a year earlier he had had to plead with his people not to ill-treat the new settlers,[1] from which we may infer that the

---

[1] Information from George K. Clarke, Esq.

Smiths soon must have had Scotch Irish neighbors.
The church reference to Mr. Smith is an interesting
record:

"Jan: 9, 1726. — *James Smith* & *Mary* his Wife
admitted into the Church. came from *Ireland* A. D.
1718, & Brought a Testimonial with them from M^r.
John Stirling Minister of the Congregation of *Belly-
kelly* in the County of *Londonderry.*"

The leaders of the Bann Valley settlers, finding
that their agent, the Rev. William Boyd, had obtained no definite grant of land, determined to spend
the winter in or near Boston until affairs were more
to their satisfaction.   Boyd, as we have seen, remained in Boston, but the Rev. Mr. McGregor's
means were not sufficient to allow him to pass the
winter in idleness, and he appealed to the Rev. Cotton Mather for influence in obtaining a position as
teacher or minister.   Mather in his diary under
October 3d writes: "Encourage ye people of Dray-
cot unto ye Inviting of a worthy Scotch minister
lately arrived here, to settle among y^m."

Mather's letter, written on the previous day, is
printed below from the somewhat illegible rough
draft at the American Antiquarian Society's library
in Worcester:

2^d VIII^m 1718

Dear Brethren

Being informed that you are desirous to hear from
us, the character of o^r Friend and Brother Mr Mc

Gregore, we do, with great Alacrity and satisfaction give you to understant that we look upon him, as a person of a very excellent character: and considerably qualified for the work of ye ministry as well for his ministerial abilities as his Christian [?] piety: [serious gravity and as far as we have heard every way unexceptionable Behaviour.][1] And we have also had it credibly Reported unto us, that from a singular goodness in his Temper, he was usually called The peace-maker, in ye countrey from whence he came. On these Accounts we cannot but hope that if you should obtain him, to become your pastor, you will enjoy in him a very precious gift of your ascended Saviour, To whose Blessing you are now commended by Your hearty Friend

[Cotton Mather].

In writing of Mr. McGregor it must be evident that Cotton Mather expressed himself after two months of intercourse with the Scotch minister. We may assume also from McGregor's marriage to a sister of the wives of James McKeen and Captain James Gregg that he must himself have been a man of ability, for they were leaders among men wherever they chanced to be.

The village of Dracut had built a little meeting house three years earlier on the river road, now Varnum Avenue. It was thirty feet long and twenty

---

[1] Mather wrote this clause as a marginal insertion.

feet wide, and to this house of worship after listen-
ing to some fifteen candidates the people decided
to summon Mr. McGregor, "the peace-maker." The
town evidently hoped that he would, if acceptable,
settle down after the admirable custom of the time
to be the father of his flock through life. The record
of the town (there are no church records until 1788)
reads:

"Dracutt, Oct. ye 15, 1718.

"Mad choice of Mr. Mackgreggor to settel in Dracutt to prech the Gospel and to do the Whole Work of
a Settled minister; and likewise Voted to give to Mr
Macgreger Sixty five pounds a year for his salary
for the first four years, and then Seaventy pound
a year till there Be fifty families in the town of Dracutt, and then it Shall Be eighty pounds a yeare;
and likewise voted for a settlement sixty pounds the
one half the Next June inseying, and the other half
the next June, in the year 1720''[1]

The Rev. James McGregor spent the winter of
1718–19 in Dracut on the banks of Beaver Brook, a
little north of the present city of Lowell, and south
of the future Nutfield; but there is no evidence that
the Scotch Irish people followed him to Dracut. In
addition to his work as the village pastor he taught
the school.

Parker in his History of Londonderry refers to a
winter settlement of Scotch Irish at Andover, a

---

[1] I consulted also papers lent by Silas R. Coburn, Esq., of Dracut.

village five or ten miles east of Dracut. "On taking their departure," he writes, "from one of the families with whom they had resided, they left a few potatoes for seed. The potatoes were accordingly planted; came up and flourished well; blossomed and produced balls, which the family supposed were the fruit to be eaten. They cooked the balls in various ways, but could not make them palatable, and pronounced them unfit for food. The next spring, while ploughing their garden the plough passed through where the potatoes had grown, and turned out some of great size, by which means they discovered their mistake."

This incident is said to have occurred on the farm of Nathaniel Walker, father of the Rev. Timothy Walker, first minister of Concord. The farm was near the boundary line between North Andover and Bradford, and several families probably spent the winter of 1718–19 there, the single men and girls finding shelter and employment in the neighboring villages.[1] The Andover taxpayers were assessed forty shillings in 1719 to provide funds to aid the poor, and part of the money thus collected was no doubt spent for provisions for the Scotch Irish. Obviously the settlers of a single winter left few records of their stay; but Miss C. H. Abbott, the indefatigable investigator, has found traces of them.

---

[1] Miss Abbott writes: "The Walker garden may have been on the Andover *line*, but I am quite as sure *he worshipped* and paid taxes mainly in Bradford town."

Thomas Grow, probably the same man who signed the petition to Governor Shute in 1718, was one of those who remained in Andover after his companions had moved to Nutfield. An order was issued the next winter for his relief, and at about the same time, with man's improvidence, he was married. His wife, Rebecca Holt came of a well known local family.[1]

Two other men from Ireland are mentioned upon the records at an early date, Robert Stuart and William Bolton, who were recorded January 30, 1718–19, as living in the town. They had come up from Boston the preceding summer or autumn, Stuart bringing a family with him. Very unreliable tradition[2] states that Robert Stuart of Edinburgh (1655–1719) was the father of Robert of Andover and of John (1682–1741), the proprietor of Londonderry, New Hampshire. Samuel Stuart of Andover, called a third son of the first Robert, was executor of the will of John in 1741. A Walter Stewart or Stuart of Londonderry married in 1722 Giziell Crumey of Boxford, and a little later John Stuart of Londonderry owned land in Boxford. These men may have been kinsmen, but there were so many early immigrants by the name of Stuart, some on Cape Cod,

---

[1] Their children mentioned upon the records were Ruth, born in 1720, and Hannah, born in 1723. In 1721 the town records refer to "Elizabeth Nichols' child that is called John Grow," for whom provision was to be made.

[2] See, however, the "Duncan-Stuart family," p. 140.

others in Connecticut, in Charlestown, Lunenburg and elsewhere that only the family historian could trace their relationship.

William Bolton, called "Scotch" by his descendants, came from the vicinity of Coleraine. He married at Andover in 1719–20, and died soon after in the adjoining town of Reading, leaving two sons William and John.

Of these immigrants Miss Abbott says: "I find many were tenants on farms held partly by dower widows and worked on shares." Land was difficult of purchase in an old town like Andover, and most of the Scotch Irish were transients only. On the Andover town records are the names of:

John Cofferin or Cochran . .	1725/6
John Telford	1725/6
John Cromme or Crombie . .	1726/7
Hugh Riddle	1726/7
William Crumney . . .	1727
Thomas Richardson, "Irishman," his son John baptized . .	1730
Joseph Waugh and wife Margaret, before	1732
Alexander Macartney, "Irishman," and Margaret his wife, about	1742
James, John and Samuel Seaton .	1748

Other members of the Scotch Irish migration may

have tarried at Haverhill, Bradford and Dracut, but the record of them is meagre.

While the Andover colonists were spending the winter in moderate comfort, the "Irish" at Casco Bay suffered great hardship. Parker writes: "The party that left Boston for Casco Bay, arrived there late in the season; and it proving to be a very early and cold winter, the vessel was frozen in. Many of the families, not being able to find accommodations on shore, were obliged to pass the whole winter on board the ship, suffering severely from the want of food, as well as of convenience of situation."

The village of Falmouth on the site of the present city of Portland, Maine, had suffered from Indian raids, from intense cold in winter, and from the poverty of its fishing population. In the Acts and resolves of the province of the Massachusetts Bay it is recorded July 16, 1718, that a committee of five was appointed to view Falmouth, give advice as to laying out of streets, placing the meeting house, and organization. The appointment of this committee probably drew the attention of Governor Shute to the lands about Casco Bay between Cape Elizabeth and the mouth of the Kennebec, roughly the land between Portland and Bath. He, it is said, spoke to McGregor and McKeen, and the latter with the Rev. Mr. McGregor's congregation, relatives, and friends, determined to go at once in the ship in which they had crossed the ocean, to explore the coast of the bay.

Meanwhile the Committee recommended that the inhabitants already there be given powers of self-government since there was "a Fair Prospect of its being in a little time a flourishing town." On No-

vember 12th the Legislature approved the suggestion on condition that fifty families more be admitted as soon as possible and settled in a compact and defensible manner. On the 19th the Legislature approved a project for a town to be laid out near Falmouth for the Scotch Irish, evidently having no thought that the Scotch Irish emigrants would settle in Falmouth.

Those who sailed into Casco Bay in the "Robert" went ashore probably between Falmouth Village and the Point on Cape Elizabeth, where they began about the month of November to build rough shelters for the winter.[1] It seems difficult to believe that the families which were on the ship could not provide rough huts before winter set in. Evidently the autumn was extremely cold and the vessel, if tradition is to be believed, was caught in the ice, so that those who did not immediately get their huts well under way were forced by the bitter weather to settle down on the "Robert" for the winter. John Armstrong and others at once sent a petition to the government at Boston.

This John Armstrong is no doubt the indigent voyager on the "Robert"; in the wild life on Cape Elizabeth his ability brought him forward. The official reference to the petition reads: "A Petition of John Armstrong & divers others, Setting forth that there are about thirty Families arrived from the North of Ireland, at Falmouth, in Casco Bay, that they are building Cottages to shelter themselves from the weather, that their good Success in these Parts will encourage many of their Brethren to transport themselves & Families into this countrey;

---

[1] Southack's "Actual survey of the sea coast" has houses and trees at "Porpolac Pt."

And therefore Praying that they may have Portions of Land allotted to them near Falmouth; & seeing they are scarce of Provisions, that they may have some thing to subsist them this Winter.''[1] There are several petitions of this period, and in reply the Council stated that Armstrong's petition could not be granted as Falmouth was ''anciently inhabited,'' and the lands were already owned.

Meanwhile the development of Falmouth languished. Samuel Moody and John Smith wrote to the government that notwithstanding the favorable report of the Committee, and the powers given to Falmouth, yet claimers and proprietors of lands could not agree upon their bounds. The petitioners asked that a constable and other officers be appointed to regulate affairs and provide for the support of a minister. They stated that the population was about three hundred,[2] most of them from Ireland, and one half so poor that they had neither provision nor money for them. They conclude by asking ''that this Hon[ble] Court would be pleased to consider the deplorable Circumstances of the said Place by reason of the great Number of poor Strangers arrived amongst them and take some speedy & Effectual Care for their supply.''

This petition was ordered to be referred to the

---

[1] Legislative Records of the Council, Vol. 10, pp. 309, 313, 314, 318, 321.

[2] The "Robert's" passengers were not the only Scotch Irish on Cape Elizabeth.

session in May, and one hundred bushels of Indian meal were to be forwarded to the Irish people.[1]

The Rev. William Cornwall had gone with the "Robert" in place of the Rev. Mr. McGregor. Mr. Cornwall was from Clogher, in County Tyrone, a day's journey south of Londonderry. He was not well, and on account of the distance of his dwelling house in Clogher from the church, and the arrears of his salary, he resigned his pastorate and joined the McGregor colony. One winter at Casco Bay seems to have chilled his ardor for pioneering and he returned to become minister at Taughboyne in 1722. The privations which threatened the "Robert's" company at Porpooduc, as the Cape Elizabeth land was called, brought from Mr. Cornwall a letter of distress. Cotton Mather, January 8, 1718–19, wrote in his Diary: "Some Letters unto ye Scotch ministers arrived in o[u]r East Countrey, may have a Tendency to hearten them in that work of God, which they have to do, in those New Plantations; and more particularly for ye Christianizing of the Indians there."[2] The following draft of a letter by Mather gives an intimation of his labors in behalf of the struggling colony "at Porpooduc, Casco Bay, Falmouth township." He writes:

"Whereas, the New Settlement at *Casco-bay,* is as yett in its feeble infancy, But Yett there is usual

---

[1] Passed December 3, 1718.

[2] I am indebted to Mr. Julius H. Tuttle for these references to Mather's Diary.

(besides yᵉ Families that have began as inhabitants) on yᵉ Lords-day a Considerable Resort of people that are from divers places on their Fishing voyages: which renders yᵉ Condition of these places a little peculiar, and Considerably calls for our care that the Lords-days may not pass without public Exercise of Religion there: Whereas also there is now a very worthy, pious & Peaceful Minister whose name is Mr. *Cornwal* much desired and invited by the people there: who are willing to do something toward the subsistence of him; which something is much too little in any tolerable measure to insure yᵉ Instruction.

" 'Tis humbly moved That yᵉ General Assembly would express yᵉ goodness usual wᵗʰ ye governmenᵗ on such occasions and allow for one year from ye public Treasury some agreeable accession to what yᵉ people there can do, towards ye support of such a minister.'"[1]

With the approach of warmer weather in the spring of 1719 most of the McGregor colony looked about for a more promising place. Those who remained at Falmouth led a miserable existence. The Rev. Thomas Smith, "pastor of the first church of Christ in Falmouth," came to his desolate field of labor in 1720. There were less than sixty families, very poor because they were so often forced through fear of the Indians to abandon their farms and live in garrison houses, and some of them, says Smith,

---

[1] American Antiquarian Society, Mather Papers.

"soldiers that had found wives on the place, and were mean animals." But the fighting in 1722 did away with the worst of them.[1]

In 1735 there were only twenty families at Porpooduc, and the Presbyterians there, at Falmouth, and at the settlement in Brunswick, to be noticed later, were ministered to by the Rev. James Woodside for several years. He was followed by the Rev. William McClenathan, who removed to Blandford in Massachusetts in 1744. During the next score of years only the aged gathered to hear a passing Presbyterian minister, to renew their faith and their memories of old Ireland.[2]

History and tradition have left some record of those who remained in Falmouth after the winter sojourners had gone on to Nutfield. John Armstrong, signer of the petition, with Robert Means, who had married his daughter, were certainly there, and Means settled at Stroudwater, a village near Falmouth. The descendants of Means became very prominent later in Massachusetts. Armstrong is said to have had brothers Simeon, James and Thomas, who had grants in or near Falmouth before 1721.[3]

---

[1] Smith's Journal, p. 15.

[2] A. Blaikie's Presbyterianism, p. 88.

[3] Armstrong had an infant son, James, and a son Thomas, born in Falmouth in 1719. His brother, James, had Thomas, born in Ireland in 1717, as well as John, born in 1720, and James, in 1721, both in Falmouth.

John Barbour[1] came with his family, a son John having come to York, it is said, as early as 1717.

Randal McDonald is also mentioned as of the company which spent the winter of 1718–19 in Falmouth, and with him William Jameson. A man named Slemons is said to have settled at Stroudwater with Means.

This list is no doubt wholly inadequate, but the establishment of settlers a few miles away at Brunswick in 1718, supposed to be the passengers by the "Maccallum," and additions in great numbers there in 1719 under Captain Robert Temple, make it extremely difficult to name those who spent the winter of 1718–19 in or near Falmouth, and remained long enough to find a place on the records.

Trouble with the Indians drove many farmers out of the country during the next five years, and from the lists of persons reaching Boston a few names of early dwellers in Casco Bay can be added. These names were incorporated into the Boston Selectmen's records.

Recorded at a meeting of the selectmen, April 27, 1719:—

Anne Hanson who came from Casco into this Town ab[t] a week before was on ye 23th of march, 1718[–19] warned to depart.

---

[1] Smith and Deane's Journal, pp. 57, 60, 92, 165; Willis's Portland, pp. 326, 788; McLellan's Gorham, p. 395. See also an article by Mrs. Alice F. Moody in *The Boston Transcript*, June 5, 1907.

HOME OF BRYCE MCLELLAN OF FALMOUTH

Now the oldest house in Portland, Maine

Robert Holmes & wife, William Holmes & child who came from Casco into this Town ab[t] 12 dayes before was on the 15th of Aprill cur[t] warned to depart.

Recorded July 25, 1719:—

Joan Maccoullah widd[o] came from Casco bay who had been then here ab[t] 5 dayes was on the 5th of June, warned to depart.

Recorded October 28, 1720:—

Noah Peck from Casco 2 moneths warned 26th of August.

Recorded July 28, 1722:—

Thomas Longworth, Lame, from Casco [warned] June 3.

Longworth was a settler long before 1718. The same may perhaps be said of Peck.

The Scotch Irish settlers at Casco Bay between 1718 and 1722, that is, at Falmouth and along the shore of Cape Elizabeth, were more numerous than these records show, but some of the earliest were:

James Armstrong.
John Armstrong.
Simeon Armstrong.
Thomas Armstrong.
? John Barbour.
Thomas Bolton.
Rev. William Cornwall.

Joshua Gray.[1]
Anne Hanson.
Robert Holmes and wife.
William Holmes and child.
William Jameson.[2]
Joan Maccoullah.
Randal McDonald.
Bryce McLellan.
Robert Means.
Andrew Simonton.
William Simonton.
William Slemons or Slemmons.

Bryce McLellan, who appears in the above list, built a house in Falmouth in 1731. Through the vicissitudes of fortune this house survived fire and storm, Mowat's attack in 1775, and the ruthless hand of progress, standing on York Street after every other house of its period had disappeared from the present city of Portland.

Among the later Scotch Irish settlers at Falmouth was John Motley, from Belfast in Ireland, who married in 1738 Mary Roberts. A son settled in Boston, where he became prominent; his descendant, John Lothrop Motley, was the historian of the Netherlands.

---

[1] So says Professor A. L. Perry. Proceedings Scotch Irish Society, 2d Congress, p. 135. He also includes William Gyles.

[2] This was probably the William Jameson who died at Rutland in 1760, leaving a sister, Martha Reed, of County Antrim, Ireland.

XII

THE YEARS 1718 AND 1719 AT MERRY-MEETING BAY

In a previous chapter the voyage of the ship "Maccallum" was described, and it was made evident that her passengers from Londonderry settled on lands at the Eastward. These lands skirted a large body of water, known as Merrymeeting Bay, which is formed by the Androscoggin River entering the Kennebec. Southack's map, covering this region, bears the inscription, "An actual survey of the sea coast from New York to the I. Cape Briton . . . by Capt. Cyprian Southack. Printed and sold by Wm. Herbert, London Bridge & Rob\ Sayer . . . Fleet Street." On the land between Brunswick and Maquoit Bay there is an inscription which states that in the years 1718, 1719 and 1720 five hundred emigrants from Ireland had come to settle; the inscription reads:

> "Kennebeck River *very Long*
> strong Tydes with all its branche
> Trade mostly is as yet Lumber
> Fish small matter came from
> the Kingdom of Ireland with
> in three Year: 1720 five Hun-

dred Inhabitants and made
new Settlements for Farm-
ing and Lumber.''

In the English Pilot, Part IV, London, 1737, the
map described as ''The Harbour of Casco Bay, By
Cyprian Southicke,'' indicates a church and several
houses between Maquoit Bay and the Androscog-

PART OF SOUTHACK'S MAP

gin River.[1] The words ''Irish new settlement''
show the character of the inhabitants.

By the depositions of David Dunning, Jane
McFadden, and her son Andrew, and John McPhetre, we learn that some of the people who settled
here in 1718 ''removed from Ireland to Boston, from
Boston down to Kennebec River and up Merrymeeting Bay to a place called Cathance.''

[1] I am indebted to Mr. John W. Farwell, Mr. Frederick L. Gay,
and Mr. John H. Edmonds for much information relating to early
New England maps.

A summary of these depositions follows:

David Dunning, gentleman, of Brunswick, deposed October 8, 1767, that on or about the year 1718 he came first to Boston, and in the same vessel with Andrew McFadden and his wife (now widow). Soon after they came down together in the same vessel to the eastern country, and lived in Brunswick ever since 1718.

Jane McFadden of Georgetown, aged about eighty-two, deposed June 19, 1766, that she with her late husband, Andrew McFadden, lived in the town of Garvo [Garvagh], County Derry, on the Bann Water, Ireland, at a place called Summersett. About forty-six years ago they removed from Ireland to Boston, from Boston down to the Kennebec River and up Merrymeeting Bay to a place called Cathance Point.[1]

Andrew McFadden of Georgetown, aged fifty-three, deposed June 22, 1768, that he was a son of the above Andrew and Jane. Daniel McFadden of Georgetown, aged forty-six, made a similar deposition. Other testimony shows that Andrew and Jane had a daughter between Andrew and Daniel, born on the Kennebec River. They christened her Summersett.[2]

---

[1] See Appendix III.

[2] John Moore, living in Philadelphia in 1712, had a child of the same name.

John McPhetre of Georgetown, aged above sixty, deposed June 22, 1768, that he knew Summersett place on the Bann Water, for he lived within about five miles of it.[1]

Colonel David Dunning was the son of Andrew Dunning, who was born in 1664, and came with his wife, Susan Bond, to the lower Kennebec, known then as Georgetown in Maine. After a year Andrew settled at Maquoit in Brunswick. He was a blacksmith, and died January 16, 1736, aged 72 years. His children were James, Andrew, Robert, William and David. He and Andrew McFadden evidently were able, thrifty settlers, not unlike those led by McGregor, and they also were from the Bann Valley.

But these were not the only early settlers on the Kennebec. Captain Robert Temple came over to Boston with his family and servants in the autumn of 1717 to settle as a gentleman farmer. He visited Connecticut and also the lands of the Pejepscot Company about the Androscoggin River in Maine. He much preferred, however, the lands on the east side of the Kennebec, opposite the mouth of the Androscoggin. Upon his return to Boston he was taken into the enterprise, and agreed to undertake the transportation of settlers from Ireland. Tem-

---

[1] Depositions given in the New England Historical and Genealogical Register, Vol. 39, p. 184; taken from the Cumberland County Court files by W. M. Sargent of Portland.

ple engaged two large ships in 1718, and three more
ships were chartered the next year. The Scotch
Irish whom he brought over settled on the east bank
of the Kennebec, between the present towns of Dresden and Woolwich. The land was called Cork. The
names of some of his people were: William Montgomery, ―――― Caldwell, James Steel, David Steel,
―――― McNut, James Rankin, William and James
Burns or Barns.[1] A few of the Temple colonists settled in Topsham, opposite Brunswick, and several in
Cathance, now part of Bowdoinham, on the Kennebec, south of Dresden.[2] Others, the larger part of
the several hundred who came under Temple, went
to New Hampshire and Pennsylvania to avoid the
wrath of Father Rasle and his Indians. Cork was
destroyed soon after.

The ships must have brought immigrants rapidly,
for Southack's map, published in London in 1720,
states that already five hundred had arrived, or
about one hundred families. The *News-Letter* for
August 17–24, 1719, prints an item from Piscataqua
dated August 21st, to the effect that Philip Bass had
arrived at the Kennebec River from Londonderry
with about two hundred passengers. Many of these
must have been friends of those who came in the

---

[1] See an interesting paper on "The Transient Town of Cork," in
Maine Historical Society Collections, 2d Series, Vol. 4, p. 240.

[2] The Rev. E. S. Stackpole has given me valuable aid on this
subject.

"Maccallum." We unfortunately have no record of the arrival of ships in 1718 and 1719 at the mouth of the Kennebec. But not all the settlers there sailed directly from Ireland; many came through the forests or by sea from Falmouth, York, and Boston. Perhaps the Spear and Harper families of Brunswick had associations farther south, since David Spear (from Coleraine) and James Harper, both of the Connecticut Valley, were early settled in and near Windsor.

The Rev. James Woodside had been preaching at Garvagh, in the Bann Valley, since 1700. Wheeler, in his history of Brunswick,[1] calls him a clergyman of the Church of England; but there is more significance in the fact that we find him mentioned in Killen's Congregations of the Presbyterian Church in Ireland, as a Presbyterian minister at Garvagh. Wind and tide drove him into Massachusetts Bay, and he went with his flock to Casco Bay and on to Brunswick, where they arrived in September, 1718. Possibly his sympathies were with the English ritual; this might have made him unwelcome to some of his Brunswick congregation and so given color to the tradition that he was an Episcopalian.

The first reference to religion at Brunswick ap-

---

[1] Mr. Wheeler in his History and also in an entertaining sketch of Brunswick at the time of its incorporation (Pejepscot Historical Society Collections) is not always to be followed in statements as to ancestry and year of immigration.

pears to be a petition to the General Court from
three Indians at Fort George, in October, 1717; and
in response to their desire the Rev. Joseph Baxter
was sent north from Medford to preach. In the
summer of 1718 Mr. Woodside, with from twenty-
five to forty families, reached Casco Bay from the
Irish Londonderry, or from "Derry Lough." The
company went from Falmouth over land or by water
to Merrymeeting Bay, as described in the deposition
of Jane McFadden. Woodside appears to have settled down, temporarily at least, with his family at
Falmouth. It is probable that the McGregor colony,
with the Rev. Mr. Cornwall, had not yet arrived at
Casco Bay, for they are known to have reached there
in cold weather. Furthermore, Mr. Cornwall dined
in Boston with Judge Sewall as late as October 16,
1718, and as he probably sailed with the rest of his
party, the departure was no doubt as late as the end
of October.

The settlers at Brunswick, having been without
Mr. Baxter's ministrations for six months, voted in
town meeting November 3, 1718, to call Mr. Woodside from Falmouth. The vote touches upon several
details of interest, and it is given here: "Att a
Leagual Town meeting in Brunswick Novm^{ber} 3^{d}
1718, It was Voted That whereas the Proprietors of
S^{d} Township in their paternal Care for our Spiritual
Good, have by there Joynt Letter Sought to ye Reverend M^{r}. James Woodside to be our Minister & in

order there to proposed Conditions for his Settlement on their part, Wee the Inhabitance of Brunswick will Give Fourty pounds pr annum toward ye support of ye s^d Mr. Woodside & a Sum in proportion there to from this time untill May next (if he Come to us) & God in his providence Should Then part us.

"It was also at this meeting Voted That Mr Baxters house on ye 6th Lott in Brunswick Be forthwith made habitable for ye s^d Mr. Woodside. That ye Charges there of ye Transporting him & his famoly from Falmouth to Brunswick be paid Equally by us ye inhabitance of s^d Brunswick & y^t Capt Gyles is here by impowered to se ye Buisness effected.

Joseph Heath Town C^lk'"[1]

In January, 1719, Cotton Mather wrote letters to the Scotch ministers at the Eastward to give them courage. Mr. Woodside certainly needed this encouragement, for matters went ill with him there. In May the town voted to continue Mr. Woodside's services for six months, "provided those of us who are Dissatisfied with his Conversation (as afore Said) Can by Treating with him as becomes Christians receive Such Sattisfaction from him as that they will heare him preach for ye Time afore s^d." Mr. Wheeler takes "Conversation" to mean character. Possibly deportment or habits would come a

---

[1] Wheeler's Brunswick, p. 354.

little nearer, although in another place Wheeler says the trouble was that he was not puritanical enough. Mather, in 1716, writing to a friend in Scotland, spoke of the transplanted clergy as too often "of a disdainful carriage," and of an "expression full of a levity not usual among oᵣ ministers." The town voted September 10, 1719, to pay Mr. Woodside to that date and to dismiss him. In 1721 the Rev. Isaac Taylor, an assistant to the Rev. Samuel Haliday at Ardstraw, County Tyrone, came over. He could not have remained long, for in 1729 he was at Ardstraw, and had conformed to the Church of England. In 1722 he lent money to the McFarlands, probably those who were later of Boothbay, to pay their passage across the Atlantic.

The Rev. James Woodside returned to Boston, and on January 25, 1720, Mather writes that "poor Mr. *Woodside,* after many and grievous calamities in this uneasy country, is this week taking ship for London." He obtained credentials from the Rev. Cotton Mather, and a note of recommendation from the governor. Mather's letter reads:

"Boston, New England
"Jan 14, 1720

"Concerning the Reverend Mr. James Woodside the Bearer hereof, we have been informed That arriving with other good people to the Eastern parts of New England from the Northern parts of Ireland with ample recommendation [?] from the presbertery of Route[1] in the year 1718 he had invitations to settle at several places, but chose a settlement at a New Town called *Brunswick*: Declaring that he had in his view the instruction of the Eastern Salvages (which he Chould have near unto him) in the primitive and Reformed Christianity. In the progression [of] that Excellent service we have been informed.''

Woodside's son, Captain William, remained in Brunswick, where he became prominent. Captain Woodside had the ready wit and resource of his people. He once agreed to outrun a very fleet Indian if the savage would when defeated give him a fur robe. The Indian was delighted with the plan, since Woodside's corpulent figure was known far and wide to be slow of movement. A great crowd gathered at the appointed time and place, and the trial began. The captain ran so awkwardly and perspired so freely that the entire company, including his rival, broke into continual roars of laughter. The Indian remained near the captain to enjoy the fun, and so far forgot his part in the sport that the captain, with a final burst of speed, came home a winner before anyone recalled the fact that he was a competitor.

In 1723 the Rev. Mr. Woodside sent a very inter-

---

[1] "Above these [i. e. The Glinnes] as far as the river Bann, the country is called Rowte."—Camden's Britannia, 1722, p. 1406.

esting petition to the king in council, which tells of
the family misfortunes :[1]

"To the Kings most Excellent Majesty in Council
        The humble Memorial & Petition of James
        Woodside late Minister of the Gospel, at
        Brunswick, in New England.

"Sheweth

"That he with 40 Familys, consisting of above 160
Persons did in the Year 1718 embarque on a ship at
Derry Lough in Ireland in Order to erect a Colony
at Casco Bay, in Your Majestys Province of Main
in New England.

"That being arriv'd they made a settlement at a
Place called by the Indians Pegipscot, but by them
Brunswick, within 4 miles from Fort George, where
(after he had laid out a considerable sum upon a
Garrison House, fortify'd with Palisadoes, & two
large Bastions, had also made great Improvements,
& laid out considerably for the Benefit of that Infant
Colony) the Inhabitants were surpriz'd by the Indians who in the Month of July 1722 came down in
great Numbers to murder Your Majesty's good Subjects there.

"That upon this Surprize the Inhabitants, naked
& destitute of Provisions run for shelter into your
Pet.rs House (which is still defended by his sons)

---

[1] From Maine Historical Society Collections.   Baxter Mss.,
Vol. X, p. 163.   Original in the Rolls office, London.

where they were kindly receivd, provided for, & protected from the rebel Indians.

"That the S^d Indians being happily prevented from murdering Your Majesty's good Subjects (in Revenge to your Pet.^r) presently kill'd all his Cattel, destroying all the Moveables, & Provisions they could come at, & as Your Pet^r had a very considerable Stock of Cattel he & his Family were great sufferers thereby, as may appear by a Certificate of the Governour of that Province a Copy whereof is hereunto annexed.

"Your Pet^r therefore most humbly begs that in Regard to his great undertaking, his great Losses & sufferings, the Service done to the Publicke in saving the Lives of many of Your Majesty's Subjects, the unshak[en] Loyalty & undaunted Courage of his Sons, who still defend the S^d Garrison. Your Majesty in Councel will be pleas'd to provide for him, his Wife & Daughter here or grant him the Post of M^r. Cummins, a Searcher of Ships in the Harbour of Boston N England, lately deceas'd that so his Family, reduced to very low Circumstances may be resettled, & his losses repair'd where they were sustain'd.

& Your Pet^r shall ever pray &c.''

"I do hereby certifie that the Rev.^d M^r. Woodside went over from Ireland to New England with a considerable Number of People, that he & they sate

down to plant in a Place they called Brunswick in
the Eastern Parts of New England there he built a
Garrison House, which was the Means of saving the
Lives of many of his People in the late Insurrection
of the Indians in July last.   That his Generosity is
taken Notice of by both Doctors Mathers & that the
Indians cutt off all his Cattle, whereby he and his
Family are great Sufferers

                                        Samuel Shute

"Copia vera

              "London June 25, 1723

  "E: Memorial & Petition of James Woodside
     to His Most Excellent Majesty in Councel.
                    June 1723"

During these days of Indian warfare, pillage and
reprisal, men were impressed for sentinel duty, and
distributed in small groups at garrison houses
throughout the frontier towns in Maine, which was
then under the jurisdiction of Massachusetts.   One
of the unpleasant experiences of young Scotch Irishmen was to be met in the street by an officer and his
attendants, and forced into military service.   Many
fell sick under the strain of such a life in the Maine
woods, and through rough usage at the hands of
officers.   This ill-treatment fell heaviest upon the
"Irish," and particularly at the outset of the Indian
troubles.   A case is on record of a Scotch Irish impressed soldier returning weak and crippled to the

place of his enlistment with no attempt at conceal-
ment, and because he could not produce papers to
show his discharge, he was whipped at the cart's
tail, and kept in jail until the Sheriff was moved
through pity to ask for his release. Not until one
half the force at the front had disappeared through
illness and desertion did the Governor take the
matter in hand. A committee then visited the frontier and brought back an unpleasant account of
garrison life in such places as Brunswick.

With the coming of militant Indians the colonists
fled, some to the New Hampshire Londonderry or to
Worcester, and many to Pennsylvania, leaving few
traces of their sojourn in Maine. William Willis,
editor of Smith and Deane's Journals, has attempted
to gather the names of these early settlers. The
Rev. Everett S. Stackpole, a student of the subject,
suggests the addition of those whose surnames appear between brackets:

[Andrew] McFadden ———— Ward
———— McGowen [David] Given
[William?] Vincent [Andrew] Dunning
[John?] Hamilton [William] Simpson
———— Johnston [David Alexander and son]
[John?] Malcome [William Alexander]
———— McLellan [James Wilson]
———— Crawford [James McFarland]
———— Graves [George Cunningham]

[Robert Lithgow]   [David Ross]
[John Welch]   [William Craigie]
          [John Young]

The last four men Welch,[1] Ross, Craigie, and
Young, witnessed a deposition at Brunswick September 4, 1718.[2]   If they were Scotch Irish they
might have come in July or August, but it seems
most natural to place them with John Barbour at
York where Scotchmen had lived since Cromwell's
wars in 1650.   Possibly they did not have any connection with the Scotch Irish movement.

At the outbreak of Dummer's war many Brunswick settlers sailed for Boston, and suffered the
customary formality of being warned out of town.
Lists of these have the virtue of being well within
the field of verity.   The settlers thus recorded undoubtedly came from the Kennebec country or settlements adjoining, and nearly all of these were Scotch
Irish.   The date at the left shows when the record of
warning was reported to the selectmen in Boston.

July 25, 1719:

    Mary Banerlen, a widd° wth 6 Children who
    came from Bronswick into this Town on ye[e]
    22th of July.

---

[1] See Monmouth, Maine.
[2] York deeds, Vol. 9, folio 238.

October 24, 1719:

>John Clark wth his wife & five children who came from Merrymeeting bay.

October 24, 1719:

>John Gray w[th] his wife & five Children

>John Newel w[th] his wife & three Children

>Robert Tark w[th] his wife & three Children who all came into this Town from Berwick in a sloop Thomas Bell mast[r]

>James Dixwell & James Wallis husb[d]men who arrived here from y[e] Eastward

>Susanna Gate who Sayes She came from the Eastw[d]

July 22, 1720:

>Eliz[a] Rylee from Arrowsack.

October 28, 1720:

>Jean Hall & child from Piscattiqua.

January 27, 1721/22:

>Humphry Taylor Wife & Six Children from Smal point, warned Aug. 7th.

>Jean Sper & three Children from the Eastward, warned August 5th.

>Mary Shertwell from Arowshick

>John Miller from Misconges

July 28, 1722 from the Eastward viz.[t] [the following who from their names, notably that of McFarland, evidently came from about Merrymeeting Bay.]

>Jean Hunter with Two Children

Katherin Carter with & 3 Children
Jean Wilson with 4 Children
Sundry from the Eastward viz[t]
Andrew Macfaden wife & 6 Children
Isaac Hunter wife & 2 Children
Alexan[r] wife and 4 Children
James Johnson wife & 4 Children
John Nelson wife & 2 Children
Mathew Acheson wife & 2 Children
Andrew Rogers
Robert Rowland
Samuel forgeson
William Hambleton

November 6, 1722. A List of Sundry Persons
Brought from Brunswick, Topsham and Towns
adjacent at the Eastward parts by Thomas San-
ders, and warned to depart the Town of Boston,
as the Law directs, August the 12th 1722. viz[t].

Charles Stuart	Susan Lithgoe
Hanna Stuart	Will[m] Lithgoe
Hana Stuart	Jean Lithgoe
Sam[ll] Stuart	Susan Lithgoe
Henry Stuart	James Ross[1]
Moses Harper	Jenet Ross
Mary Harper	Eliza[th] Ross
Jenat Harper	Mary Ross
Robert Lithgoe	Isb[ll] Ross

[1] Wheeler thinks he was not Scotch Irish.

John Ross
Mary Thorn
Thomas Thorn
Hugh Minsy [Menzies?]
Sarah Minsy
John Young
Katherine Young
Margaret Young
Mary Young
Easter Young
Sarah Young
James Harper
James Miller
Margaret Wadburn
Mary Wadburn
George Wadburn
David Evins
Will[m] Evins
Thomas Rogers
Eliza[th] Rogers
Isabella Rogers
John Hamilton
John Hamilton
James Rodgers

James Beverly
Agnus Beverly
James Beverly
Sam[ll] Beverly
Joseph Beverly
Mary Smith
John Smith
Aubia Smith
Mathew Smith
Robert Wallis
Martha Wallis
John Wallis
Anbah Wallis
Jonas Stanwood[1]
Sam[ll] Stanwood[1]
David Stanwood[1]
M[r] Salter
Mary Salter
Thomas Salter
Mary Salter
M[r] Swwanan &
   Maid
M[r] Cary & wif

April 26, 1723:
Daniel Hunter & His Wife
James Savage His Wife & five Children—
Irish people from Smal Point. Ap[r] 10th.

---

[1] Not Scotch Irish.

October 28, 1723:

> Tho. Hogg his wife & Two Children from Arowshick.

June 29, 1724:

> Mary Thomas & one Child from St. Georges.

We may summarize the Merrymeeting Bay Scotch Irish settlers of 1718–1722 somewhat in this way, using Wheeler's list of early settlers, pages 865–874; the warnings above; and various facts found elsewhere. Some names are no doubt English, but as yet they cannot safely be eliminated.

Merrymeeting Bay Scotch Irish Settlers, 1718–1722.

> Matthew Acheson, wife and two children
> ———— Alexander, wife and four children
> David Alexander and son
> William Alexander
> Mary Banerlen, widow, and six children
> James and William Barns or Burns
> Agnes Beverly
> James Beverly
> Joseph Beverly
> Samuel Beverly
> ———— Calwell
> Katherine Carter and three children
> ———— Cary and wife
> John Clark, wife and five children

John Cochran
  Selectman at Brunswick in 1719? "Ireland"
    in muster roll
William Craigie
  At Brunswick September 4, 1718
———— Crawford
George Cunningham
James Dixwell
Andrew Dunning
  "Ireland" in muster roll
David Evans
John Evans
William Evans
Samuel Ferguson
  Alexander and James Ferguson were at Kit-
    tery in 1711
Thomas Fleming
David Given or Giveen
John Graves
John Gray, wife and five children
Jean Hall and child
John Hamilton
  Abel and Gabriel Hamilton at Berwick in
    1711
Patrick Hamilton
Robert Hamilton
Robert Hamilton, Jr.
William Hamilton
William Handsard

James Harper
  "Ireland" in muster roll
Jenet Harper
Joseph Harper
Mary Harper
Moses Harper
William Harper
Thomas Hogg, wife and two children; from Arrowsic, 1723
?Adam Hunter
Daniel Hunter and wife
  "Irish people from Smal point," 1723
Isaac Hunter, wife and two children
James Hunter
Jean Hunter and two children
John Hunter
James Johnson, wife and four children
Jean Lithgow
Robert Lithgow
Susan Lithgow
William Lithgow
Andrew McFadden, wife and six children
James McFarland
———— McGowen
———— McNut
John Malcom
James Miller
John Miller
  From Miscongus

Dr Hugh Minnery or Minory
Hugh Minsy
Sarah Minsy
Henry Mitchell
    "Ireland" in muster roll
Hugh Mitchell
    "Ireland" in muster roll
William Montgomery
John Nelson, wife and two children
John Newel, wife and three children
James Rankin
Elizabeth Riley
    From Arrowic
Andrew Rogers
Elizabeth Rogers
Isabella Rogers
James Rogers
Thomas Rogers
David Ross
Elizabeth Ross
Isabella Ross
James Ross
Jenet Ross
John Ross
Mary Ross
Robert Rowland
Mr ———— Salter
Mary Salter
Thomas Salter

James Savage, wife and five children
  "Irish people from Smal point," 1723
Mary Shertwell
  From Arrowsic
William Simpson
Aubia Smith
James Smith
John Smith
Mary Smith
Matthew Smith
Jean Spear and three children
David and James Steel
James Stinson or Stevenson
  "Ireland" in muster roll
John Stinson
Robert Stinson
Charles Stuart
Hannah Stuart
Henry Stuart
Samuel Stuart
William Tailer
Robert Tark, wife and three children
Humphrey Taylor, wife and six children
  From Small Point
Mary Thomas and one child
  From Saint Georges, 1724
Peter Thompson
Mary Thorn
Thomas Thorn

James Thornton
Thomas Tregoweth
John Vincent
Anbah Wallis
Daniel Wallis
James Wallis
John Wallis
Martha Wallis
Robert Wallis
———— Ward
John Welch
James Wilson
Jean Wilson and four children
George Woodburn
Margaret Woodburn
Mary Woodburn
Samuel York
Easter Young
John Young
Katherine Young
Margaret Young
Mary Young
Sarah Young

These are the settlers who fulfilled the Rev. Cotton Mather's dream of a line of emigrant outposts. They suffered grievous hardships, but who shall say that they and theirs did not in the fulness of time reap a just reward of prosperity, influence and honor?

CHAPTER XIII

NUTFIELD AND LONDONDERRY, 1719–1720

The Scotch Irish petition, signed in Ireland, bears the date "this 26th day of March, Annoq. Dom. 1718," a few weeks only before the Rev. Mr. Boyd set sail for New England, where he arrived about July 25th. While his friends were crossing the ocean, Mr. Boyd endeavored to interest Governor Shute, Judge Sewall and the Rev. Cotton Mather in their behalf. Evidently he could do little more in Boston than call upon persons of influence before his flock came into the harbor.

We have seen that many of the settlers went to the frontier settlement at Worcester, and still others to Casco Bay, where Governor Shute was endeavoring to foster the growth of Falmouth. James Smith went to Needham, Walter Beath to Lunenburg, and Matthew Watson to Leicester, although it is not always possible to say that these or others went immediately to the towns where they eventually settled. The followers of the two clergymen, Boyd and Mc-Gregor, desired a grant of land which they might control rather than permission to settle among the old stock that had founded the colony. These men remained in Boston while negotiations went on. The

Rev. Mr. McGregor and Archibald Boyd,[1] perhaps a brother of the clergyman of that name, sent the following petition to the General Court:

"A Petition of Archibald Boyd, James MacGregory & sundry others Setting forth that the Petitioners being under very discouraging circumstances in their own Countrey (viz. the Kingdom of Ireland) as well on the Account of Religion, as the Severity of their Rents & Taxes; & having heard of the great Willingness to encourage any of his Majestys Protestant & loyal Subjects of sober conversation to settle within this Province they have this last Summer, with their Families, undertaken a long & hazzardous Voyage to the sd Parts & are now residing in & about Boston, & have been waiting the Meeting of this Honble Assembly: And Praying that the Court would be pleased to grant unto them a convenient Tract of their wast Land, in such Place as they shall think fit, where they may without Loss of time, settle themselves & their Families, as over forty more Families who will come from Ireland as soon as they hear of their obtaining Land for Township; which they apprehend will be of great Advantage to this Country by strengthening the Frontiers & out Parts & making Provisions Cheaper.

"In the House of Represent^ves October 31, 1718: Read and Committed. In Council; Read."

---

[1] A Rev. Archibald Boyd, of Maghera, ordained October 28, 1703, was "set aside" in 1716.

The above petition shows that the rigorous laws relating to religion, and the rise in rents and taxes about Coleraine in Ireland, brought about the Scotch Irish migration. The reference to forty families soon to follow may indicate some connection in the plans of the McGregor company and the Rev. James Woodside's party which finally settled at Brunswick. The petition was granted November 20, 1718, and a committee of six was appointed to lay out a town for the people from Ireland. It was to be six miles square, of unappropriated lands "in the Eastern parts." Eighty house lots were to be laid out in a defensible manner, and not exceeding one hundred acres more to each lot. When forty lots had been taken the owners would manage all their own prudential affairs, and upon the settlement of eighty families they could then dispose of common lands. With true New England spirit, provision was made for two hundred and fifty acres to be set aside for the ministry before any other allotments were made, and a like amount for a school.[1]

Parker states that the company which passed the winter of 1718–19 on shipboard in Casco Bay explored the country to the eastward, and finding nothing satisfactory that had not been claimed they ascended the Merrimac to Haverhill, April 2, 1719; at this point they were told of a fertile tract of land covered with nut trees, lying about fourteen miles

[1] Province Laws, 1718–19, Chapters 99, 104.

north west of the meeting-house at Haverhill. Leaving their families there, or across the river at Bradford, the men of the party, James McKeen, Captain James Gregg and others, at once mounted horses and rode over to examine the land. They found it satisfactory and named the place Nutfield, on account of the trees growing there. They remained to build a few temporary huts near a small tributary of Beaver Brook, which they called West-running Brook. They then returned to Haverhill for their wives and children. Those who had remained on the south side of the Merrimac at Bradford or Andover crossed over the river in boats. The Haverhill rabble had no love for the "Irish," and greeted them with jeers and ridicule. When nearing the shore for a landing one of the boats turned over, so that women and children were thrown into the water. This afforded boundless delight to the onlookers, and at last inspired a local bard, who sang:

> "Then they began to scream and bawl,
> And if the devil had spread his net
> He would have made a glorious haul."[1]

Several of the company went to Nutfield by way of Dracut, a town near the mouth of Beaver Brook, where it joins the Merrimac. They met the Rev.

---

[1] B. L. Mirick's Haverhill, 1832, pp. 140–141.

Mr. McGregor and asked him to go with them. The two parties journeying to Nutfield met on April 11th, at the little hill where the men had on the previous visit tied their horses. This happy and memorable occasion was made impressive by an address from the Rev. Mr. McGregor. He congratulated his friends on the termination of their wanderings after enduring the perils of a voyage across the ocean and a pitiless winter. He besought them to be steadfast in their faith in the midst of a strange people and unknown dangers.

Before he returned to Dracut the next day he preached from Isaiah xxxii. 2, "And a man shall be a hiding-place from the wind, and a covert from the tempest; as rivers of water in a dry place; as the shadow of a great rock in a weary land." He stood under a large oak tree, east of Beaver Pond and within sight of the first rude cabins of his people, who now gathered round him. His tall figure was erect and commanding, his dark face serene and strong. It was a time for courage and for prayer. They had come over the sea to escape persecution and had met everywhere in the new world intolerance and distrust. They had not only to subdue the wilderness but to kindle a brotherly Christian spirit in the grandsons of those who founded Plymouth and Boston.

The settlers decided to build on either side of West-running Brook, each home lot to be thirty rods

wide, fronting the brook, and extending back from
the bank to a distance sufficient to make each lot
contain sixty acres. In this way they were able for
a few years to live in a close community as a protection from the Indians. Two stone garrison houses
were built for further safety, although as it happened the town was never attacked, and one man,
James Blair, never sought their sheltering walls.

There is a tradition that this immunity from Indian assault was due to a bond of friendship between
McGregor and Philippe, Marquis de Vaudreuil, Gov-
ernor-general of Canada. It has been said that the
two men, the Catholic nobleman and the Protestant
commoner, attended the same college. The improb-
ability of the story is apparent, although some form
of intercourse between the two may be inferred
from the fact that a manuscript sermon in McGreg-
or's hand bears on the margin Vaudreuil's name
and titles. The following paragraph in Sewall's
Diary, under date of March 5, 1718–19, refers to
news obtained by Boyd, possibly from a letter written by Vaudreuil, although there is not the slightest
evidence that it was sent to McGregor. The passage
reads: ''Mr. Boyd dines with me: he says there is
a Report in the Town that Govr Vandrel [Vaudreuil]
has written that he can no longer keep back the Indians from War.''

In these days of hewing and building at Nutfield
we get a pleasant bit of humor in the story of the

MEETING HOUSE AT LONDONDERRY, N. H.

construction of John Morison's log cabin. John
was at work on the bank of West-running Brook,
selecting from his pile of logs those that he preferred for front wall and for sides, and those best
suited for beams to support the roof. His wife
Margaret, engrossed by her share of the home du-
ties, nevertheless found time to watch his progress
and also to cast an eye about upon the work being
done by other women's husbands. As the cabin
grew she became anxious, and approaching him in
a manner unusually affectionate she said: "Aweel,
aweel, dear Joan, an it maun be a loghouse, do make
it a log heegher nor the lave" (higher than the rest).
It was her grandson, Jeremiah Smith, whose inherited desire to excel made him a member of Congress
and chief justice of his state.

But there was in these settlers something more
vital than even a proper pride. They were everywhere devout. When a religious organization was
needed the Bann company at once thought of the
Rev. Mr. McGregor. He accepted their invitation
to settle at Nutfield and in May, 1719, removed with
his family from Dracut to the new village. This
must have been a contrast indeed, leaving the well-
established town for a large field covered with
stumps of trees, intersected by a brook, and dotted
with log cabins. But between the stumps potatoes
and beans and barley grew, and where the smoke
curled from the clay chimneys he knew that there

he should recognize voices, and should meet eyes that were familiar with Coleraine in old Ireland, with the Salmon Leap, the Giant's Causeway, Boyd's mountain, and even with God's house in far-away Aghadowey church-yard. There he had been known as the "Peace-maker," and he lived to be revered anew in his New England home.

The settlement had been made at Nutfield under the impression that the lands were in Massachusetts, but in May, 1719, the General Court decided that New Hampshire had jurisdiction over them. James Gregg and Robert Wear, in behalf of the Scotch Irish at Nutfield, then asked the governor and court assembled at Portsmouth, New Hampshire, for a township ten miles square. Meanwhile, to obtain a title to the lands of Nutfield, which were claimed by several persons, they applied to Colonel John Wheelwright, the chief claimant. By virtue of a deed or grant made to his grandfather and others by representatives of all the Indians between the Merrimac and the Piscataqua, the colonel held a title which commanded attention. His deed to James McGregor, Samuel Graves, David Cargill, James McKeen, James Gregg, "and one hundred more" was dated October 20, 1719.[1]

Lieutenant-Governor Wentworth, on account of a dispute as to the title, refused to make a grant, but by advice of his council extended to the people the

---

[1] See Parker's Londonderry, page 321.

benefits of government and appointed James McKeen a justice of the peace and Robert Wear a sheriff. The petition[1] reads: "The Humble petition of the People late of Ireland now settled at Nutfield to his Excellency the Governor and General Court assembled at Portsmouth Sep^t 23^d 1719.

"Humbly Sheweth, That your Petitioners having made application to the General Court met at Boston in October last[2] and having obtained a grant for a Township in any part of their unappropriated lands took incouragement thereupon to settle at Nutfield about the Eleventh of Aprile last which is situated by Estimation about fourteen miles from Haverel meeting House to the North West and fifteen miles from Dracut meeting House on the River merrimack north and by East. That your petitioners since their settlement have found that the said Nutfield is claimed by three or four different parties by virtue of Indian Deeds, yet none of them offered any disturbance to your petitioners except one party from Newbury and Salem. Their Deed from one John Indian bears date March the 13th Anno Dom: 1701 and imports that they had made a purchase of the said land for five pounds, by virtue of this deed they claim ten miles square Westward from Haverel

---

[1] New Hampshire Town Papers, Vol. IX, p. 480.

[2] The petition from John Armstrong at Falmouth was not granted. That from Archibald Boyd led to the grant of a township, and so appears to be the one here referred to.

line and one Caleb Moody of Newbury in their name discharged our People from clearing or any wais improving the said land unless we agreed that twenty or five and twenty families at most should dwell there and that all the rest of the land should be reserved for them.

"That your petitioners by reading the Grant of the Crown of Great Britain to the Province of the Massachusetts bay, which determineth their northern line three miles from the River merrimack from any and every part of the River and by advise from such as were more capable to judge of this Affair, are Satisfied that the said Nutfield is within his Majesties Province of New Hampshire which we are further Confirmed in, because the General Court met at Boston in May last, upon our renewed application did not think fit any way to intermeddle with the said land.

"That your petitioners therefore imbrace this opportunity of addressing this honorable Court, praying that their Township may consist of ten miles square or in a figure Equivalent to it, they being already in number about seventy Families & Inhabitants and more of their friends arrived from Ireland to settle with them, and many of the people of New England settling with them, and that they being so numerous may be Erected into a Township with its usual Priviledges and have a power of making Town Officers and Laws, that being a frontier place they may the better subsist by Government amongst them, and may be more strong and full of Inhabitants:

"That your Petitioners being descended from and professing the Faith and Principles of the Establist Church of North Britain and Loyal Subjects of the British Crown in the family of his Majesty King George and incouraged by the happy administration of his Majesties Chief Governour in these provinces and the favourable inclinations of the good people of New England to their Brethren adventuring to come over and plant in this vast Wilderness, humbly Expect a favorable answer from this honourable Court and your Petitioners as in duty bound shall ever pray &c, Subscribed at Nutfield in the name of your people Sep^t ye 21st 1719

"James Gregg
"Robertt Wear"

Nutfield was incorporated as the town of Londonderry in June, 1722, and an interesting list of proprietors was appended to the act.[1]

It would be fruitless to follow longer the fortunes of the New Hampshire Londonderry, since Parker has written the story in all its detail. The people throve and multiplied, they tilled the soil, fished at the Amoskeag falls, and made linens and hollands that became known far and wide.

---

[1] See Parker's Londonderry, pp. 322–326; also New Hampshire Town Papers, Vol. IX, p. 484.

It is said by Parker that sixteen men with their families first settled on the "common field" about the mouth of West-running Brook. Perhaps they should be defined[1] as the immediate friends of Mr. McGregor. The town in December, 1719, voted to grant a lot to each of "the first Comers to the town which is the number of *twenty.*" The sixteen men were:

James McKeen, of Ballymoney,[2] County Antrim: he married 1st Janet Cochran, 2d Annis Cargill. His daughter married James Nesmith. He died November 9, 1756, at the age of 91 years.

James Gregg, of Macosquin, County Londonderry: he married Janet Cargill, sister of Mrs. McKeen above and of Mrs. James McGregor.

John Barnett, Captain, and Jean his wife. Their children are mentioned in the records as early as 1722. He died in 1740 at the age of 86. Jean or Janet was the widow of John McKeen, a brother of James McKeen.

Archibald Clendenin, and Miriam his wife. Their children are given in the birth records as early as 1720.

---

[1] "More strictly defined as members of Rev. James McGregor's congregation."—Willey's Nutfield, p. 91.

[2] The townland of Ballynacree in the parish of Ballymoney was also a center of Quaker influence. From the Ballynacree monthly meetings there went out to Pennsylvania Daniel, Andrew and Alexander Moore, William McCool, Samuel Beverly, Samuel Miller, John Boyd and Thomas McMillan.

John Mitchell, Captain, died in 1776, aged 80. His
wife Eleanor died in 1771, aged 74.

James Sterrett, of whom little is known. His home
lot was isolated, and next to it he had a grant of
80 acres laid out in 1729.

James Anderson, and Mary his wife. Their children
are mentioned as early as 1720. He died in 1771,
aged 88. His grand-daughter Alice married the
Rev. Joseph McKeen, first president of Bowdoin
College, grandson of James McKeen.

Allen Anderson, married a daughter of Hugh Rankin but died childless. Land was laid out to him
in 1728.

Randal Alexander, and Jenet his wife. Their children are mentioned on the birth records. He died
in 1770, aged 83. The "Randal" in Scotch Irish
names came from the great Earl of Antrim.

James Clark, and Elizabeth his wife, had a child
whose birth is recorded in 1726. He became a
deacon, and had four sons and a daughter.

James Nesmith, married Elizabeth, daughter of
James McKeen. He died in 1767, aged 75. She
died in 1763, at the age of 67.

Robert Weir or Wear, and Martha his wife. A
daughter Elizabeth was born in 1723.

John Morison, and Margaret his wife. He died in
Peterborough in 1776, aged 98. She died in 1769,
aged 82.

Samuel Allison, and Catherine his wife. Their

children are mentioned as early as 1721. He died
in 1760, at the age of 70.

Thomas Steele, married Martha Morison, sister of
John Morison above. He died in 1748, aged 65.
She died in 1759, aged 73.

John Stuart, and Jean his wife.

The records speak of twenty "first comers," so
that we should, perhaps, add four others to the above
list. These might be Goffe, Graves, Simonds and
Keyes, or the first two, with the Rev. Mr. McGregor
and a fourth. At best we can only offer a surmise.

With the sixteen settlers should be associated the
Rev. James McGregor who married Marion Cargill,
the sister of Mrs. McKeen and Mrs. James Gregg.
These people were all from the banks of the Bann
River, or the Bann Water, as it was called, and had
ties of blood or social intercourse to hold them
together. James McKeen and his brother John were
in business together at Ballymoney,[1] county Antrim,
in 1718, and had prospered. They determined to
emigrate to America, influenced perhaps by James's
brother-in-law McGregor who felt keenly the effects
of commercial depression and religious strife in Ire-

---

[1] The accompanying sketch of Ballymoney, reconstructed from
a plan, shows its four streets. In the foreground is Meeting
House Lane, with the Gate Cabin (near Gate End and the Castle)
at the extreme left, and Fort Cabin at the right, with the Meeting House opposite to it. The Main Street leads to Coleraine.
From it to the right is Church Street; to the left is Piper's
Row, with the Market on the corner.

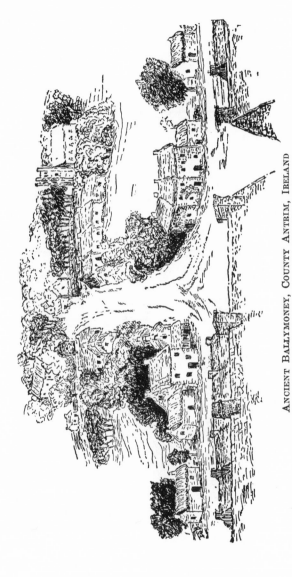

ANCIENT BALLYMONEY, COUNTY ANTRIM, IRELAND

Home of the McKeen family. Reconstructed from a plan and description

land.[1] John McKeen died a short time before the ship was to sail; but his widow with her four children continued with the party, which was evidently composed of families allied by marriage or closely associated with the McKeen business interests in Ballymoney, or with the Rev. Mr. McGregor's religious life across the Bann at Aghadowey and Macosquin. We are not surprised therefore to hear that McKeen's daughter said to *her* granddaughter one day that "James McKeen, having disposed of his property embarked with his preacher, Rev. James McGregor and sixteen others, who had bound themselves to him for a certain time to pay for their passage to America."[2] He no doubt engaged the ship and became responsible for most of the expense of the enterprise.

The news that the Scotch Irish were to have a tract of land ten miles square for a town of their own soon attracted settlers from Boston, Worcester, and Falmouth. In September, 1719, there were seventy families at Nutfield, not all, however, of Scotch Irish connection. The list of proprietors of Londonderry in 1722 records about one hundred Scotch Irish land owners, and also several of English descent, John Wheelwright, Benning Wentworth, Richard Wal-

---

[1] His parish had become poor and his salary was greatly in arrears.

[2] Mrs. Thom's statement, L. A. Morrison's Dinsmoor Family, Lowell, 1891, p. 41.

dron, Edward Proctor, Benjamin and Joseph Kidder.

It is difficult to name the seventy families who settled at Nutfield before September, 1719; there must have been in addition to the sixteen original families at least twenty five who came during the summer of 1719. Some of these twenty five or more we know: others are to be found probably in the list of proprietors of 1722.[1]   One might name:

David Cargill, a selectman in 1719; he may have been the father of Mrs. McKeen, Mrs. Gregg and Mrs. McGregor: he was elected as the first selectman, a courtesy perhaps to his distinguished sons-in-law, for he served but one year. He had been a Ruling Elder of the church in Aghadowey, Ireland, and died in 1734, at the age of 73. His wife Jenet survived him for eleven years.

Alexander McMurphy, mentioned very early. His son John was a Justice of the Peace, and the town's first representative.[2]

James Reid, a graduate of the University of Edinburgh; among the first settlers, and prominent. He died in 1755, at the age of sixty.

John Wallace, who came in 1719 or 1720, and married in 1721 Annis Barnett. They had four sons and four daughters.

[1] I am indebted to Mrs. Charles F. White, Mrs. Henry S. Tufts and Miss Virginia Hall for many genealogical facts of value in connection with these families.

[2] See Willey's Nutfield, p. 231.

ABRAHAM HOLMES'S LETTER FROM THE CHURCH AT AGHADOWEY, IRELAND

John Bell, from Ballymoney in 1719 or 1720. The grandfather of Governor Bell of New Hampshire.

Abraham Holmes came with his wife and children in 1719. He died in 1753, at the age of 70. His wife

Mary Morison was probably a sister of David and Samuel Morison. They brought a very interesting letter from the church in Aghadowey, Ireland, signed by John Given and David Cargill. This letter reads:[1]

"The bearer, Abraham Holmes, Janet Givens his mother-in-law, Mary Morison his wife, and their two Children has lived in this Congregation the most part of them from their Infancy, and all along, and now at their departure they were not only sober and free of publick scandle, But also of good Report and Christian Conversation (Children exepted) now Communicants with us. And now being about to transport themselves to New England in America we have nothing to hinder their being received as members of any Christian Society, and may be admitted to sealing ordinances wherever providence may order their lot; all of which is certified at Ahadonia [Aghadowey] this 12ᵗʰ day of June 1719.

Witness by
"John Givens
"David Cargill"

The following men are mentioned in the historical statement with which the first town clerk opened his book of records:

---

[1] I am indebted to Mr. J. Albert Holmes for a copy of this paper. The original is owned by Mr. Charles D. Page of New Haven.

Robert Boyes, a prominent pioneer, who was sent to Ireland after Mr. McGregor's death to secure a successor in the pulpit;

Alexander and James Nichols, both useful men;

Alexander McGregor, doubtless a relative of the clergyman;

James Blair, the man who lived without fear of Indians and was never molested;

Alexander Walker, and

James Morison.

Among those who may have been of English origin, but were very early in Nutfield two appear on the town records in 1719:

John Goffe was town clerk from 1719 to 1722. He probably belonged to the Charlestown family of the same name.

Samuel Graves, a selectman as early as 1719. One might expect him to be a relative of the McKeen connection, for he was a grantee from Wheelwright of the Nutfield township, and the other four grantees mentioned, McKeen, McGregor, Cargill and Gregg were all related one to another by blood or marriage.

Two other men are noted by the editor of the printed Londonderry records as early settlers, Joseph Simonds, who appears in the historical statement, and Elias Keyes, who, like Goffe and Graves, fails of mention in the statement.

So ends a list which is far from satisfactory since many others may have been in Londonderry during the summer of the year 1719. Goffe, the town clerk, placed upon the Nutfield records birth dates which antedate 1718. It cannot be assumed that settlers reported these facts before the settlement was made at West-running Brook. Probably Goffe, who recorded his own early family statistics, did a like service for his friends the Graveses, MacMurphys, Leslies and Smiths.[1] They were, perhaps, all in Nutfield in 1719.

The early settlers of Londonderry comprised many who remained but a short time and moved on to new plantations.[2]

William Aiken	James Anderson‡
Edward Aiken	John Anderson
James Aiken	John Archibald
William Adams	John Archibald, Jr.
James Alexander	Robert Armstrong
(called "early" by	Robert Actmuty or
Jesse McMurphy)	Auchmuty
Randal Alexander‡	John Barnett‡ °
Samuel Allison‡	John Barnett, Jr.
Allen Anderson † ‡ °	John Bell

[1] Willey's Nutfield, pp. 63, 237.

[2] Robert Boyes and David Cargill in 1729 sent a petition to Colonel Dunbar in behalf of 150 families who desired lands about Pemaquid, Maine, for settlement. Maine Historical Society Collections, Baxter MSS., Vol. X, p. 439.

* † ‡ °. For explanation see p. 265.

James Blair† °
John Blair
David Bogle
Thomas Bogle
Dr. Hugh Bolton
William Bolton
Robert Boyes† °
Thomas Caldwell
William Campbell
David Cargill* °
David Cargill, Jr.°
George Clark
James Clark‡ °
John Clark
Matthew Clark
Robert Clark
Thomas Clark
Archibald Clendenin‡ °
Andrew Cochran
John Cochran
Peter Cochran
William Cochran
David Craig
John Crombie
David Dickey
Samuel Dickey
James Doak
John Doak
Robert Doak

George Duncan
William Eayers
James Gilmore
Robert Gilmore
William Gilmore
John Given
John Goffe*
Samuel Graves* °
John Gray
Henry Green
David Gregg
James Gregg* † ‡ °
John Gregg
Samuel Gregg
William Gregg
Nehemiah Griffin
Abraham Holmes
Samuel Huston
William Humphra or
    Humphrey
James Lesly or Leslie
James Liggit
James Lindsey [of
    Mendon, turner,
    1731]
John McClurg
Alexander McCollum
John McConoeighy
Daniel McDuffee

James McGlaughlin	Peter Patterson
Rev James McGregor* † °	John Pinkerton
Alexander McGregor† °	Hugh Ramsey
John Mack	Hugh Rankin
James McKeen* † ‡ °	James Reid
Janet McKeen	John Richey
John McKeen	James Rogers
Robert McKeen	John Sheales
Samuel McKeen	William Smith
Alexander McMurphy	Archibald Stark
John McMurphy	Thomas Steele† ‡ °
Alexander McNeal	James Sterrett‡
James McNeal	John Stuart‡
John McNeal	Jonathan Taylor
Abel Merrel	Matthew Taylor
John Mitchell‡	William Thompson
Hugh Montgomery	Andrew Todd
James Moor	Alexander Walker† °
John Moor	John Wallace
Samuel Moor	Robert Weir or Wear
David Morison	Benjamin Williams
James Morison† °	Benjamin Willson
John Morison, d. 1736	Elizabeth Willson
John Morison (Jr.) * † ‡ °	Mary Willson
Robert Morison	Thomas Willson
Samuel Morison	William Willson
James Nesmith‡ °	James Wilson
Alexander Nichols† °	Robert Wilson
James Nichols† °	John Woodford

* indicates that the name will be found on the town records of 1719.

† indicates that the name appears in the historical statement with which the town records open.

‡ indicates one of Parker's "first sixteen settlers."

° indicates an early settler in the judgment of the editor of the printed Londonderry records.

The following proprietors of Londonderry in 1722 have not been included above; few if any were Scotch Irish: Col. John Wheelwright, Edward Proctor,

BEARDIVILLE, BALLYWILLAN, COUNTY ANTRIM

Seat of the Leckys, distinguished at the Siege of Derry

Benjamin and Joseph Kidder, Joseph Simonds, Elias Kays, John Robey, John Senter, Stephen Perce, Andrew Spaulden, Benning Wentworth, and Richard Waldron. The Scotch Irish had their wish fulfilled, the desire for a town to be ruled by their own kith and kin.

XIV

THE SCOTCH IRISH IN DONEGAL, DERRY AND NESHAMINY, PENNSYLVANIA AFTER 1718

After the development of Londonderry, Rutland, and Pelham the New England Scotch Irish spread gradually into other towns, Windham, Antrim, Peterborough, Colerain, Blandford, Palmer and many more. Upon each they left a mark of thrift and piety. From these towns the more venturesome moved westward into New York, and one of their settlements, Cherry Valley, became famous later as the scene of an Indian massacre. Receiving fewer immigrants from Ireland to swell their numbers than like communities at the South received, the Scotch Irish of New England had less power, both to exercise in civil affairs, and to aid them to maintain their transplanted faith. If they may be said to have been unfortunate in this respect they have been peculiarly favored in their historians. Londonderry, Windham, Peterborough and Pelham are represented by local histories that treasure the Scotch Irish tradition. The life of Judge Jeremiah Smith, and the family histories of the Blairs, Smiths and Morrisons, are typical of the record of Scotch

Irish life that New England has preserved. If it be true that history must achieve vitality to reclaim a dead past, we may say, viewing these vital historical works, that New England in the days of the Scotch Irish pioneers still lives. Of the Scotch Irish at the South much of this can also be said with equal emphasis. Theirs is a record of influence still to be traced in history.

A southern stronghold of Presbyterianism was in the neighborhood of Newcastle, Delaware. The narrow tongue of land between the upper shore of Chesapeake Bay and the Delaware River is shared by Maryland and Delaware. Maryland's portion includes the Elk River and is known as Cecil County. Delaware's portion is called Newcastle County, with Wilmington, its chief city, at the mouth of Christiana Creek. North of these two counties and across the Pennsylvania line are Lancaster and Chester counties (all known as Chester County from 1682 to 1729), extending from the Delaware River to the Susquehanna River. This territory, south a few miles from Philadelphia, became the mecca for Scotch emigrants from Ireland. These emigrants pushed up through Newcastle County to cross the Pennsylvania line, hoping to escape from Maryland and its tithes.[1] Unfortunately at this very time the exact line of the boundary was in dispute between Lord Baltimore and the heirs of William Penn, and

---

[1] Pennsylvania Magazine of History, January, 1901, p. 497.

many of the settlers flocked in and preëmpted land in dispute, without obtaining right or title. To add to the confusion the Penn family were in a state of domestic discord, so that their agent James Logan allowed very few grants in any place after the year 1720. An exception was made however in the case of the Scotch Irish, people who, said Logan, "if kindly used, will I believe be orderly, as they have hitherto been, and easily dealt with; they will also, I expect, be a leading example to others." These grants were made for a settlement which was called Donegal.[1]

At this early period when the business of sending "runners" into the rural communities in Ireland to stimulate emigration[2] had not begun, we must not expect to find any noticeable increase in the number of ships entering the Atlantic ports. At Boston trading vessels from Dublin were not infrequent visitors, but aside from servants their passengers were few. At Charleston the number of ships entering the port scarcely varied between the years 1714 and 1724, except for a falling off when the pirates injured commerce in 1717–18, and a temporary increase in 1719.

Few Scotch Irish came to New York in the early part of the eighteenth century because the Governor of New York and New Jersey, Lord Cornbury, dealt

---

[1] Pennsylvania Magazine of History, Vol. 21, p. 495.

[2] *Ibid*, p. 485.

harshly with dissenters. The Rev. Francis Makemie and the Rev. John Hampton visited the city on a missionary tour to New England in January, 1706-7. Makemie was refused permission to preach in the Dutch Church, but conducted a service openly at the home of William Jackson in Pearl Street on Sunday, the 19th. He was arrested and thrown into prison for preaching without a license. Makemie petitioned for a speedy trial, but the legal proceedings were permitted to drag on until the seventh of June when a verdict of not guilty was brought in. The financial burden of imprisonment and trial, amounting to more than eighty three pounds, fell entirely upon Makemie, although he is known to have had firm friends in New York. His sureties John Johnstone, gentleman, and William Jackson, cordwainer, both recorded in 1703 as residents of the South ward, no doubt had listened to this famous sermon; and we know of four others who were present: Captain John Theobalds, John Vanhorne, Anthony Young and one Harris, Lord Cornbury's coachman.[1] The Governor, soon after the trial, was removed from office and imprisoned for debt. Late in 1718 the *News-Letter* furnishes evidence of the arrival of passengers from Ireland at the port of New York.[2] Whether Celts or Scots

---

[1] For a list of Presbyterians in New York in 1755, see Journal Presbyterian Historical Society, Vol. 1, p. 244.

[2] A pink from Ireland, John Read, master, arrived with passengers November 10, 1718.

we have as yet no information. But in forty years we find the Scotch Irish in New York to be wealthy and of great political influence.

Philadelphia seems to have had a considerable immigration from Dublin, Belfast and Glasgow from the time of the arrival of the first Quakers in 1682. What are we to think of over seventy passengers from Waterford, Ireland, who arrived in the ship Cezer, Matthew, Cowman, commander, in July, 1716,[1] or of fifty passengers from Cork in March 1718?

Again, of what character were the one hundred and fifty passengers which the Elizabeth and Margaret, after a voyage of twelve weeks from Dublin, left at Philadelphia in August, 1718?   Were these people Presbyterian Scotch Irish? A few may no doubt have claimed their faith and their blood, but I cannot but believe that up to the year 1719 most of the passengers were English and Celtic servants and mechanics, with a number of prosperous Scotch and English Quakers. Very few Ulster weavers and farmers came to the South until word reached Ireland late in 1718 that Boyd, the Bann Valley envoy, had found serious difficulty in obtaining land in New England for settlement. In 1719 hundreds of Scotch Irish immigrants turned to lands in Chester

---

[1] *News-Letter*, August 6, 1716. Captain Cowman arrived from Dublin in September, 1717, with about one hundred passengers. Captain Gough in the Dove brought passengers a month later.

County and to the fields south of the Pennsylvania line for their homes.[1]

The Scotch Irish migration of Presbyterians to Chester County[2] began in 1719 and thus came long after the English-Irish migration of Quakers which had begun in 1682. These Presbyterians became of sufficient influence in Chester County in 1722 to obtain the name Donegal for their township. Chief among them at this time were:

James Galbraith, Senior, and his sons Andrew, James and John

Robert Wilkins and his sons Thomas, William, Peter and John

Gordon Howard and his sons Thomas and Joseph

George Stuart and his son John

Peter Allen

James Roddy

James and Alexander Hutchinson

John and Robert Spear

Hugh, Henry, and Moses White

Robert McFarland and his sons Robert and James

James Paterson

Richard Allison

---

[1] The curious reader may be interested in Charles Clinton's Journal of his voyage from Dublin via Glenarm and Derry Lough in 1729 when over one hundred passengers died on board. See the Pennsylvania Magazine of History, 1902, p. 112.

[2] Futhey and Cope's Chester County, p. 248.

Patrick Campbell
Robert Middleton
Thomas Bayly
Jonas Davenport
James and Samuel Smith
James Kyle
James and Thomas Mitchell
John and Benjamin Sterrett
Joseph Work
Ephraim Lytle
David McClure
Samuel Fulton
Alexander McKean
Robert and Arthur Buchannan
James Cunningham
William Maybee
William Hay
Henry Bailey
John Taylor
William Bryan
John and Malcom Karr
Edward Dougherty
John and Hugh Scott

The place names in old Chester County, Pennsylvania, such as Derry, Donegal and Toboyne, suggest that the early emigrants came for the most part from lands west of the River Foyle.

These pioneers built their log cabins in the pleas-

MEETING HOUSE AT DONEGAL, PENNSYLVANIA

ant meadows and woodlands near John Galbraith's mill, and in due time they gave of their prosperity to maintain a well-built "ordinary" or tavern, for which the same thrifty John obtained a license in 1726. Here Rebecca, his daughter, was born, to become at the age of eighteen the wife of Colonel Ephraim Blaine whose untiring efforts as Commissary of Provisions kept body and soul together through the terrible winter at Valley Forge. Thus the Scotch Irish of Donegal were to have their influence upon the greater events of the world.

The fine old church at Donegal became a center of religious influence. Its plain walls, high windows, and great gambrel roof symbolizes the plain manners and large hearts of its worshippers. Beneath the even turf within the graveyard wall these pioneers now lie, protected from the summer's heat by spruce and cedar. The heirs of their blood and brain are building the great west, while strange hands trim the sod, and children with unfamiliar names play among the ancient head stones.[1] After the Galbraiths and their friends had moved westward or had become less dominant in their influence other men of the same race came into prominence, the Semples, Andersons, Lowreys, Pedans, Porters, and Whitehills.

---

[1] A picture of the church may be seen in Gail Hamilton's Biography of James G. Blaine, 1895, and both the Church and Galbraith's "ordinary" in the Scotch Irish Society, 8th Congress, pp. 80, 336.

Donegal was only one of four townships along the east bank of the Susquehanna, all of them Scotch Irish settlements, which extended south and north of the present city of Harrisburg.   Perhaps the most interesting of these is Derry since its ancient meeting house brings to the present generation a flavor of those pioneer times.   Built on the "barrens of Derry" as early as 1729, its walls were of hewn oak logs, two feet thick, covered by rough hemlock boards, and sheathed within with yellow pine and cherry.   The nails and fastenings were

MEETING HOUSE AT DERRY, PENNSYLVANIA

primitive examples of hammer and anvil; the thirty eight panes of glass over the pulpit were set in pewter, and the communion service was of the same metal — mugs and platters sent over from London by sympathizing dissenters in 1733.

The pulpit was small and crescent shaped, with

narrow steps leading up from the east side. Along the wall were stout pegs on which to sling the muskets of the male worshippers. Close by the meeting house was the session-house with the pastor's study, and a few rods away within a neat wall about God's acre slept the dead.[1]

Derry, early known as Spring Creek, received its first settlers about 1720. As the Scotch Irish began to increase in numbers a Presbyterian minister was needed, and in 1726 the Rev. James Anderson of Donegal gave one fifth of his time to Derry, and another fifth to Paxtang.

One of the founders of the church was James Galbraith whose father James had crossed the ocean, some say, as early as 1718. The younger James had fallen in love with Elizabeth Bertram, the daughter of a clergyman from Bangor, County Down, who came to the church at Derry. Elizabeth's mother, Elizabeth Gillespie, tradition claimed, had a fine estate in Edinburgh. James settled on Swatara Creek, next to the farm of three hundred and fifty acres which the Derry people had deeded to their minister upon his arrival. Here a prosperous farm and grist-mill brought food and clothing for James's growing family and for his aged father, who came to dwell under his roof.

Another settler, David McNair, came over from

---

[1] W. H. Egle's History of Pennsylvania, 1883, p. 644. Also his address at the church October 2, 1884.

Donaghmore, County Donegal, the ancestral town of the Rev. William Homes of Martha's Vineyard. David's nephew became governor of Missouri. In the Derry grave yard lie the Boyds, Campbells, Chamberses, Clarks, Harrises, Hayses, Logans, Martins, Mitchells, Moodeys, McCords, Roans, Rodgers, Snoddeys, Thompsons, Wilsons and Wallaces.

In Hanover township were William Crain, John Barnett, William Allen and others. At Paxtang were John Wiggins, John Gray, Robert Elder, John Forster, Matthew Cowden, Hugh McCormick and Thomas Rutherford. The last mentioned emigrant left a record of his birth and marriage in old Tyrone.

Across the river in Allen township lived the families of Wilson, Wallace, Parker and Linn, as well as Andrew Gregg who is said to have had a brother David amid the ungracious rocks of New Hampshire, another brother Samuel in Massachusetts, and a brother John in South Carolina. A study of the marriages in the various families given in Dr. Egle's Scotch Irish genealogies, will yield names of many neighbors along the banks of the Susquehanna.

North of Philadelphia the Presbyterians, chiefly Dutch settlers with a few Welshmen, had worshipped at Neshaminy Creek, Bensalem, and other near-by towns since 1710. The Neshaminy records are of especial interest in 1722 when persons from ''Eerlant'' (Ireland) were recorded as admitted by certificate.

These persons were:

> William Pickins and his wife (Margaret?)
> George Davis and his wife
> Hugh White and his wife
> Andrew Reed and his wife
> John Anderson and his wife
> Moses White and his wife
> Humphrey Eyre and his wife
> Israel Pickins
> Matte Gillespie
> Joanna Bell (or Jane who married George Logan?)
> Thomas Foster, his wife, daughter Margaret and the rest of his children; also his wife's brother, George Logan [1]

Neshaminy became famous in the annals of the Presbyterian Church as the site of the Log College in which the Rev. William Tennent trained young men for the ministry.[2] Tennent had married in Ireland a daughter of the Rev. Gilbert Kennedy, a fine type of the sturdy old Scotch Irish clergy, a man whose tomb still remains to record his ancient blood and virile inheritances. Tennent's four sons brought

---

[1] Journal Presbyterian Historical Society, Vol. 1, p. 111.
[2] *Ibid*, p. 345.

to America great zeal and much needed high standards of ministerial culture.

In looking over the map of Pennsylvania we find that these townships, Donegal, Paxtang, Derry and Hanover (near the Susquehanna), and Drumore, Colerain, Fallowfield and Sadsbury (along Octorara Creek, which marks the western line of Chester County after 1729), together with the Brandywine farms a little north of Wilmington, the Neshaminy lands north of Philadelphia, and Allen township, ten miles west of Easton, comprise the earliest settlements of the Scotch Irish in Pennsylvania.   The settlers who first occupied these fertile lands entered America at the ports of Philadelphia and Newcastle.

At Philadelphia the Rev. Jedediah Andrews had begun about 1701 to preach in the "Barbadoes store." His followers were Presbyterians, and to his church came the strangers of that faith. From Philadelphia the immigrants spread out over the county of Lancaster.[1]   From Newcastle as another center they pushed along the Christiana to its con-

---

[1] I. D. Rupp's Lancaster County, 1844, p. 185.   For a list of landholders before 1735 in the present County of Lancaster, which comprised that part of old Chester County settled largely by Scotch Irish, see Rupp, p. 233.   The list includes the Craigheads, Cooksons, McCawleys, Storys, Greens, Blacks, Steels, Montgomerys, McCardys, Templemans, McConnels, McNealys, McClellands, Sherrards, Stinsons, McKimms, Dyers, Lambs, Bishops, McPhersons,

tributing sources, White Clay Creek and Red Clay Creek.

Along the banks of these creeks, and down the Brandywine and the Elk, the Rev. George Gillespie, a Scotch preacher, had ridden from house to house on his lonely circuit as early as 1713, when he was stationed at the church at the head of the Christiana.[1] Scotch and English chiefly composed the congregations until between 1718 and 1720, although the presence of ministers from Ireland would seem to suggest an occasional layman also from Irish soil.[2] On White Clay Creek were the Steels, Gardeners and Whites, of early importance, although their church of that name was not founded until 1721.

The purchasers of land for the joint church at

Robinsons, Murrays, Bensons, Blyths, Allisons, McClenns, Shennon, McClures, Hugheses, Duffields, Crawfords, Dennys, Scotts, Pennocks, Blackshaws, Buchanans, Gilmores, Musgroves, Higgenbothems, Livingtons, Painters, Saunderses, Stileses, Watsons, Webbs, Irwins, Palmers, Owens, Pendalls, Thornburys, Marshalls, Jacksons, Beesons, Nessleys, Herseys, Astons, Steers, McNabbs, Smiths, Lindseys, Longs, Kings, Moores, Fullertons, Francises, McKanes, Douglases, Darbys, Knowleses, McClanaghans, Burtons, Gales, Cowens and others.

A few of these families were doubtless Quakers.

[1] Mackey's White Clay Creek, p. 4; G. E. Jones's Lower Brandywine Church, 1876, p. 9.

[2] The Rev. Robert Cross of Newcastle, 1719, and Jamaica, Long Island, 1723, was born near Ballykelly, Ireland.

Lower Brandywine in 1720[1] were John Kirkpatrick, James Houston, James Mole, William Smith, Magnus Simonson, Ananias Higgins, John Heath and Patrick Scott. The surnames of the members of the Upper Octorara Church[2] before the middle of the eighteenth century were:

Alison, Blelock, Boggs, Boyd, Boyle, Clingan, Cochran, Cowan, Dickey, Filson, Fleming, Gardner, Glendenning, Hamill, Henderson, Heslep, Hope, Kerr, Kyle, Liggett, Lockhart, Luckey, McAllister, McNeil, McPherson, Mitchell, Moody, Park, Richmond, Robb, Rowan, Sandford, Scott, Sharpe, Sloan, Smith, Stewart, Summeril, Wiley, Wilkin, and Wilson.

The Rev. Samuel Young, a successor of Gillespie in this field, came to the Elk River in 1718, having preached at Magherally in County Down for fourteen years. He had been ordained by Armagh Presbytery in 1703.

The following extracts from a very long letter written by Robert Parke, an Irish Quaker of the original Chester county, Pennsylvania, to his sister in Ireland, describe life in the colony in 1725. Mr. Parke makes it evident that there was no disappointment upon their arrival in America, when he

---

[1] Jones, p. 12.

[2] Futhey's Upper Octorara Church, p. 151. The church was organized in 1720. The first minister, the Rev. Adam Boyd, Craighead's son-in-law, was ordained in 1724.

vrites: "There is not one of the family but what likes the country very well and wod If we were in Ireland again come here Directly it being the best country for working folk & Tradesmen of any in the world. . . My father bought a Tract of Land consisting of five hundred Acres for which he gave 350 pounds, it is Excellent good land but none cleared, Except about 20 Acres, with a small log house & Orchard Planted." A little later he contrasts the farmer's labor in Pennsylvania with his work in Ireland: "We plowed up our Sumer's fallows in May & June, with a Yoak of Oxen & 2 horses & they goe with as much Ease as Double the number in Ireland. . . Dear Sister I desire thee may tell my old friend Samuel Thornton that he could give so much credit to my words & find no Iffs nor ands in my Letter that in Plain terms he could not do better than to Come here, for both his & his wife's trade are Very good here, The best way for him to do is to pay what money he Can Conveniently Spare at that side & engage himself to Pay the rest at this Side & when he Comes here if he Can get no friend to lay down the money for him, when it Comes to the worst, he may hire out 2 or 3 Children. . . I wod have him Procure 3 or 4 Lusty Servants & Agree to pay their passage at this Side he might sell 2 & pay the others passage with the money." Parke closes his letter with a touch of brotherly gallantry:

"I wod not have thee think much at my Irregular way of writing by reason I write as it offer'd to me, for they that write to you should have more wits than I can Pretend to."[1]

---

[1] A. C. Myers's Immigration of the Irish Quakers, 1902, p. 70.

XV

THE SCOTCH IRISH IN SOUTH CAROLINA AFTER 1718

Settlements which were so far to the south that they were constantly menaced by the Spaniards and their Indian allies grew slowly. At Port Royal and Charleston the Scotch, both free men and deported prisoners taken in battle, were very early in residence.

About the year 1685 an Independent, or as some called it, a Presbyterian church was organized, and it had a prosperous history for half a century. The career of its chief minister, the Rev. Archibald Stobo, has already been referred to. His successor, the Rev. William Livingston, from the North of Ireland, preached from 1704 to 1720, when he died.[1]

In 1731 or 1732 about a dozen members of this first church, including James Abercrombie, John Allen, Daniel Crowford,[2] John Bee,[2] John Fraser,[2] George Ducaff or Ducat,[2] and James Paine or Payne,[2] withdrew and formed a new organization,

---

[1] His descendants bear the names of Tunno and Stewart. Charleston Year Book for 1882, p. 381.

[2] Assigned pews in the old church in 1732, and thus were not as yet known as seceders. Fraser and Ducat were members in 1724.

worshipping in a small wooden building, with the Rev. Hugh Stewart for their minister. These families were alarmed by an evident trend in the sentiment of the majority toward Congregationalism, and since they adhered loyally to the Westminster Confession they wished to be free to maintain a minister of their own faith.

Some of the founders of this seceding or Scotch Presbyterian church in Charleston in 1732 were probably Scotch Irish. The statement that John Witherspoon's daughter, who had died immediately after his arrival from Ireland, was the first person buried in the new church field implies that there were religious and perhaps racial ties which governed this choice of a spot; although in the older church there continued members bearing Scottish names.

In 1717 the town of Beaufort on the Island of Port Royal was laid out. To the west of this town were lands lying along the northern bank of the Savannah River; they had recently been left uninhabited by the retreat of the Yamassee Indians after their rebellion and defeat. These lands the Assembly opened up to Protestants in 1719, increasing the usual allotment of fifty acres to two hundred acres for each settler. It is said by Rivers, the historian, with how much authority is not known, that several hundred emigrants from Ireland were to take possession of these and other lands the same year;[1] but

---

[1] Howe's Presbyterian Church in South Carolina, p. 177.

the grants were soon after annulled by the Colonial Proprietors, the territory was surveyed, and from it fifteen baronies were erected.

Mr. A. S. Salley, Jr., secretary of the Historical Commission of South Carolina, writes that Mr. Rivers[1] "did not mean (for that would not have been true) that these Irishmen settled in a body on the Yamassee lands or expected to do so. They would have taken their grants anywhere in the province, just as hundreds of other settlers from England, Scotland, and Ireland had been doing. It is even doubtful if these Irishmen came in a body, or dispersed in a body." Many of them, if many there were, died of fever or privation, and the others were forced to look elsewhere for homes. At this time civilization in South Carolina did not extend beyond the Port Royal neighborhood at the south, and to the north it was limited to the territory between the Santee and the Edisto rivers. Some probably wandered into Charleston, where they remained until a strong Scotch Irish colony took possession of the township of Williamsburg.

This colony arrived in 1732 or the year following, the Council having granted the petition of James Pringle and other Irish Protestants that their passage be paid. A township twenty miles square, along the Black River, was laid out for them, and

---

[1] See pp. 293–294 of his South Carolina.

was given the name Williamsburg.[1] To this colony came John Witherspoon, James McClelland, William Sym, David Allan, William Wilson, Robert Wilson, James Bradley, William Frierson, John James, William Hamilton, Archibald Hamilton, Roger Gordon, John Porter, John Lemon, David Pressley, William Pressley, Archibald McRae, James Armstrong, the Erwins, Plowdens, Dickeys, Blakelys, Dobbinses, Stuarts and McDonalds.[2]

In August, 1736, a church was organized and the Rev. Robert Heron of Ireland became the first minister.   From the church at Williamsburg sprang that at Indian Town, with Major John James and William, Robert and David Wilson among its founders; also that at Salem, founded by Samuel and James Bradley.   At Mount Zion Church were Roger and James Wilson, with Captain William Erwin; at Jeffries Creek were John and Gavin Witherspoon; and John and Hugh Erwin joined the Hopewell Church which others directly from Ireland had founded.   The Plowden, Nelson and Gamble families were identified with the earliest days of the Church at Brewington.[3]

The Scotch Irish at Williamsburg, or perhaps later companies of immigrants, did not all fare prosperously, and in 1738 Charleston was forced to pro

---

[1] McCrady's South Carolina under the Royal Government, p. 132; also, Scotch Irish Society, 1st Congress, p. 202.

[2] Wallace's History of Williamsburg Church, 1856, pp. 18, 36.

[3] Wallace's History of Williamsburg Church, pp. 35, 36.

CHARLESTON HARBOR IN 1740

(From Winsor's Narrative and Critical History of America)

vide for poor Protestants from Ireland who swarmed the streets, begging from door to door.[1]

John Witherspoon came from County Down in 1734, with his children David, John, Robert and Sarah. Robert has left us an account of his early experiences, typical of the pioneer hardships of those who settled in South Carolina.[2] After lying becalmed in Belfast Lough for two weeks the ship with Robert's grandmother very ill on board, got under way on the 28th of September, 1734. It soon encountered rough weather and the aged lady died. Her interment in a roaring storm made a deep impression upon the boy. About the first of December the ship reached Charleston with a crew exhausted by almost incessant toil at the pumps. There the child Sarah died and was buried in the new Scotch graveyard. The settlers were kindly received by families that had come over in earlier years, but were soon sent up the river in an open boat to ''Potatoe Ferry,'' where the women and children were put ashore to find what protection they could in a barn-like hovel. Meanwhile the men with their tools and baggage pushed up stream, and then went forward through flooded woods and meadows to find a

---

[1] Hewit's Historical Account of South Carolina, Vol. 2, pp. 316, 324; in Carroll's Historical Collection.

[2] Witherspoon was not harassed by local Irish port officers as were many in 1736 when the Government had become alarmed by the magnitude of the migration. See Pennsylvania Magazine of History, Vol. 21, p. 485.

suitable spot for their houses. They had no timbers, and they soon discovered that boughs of trees covered with sods were but a poor protection against the fierce winter storms. Soon however a fire blazed upon the rude hearth, the smoke dried the branches overhead, and with one of Queen Anne's great muskets loaded with swan-shot close at hand, even the night in an endless waste of forest and marsh lost some of its terror. Although they had to wait long for their spring planting they were given time to become acclimated before the warm and sultry weather set in. They thus escaped the sickness which carried off great numbers of the early settlers in South Carolina.[1]

The great tide of migration, however, did not all come through the port of Charleston. Many of the Scotch Irish of the Carolinas came from Ireland to Pennsylvania, and then went through Virginia and North Carolina to the Waxhaws in South Carolina.[2] Of this stock was John C. Calhoun, and — somewhat later — Andrew Jackson. Mr. McCrady, the historian of South Carolina, in a note on this migration, says that from the Waxhaws the Scotch Irish crossed the Catawba and spread over the counties of Lancaster, York, Chester and Fairfield. Prominent among them were the Adairs, Allisons, Brattons, Adrians, Blacks, Boggs, Broones, Buchan-

---

[1] Hanna's Scotch Irish, Vol. 2, p. 26.
[2] McCrady, p. 624.

ans, Boyces, Bryces, Crawfords, Crocketts, Carrols, Carsons, Chamberses, Dunlops, Douglasses, Erwins, Flemings, Irwins, Hancocks, Kirklands, Laceys, Lathams, Loves, Lyles, Masseys, McCaws, McDaniels, McCans, Millses, McKenzies, McIllhennys, McMullans, McLures, McMorrises, Martins, Neelys,

Wylies, Witherspoons, Rosses, and Youngs.[1]   In Union County, as it now is, were the Brandons, Bogans, Jollys, Kennedys, McQunkins [McQuak-

---

[1] McCrady's South Carolina, 1719–1776, p. 317.

ins?], Youngs, Cunninghams, Savages, Hughs, Vances, and Wilsons.[1]

The McCrerys (or McCrearys), Greens, Hannahs, Abernathys, Millers, Beards, Wellses, Coffees, Gishams, Bartons, Youngs, McClures, Adamses, and the McDaids settled in Newberry between the Broad and the Saluda.[2] After them came the Caldwells, Thompsons, Youngs, Fairs, Carmichaels, Hunters, McClellans, Greggs, Wilsons, Conners, Neals, Camerons, Flemings, McCallas, Montgomerys, Sloans, Spencers, Wrights, Glenns, Chalmerses, McCrackenses, and Glasgows.

At Nazareth Church in Spartanburg were the Andersons, Millers, Barrys, Moores, Collinses, Thompsons, Vernons, Pearsons, Jamisons, Dodds, Rays, Pennys, McMahons, Nicols, Nesbitts, and Patons.[3] In the bounds of Abbeville and Edgefield were the Meriwethers, Wardlaws, Moors, Browns, McAlasters, Logans and Calhouns.[4]

These many surnames survive everywhere along the rivers and in the mountain settlements.

By the middle of the eighteenth century the Scotch Irish, through industry and intelligence even more than by force of numbers, had come to have a con-

---

[1] Southern Presbyterian Review, Vol. 14, p. 482. Quoted by McCrady.

[2] Mills's Statistics of South Carolina, p. 639. O'Neall's Annals of Newberry, pp. 47, 49.

[3] Southern Presbyterian Review, Vol. 14, No. 3, p. 483.

[4] Logan's History of Upper South Carolina, p. 25.

trolling voice in the management of much of the southern country. And this voice was heard a generation later when a rider brought into the Carolinas a paper which had told the people of New York, of Philadelphia and of farms along the shores of Chesapeake Bay that New England farmers had dared to fire upon British troops at Lexington.

XVI

THE SCOTCH IRISH CHARACTER

In this attempt to give some impression of the Scotch in Ireland and in America, so much emphasis has been placed upon documentary history that race characteristics have played only a small part in the story. But these people of Coleraine on the Bann, of Strabane and Londonderry, came into the rural settlements of the New World with so distinct a personality, with customs and habits so marked, that they left an enduring impress. Since the days of the battle of Dunbar (1650), or for nearly a century, the Scotchman had lived in the Atlantic colonies. How did his influence differ from that of his Scotch cousin of Ulster who came to America in 1718? Did the life in Ulster really effect a change? Certainly orators and writers have from time to time made this claim.

The lowland Scotch and their borderland English neighbors left heather-clad mountains and grazing flocks to cross the narrow waters of the North Channel into Antrim and Down. They abandoned pastoral land for flax fields and bleach-greens, surrendering an isolated existence to live close together upon small farms. Speaking of Aghadowey Miss

The Parish Church, Aghadowey

From a photograph by Miss Pauline Marian Stronge

Mary Semple of Larne writes: "The whole region is quite level, with a gentle slope to the river. The southern end of the village joins Kilrea, and throughout its length can be traced houses built by its first Scotch settlers. These are in clusters and are termed 'clackens,' Gaelic for village. The people are a strong-looking race, the men tall and well formed, the women rather above medium height. They are principally farmers, but many work on the bleach-greens, while others spend their lives in weaving on looms which stand in their own homes."[1]

New scenes must have quickened the mental processes of the transplanted Scot, and the greater community life enlarged the social instinct. The Episcopalians, all-powerful in government, and the Roman Catholics, strong in numbers, pressed in upon every side, and forced the Presbyterians to an exercise of their loyalty and patience, while the spirit of proselyting which existed everywhere in Ulster sharpened their wits. Under a century of these social and religious influences the Scotch character must have changed.

"It was," said Mr. Morison in his life of Jeremiah Smith, "the sternness of the Scotch covenanter, softened by a century's residence abroad amid persecution and trial, wedded there to the pathos and comic humor of the Irish."[2] And Presi-

---

[1] Blair Family of New England, 1900, p. 21.
[2] Page 8.

dent McKinley, another scion of the same stock, said of the Scotch Irishman, "He was the result of a slow fusion of diverse characteristics."[1] Time and trial had given to the Scot in Ireland memories, both of bloody Claverhouse in Scotland and of Tyrconnel in Ireland, that became a part of his fibre. The illiterate mother in the hills of Kentucky today passes on her burden of tradition when she exclaims to her unruly son: "Behave yourself, or Clavers will get you!" To her Clavers is but a bogey; to her ancestors Graham of Claverhouse was a very real cause for terror[2]. If that is an inheritance from the days of religious warfare what shall we say of Gabriel Barr and Rachel Wilson, lovers for forty years, who would not or could not marry because there were two warring Presbyterian churches in Londonderry and neither lover would abandon an allegiance of faith for the ties of affection?[3]

The Rev. Dr. MacIntosh in his charming essay on "The making of the Ulsterman" calls the transplanted Scot more versatile and more fertile in resource, less clannish and less pugnacious, or in other terms a man of wider vision. His beliefs were consistent and well defined. Against the Puritan's town meeting the Scotch Irishman placed the legislature; for the congregation he substituted the as-

---

[1] Proceedings Scotch Irish Society, 5th Congress, p. 19.
[2] The Berea Quarterly, October, 1908, p. 9.
[3] Willey's Nutfield, p. 91.

sembly; instead of laying stress upon personality, he emphasized partnership.[1]

Since the denial of the franchise to non-conformists in Ireland threw the Scotch Irish back upon their church assemblies for exercise in government they were perhaps the more eager for participation in affairs of state when they reached America. Accustomed to close reasoning in debate the Scotch Irish leaders from Maine to Georgia accepted political responsibility promptly and successfully.

Oppression commercially, politically and religiously in Ireland prepared those who emigrated to the colonies to enter the civic school of Patrick Henry and Samuel Adams. Nor were they unprepared for the inevitable result. Whatever of military science the Scotch Irish did not learn at the siege of Londonderry they acquired in the French and Indian wars in the New World. Their rugged life fitted them to endure camp and march; and their inborn hostility toward England led them to forge to the front in the early weeks of the year 1775 when many good men of the old English race wavered in the face of war with Great Britain.

The Scotch Irish have never claimed that they brought literature or art to these shores. They knew little of the former and nothing of æsthetics. Diaries and letters of the migration period do not exist and perhaps never did exist. Let us speak

---

[1] Proceedings Scotch Irish Society, 2d Congress, p. 102.

frankly. Every race brings to our western civilization a gift of its own. These people from Ulster cared very little for the beautiful, with the single exception of the wonderful and beautiful Bible story. Even the New Testament they handled as a laborer might touch a Sèvres vase — reverently

RUINS OF A CHURCH IN KILREA
County Londonderry

but rudely. The Rev. Matthew Clark of Kilrea, a veteran of the Londonderry siege and a popular minister at the American Londonderry, was a type of the patriot soldier, rough, sturdy, independent. Preaching from Philippians iv. 13 he began with the words: " 'I can do all things.' Ay, can ye, Paul? I'll bet a dollar o' that!" whereupon he drew a Spanish dollar from his pocket and placed it beside his Bible on the pulpit. Then, with a look of surprise he continued: "Stop! let's see what else Paul says: 'I can do all things through Christ, which strengtheneth me.' Ay, sae can I, Paul; I draw my bet!" and he returned the dollar to his pocket. We may wonder that such preaching fostered the simple trust and abiding faith evident in the dying words of Mrs. Morison of Londonderry. When asked what she would have more, she replied: "Nothing but Christ."[1]

The Scotch Irish could not see that the severe lines of a cabin are softened by a sumac against the south wall or a creeper at the corner. They did not trim the edge of the roadway that led to the front door. In short, utility required nothing of these things and utility was their law. For the same reason, if the soles of their feet were tough they saw small need of shoes in summer. Their bare feet, however, gave something of a shock to century-old New England.

This rude development of taste was based possibly upon a primitive state of education. Although many served as local school-masters, it is evident that few even of the scant number who attained a college education ever learned to write well or to spell correctly their English language.[2] William Smith of Moneymore, Ireland, was a bright lad in

---

[1] Morison's Smith, p. 11.
[2] *Ibid*, p. 19.

his use of the pen, and his school-master wrote in his copy book:

> William Smith of Moneymar
> Beats his master far and awar:
> I mean in writing
> Not inditing.

William's son Judge Smith of Peterborough, New Hampshire, after copying these and other lines upon birch bark became so proficient that he was employed to write letters, basing commissions from young lovers upon the burning phrases in the Song of Solomon.[1]

The earliest emigrants knew Gaelic, and some may even have had no other language until they settled among English and Dutch colonists in America. I have found no direct mention of Gaelic in New England, but Rupp the Pennsylvania historian speaks of the disappearance of the language before his day.[2] The authorities in Georgia in 1735 applied to the Society in Scotland for Propagating Christian Knowledge for a minister to preach in Gaelic and to catechise the children in English. John Macleod of the Isle of Sky was sent out in response to this request.[3] Gaelic lingered among the old Scotch emigrants very much as Presbyterianism in New Eng-

---

[1] Morison's Smith, pp. 2, 12.
[2] Rupp's History Counties of Berks and Lebanon, 1844, p. 115.
[3] Journal Presbyterian Historical Society, Vol. 1, p. 206.

land remained with the aged after their children and grandchildren had turned to Congregationalism.

In the industrial field the Scotch Irish at the outset contributed to New England's economic life; they taught their new neighbors the value of the "Irish" potato as a common article of food, and to make fine linen out of flax. The potato which now is a large part of the annual crop of every Northern farmer was rare in the colonies before 1718.[1]

The spinning industry soon became so popular that a public school of spinning was proposed in Boston[2] in 1720, and the following year the selectmen, together with a special committee, were empowered to let out without interest three hundred pounds to any one who should establish a school for instruction in spinning flax and weaving linen.[3] In 1732 the Hon. Daniel Oliver, who had been a member of the Committee in 1720, died, leaving the old Spinning House adjoining Barton's Ropewalk, with its "Proffits and Incomes . . . for learning poor children of the Town of Boston to Read the word of God and to write if need be."[4]

In time, when they had grown accustomed to their new environment, the Scotch Irish did more than to

---

[1] Parker's Londonderry, p. 49; Lewis and Newhall's Lynn, 1865, p. 312.

[2] Drake's Boston, pp. 560, 591.

[3] Town Records, March 1720-21.

[4] Suffolk deeds, Vol. 31, p. 53.

defend the frontier and fight the battles of the Revolution, for they excelled also in letters and in art.

It is evident that whether we view the Scotch Irish pioneers from the standpoint of education, or culture, or material success of the larger kind, they were in 1718 in their proper place when Cotton Mather consigned them to the frontier. The life there conformed to their standards, as measured by their opportunity at that time. Those who remained in Boston, Philadelphia, and Charleston were very generally tradesmen, and on account of the Ulster industries many naturally were tailors. But they were none the less virile, earnest and ambitious. A line of settlements extending from the Maine seacoast westward through New Hampshire and south westerly through western Massachusetts into a part of New York, and thence through Pennsylvania and the Carolinas, might be expected to produce much when a second generation had come to manhood on American soil. And the roll of statesmen, preachers and soldiers proves that these Scotch Irish did possess latent power of a high order.

All that has been said of the character of those who constituted the great migration to New England in 1718 applies equally to the brothers, cousins and neighbors in old Ireland who swarmed across the sea into the middle and southern colonies. For every one who landed at Boston a dozen set foot in Philadelphia and Charleston. In Massachusetts they were an incident in history; at the South while they did not outnumber the natives they helped to make history. In 1790, following the Revolution, the Scotch Irish in Maine still clung in greatest numbers about the Kennebec; in New Hampshire on both sides of the Merrimack; and in Massachusetts they were to be found along the Merrimac, in the valley of the Connecticut and around the ancient settlements of Worcester and Rutland. In New York state they inhabited the banks of the Hudson near Albany. Pennsylvania still held a great Scotch Irish population, not only on the fertile shores of the Schuylkill and the Susquehanna, where they first found homes, but now all about the source rivers of the great Ohio.

Farther south the Scotch Irish were very numerous in North Carolina, between the upper waters of the Great Pedee and the Catawba. Across the border in South Carolina the Scotch Irish found homes along the Saluda, the Broad and the Catawba, in two districts which then bore names made famous in Revolutionary history, Camden and Ninety six.[1]

It cannot but be evident that the great water courses were in those days as vital in their influence upon colonization as they were to be upon the commerce which follows permanent settlements.

In no state did the Scotch Irish population in 1790

---

[1] See W. S. Rossiter's A Century of Population Growth, Chapter XI.

equal the English, averaging only 6.7 per cent. of the
whole, but in every state except New York and Pennsylvania it stands second. The Scotch Irish were
largely responsible for phenomenal increases in the
population of New Hampshire and North Carolina
between 1720 and 1740. Massachusetts, Pennsylvania and Maryland already had a considerable population and new settlers made less impression on
the per cent. of increase.[1] The Scotch Irish family
averaging 5.67 members, fell short of the English
family of 5.77, a fact not expected of the later
comer[2]; but in energy, resource and endurance, in a
desire to excel in arms and in political leadership
the smaller family held its own.

The statement that the Scotch Irish in 1790
amounted to 6.7 per cent. of the entire population,
although 7 per cent. would probably be nearer the
truth, at least gives a vague basis for the compari-
son of Scotch Irish ability with that of other strains.
We may turn then with some curiosity to a group of
figures prepared by Senator Henry Cabot Lodge for
the *Century Magazine* of September, 1891, under the
title "Distribution of ability in the United States."
These figures are founded on 14,243 biographies of
Americans of more than average ability, as given in
Appleton's Encyclopædia of American Biography.
The results were so much discussed in the press of

---

[1] Rossiter, pp. 9, 10.
[2] *Ibid*, pp. 274, 275.

that winter that Senator Lodge printed similar ta-
bles in the *Century* for July, 1892, based upon names
selected in a different manner.   The results were not
unlike those first obtained.

The Scotch Irish he describes as the descendants
of the Scotch and English who settled in the North
of Ireland, with an infusion of Irish blood in some
few instances.

Of the 14,243 influential people recorded, there
were biographies of the

Race.	No. and per cent. of all biographies.		Per cent. of the population in 1790.
English	10,376 or	72.8 per cent.	83.5
Scotch Irish	1,439 or	10.1 " "	6.7
German	659 or	4.6 " "	5.6
Huguenot	589 or	4.2 " "	.5
Others	1,180 or	8.2 " "	3.7

We find that the Germans, with a little less than
one half as many biographies as the Scotch Irish,
had more representatives in art, music and science;
but in education, government, law, the stage, inven-
tion, exploration and war the Scotch Irish exceeded
the Germans by more than three to one.   As com-
pared with the Huguenots the Scotch Irish were
weaker in art and music, but were three times as
strong in government, theology, exploration, inven-
tion and the stage.   In careers devoted to government, war and exploration, just as one is prepared to
expect, the Scotch Irish exceed their natural propor-

tion; in literature, art, science, business, philanthropy and music — careers ill suited to a pioneer life, they fall far short.

Those who are represented in the work by portraits, an indication of conspicuous ability, number 1,258. Of these, the men of Scotch Irish extraction number 137, or 10.9 per cent.; the English 897, or 71.3 per cent. If this increase from 10.1 (non portrait class) to 10.9 per cent. (portrait class) means anything it suggests that among English and Scotch Irish men of ability the Scotch Irish more often produce men of the first rank.

New England may well be proud of General John Stark and General Henry Knox of the Revolution, and of General George B. McClellan of the Civil War; of Matthew Thornton, the signer of the Declaration of Independence; of Horace Greeley, the editor; of Asa Gray the botanist; and of John Lothrop Motley the historian, all scions of the early Scotch Irish migration.

Further south were other great figures in our national life — Governor Edward Rutledge, Vice President Calhoun, President Jackson, and also William McKinley, whose ancestors lived at Conagher's Farm in County Antrim, only a few hours walk from the homes of our Bann Valley settlers. We should like to believe that McKinley stands as a type of the best Scotch Irish manhood, simple in his habits, gentle in his demeanor, strong in control of himself and a peace maker among his fellows.

CONAGHER'S FARM, NEAR BALLYMONEY, COUNTY ANTRIM

Home of President McKinley's Ancestors

Dr. MacIntosh has said: "The plantation of the Scot into Ulster kept for the world the essential and the best features of the lowlander. But the vast change gave birth to and trained a somewhat new and distinct man, soon to be needed for a great task which only the Ulsterman could do; and that work — which none save God, the guide, foresaw — was with Puritan to work the revolution that gave humanity this republic."[1]

[1] Proceedings Scotch Irish Society, 2d Congress, p. 91.

THE AGHADOWEY RIVER

APPENDICES

APPENDIX I

1714

GRAY-HOUND, sloop, Benjamin Elson, master, from Ireland; arrived April, at Boston (News-Letter, Apr. 19–26, 1714).

ELIZABETH & KATHRIN, ship, William Robinson, master, from Ireland; arr. June, at Boston (N. L. May 31– June 7, 1715). Sick put on shore at Spectacle Island (Province Laws 1714, chapter 45).

MARY ANNE, John Macarell, master, from Ireland; arr. August, at Boston (N. L. Aug. 2–9, 1714). Goods on sale at Steele and Bethune's ware house, Merchants Row.

YORK MERCHANT, ship, John Beach, master, from Cork; arr. September, at Boston (N. L. Sept. 13–20, 1714). Irish servants (N. L. Sept. 6–13, 1714). Outward bound (N. L. Oct. 11–18, 1714).

THOMAS & JANE, ship, William Wilson, master, from Londonderry; arr. Oct. at Boston (N. L. Oct 4–11, 1714). Outward bound for Holland (N. L. Oct. 18–25, 1714).

1715

AMITY, snow, Nathaniel Breed, master, from Ireland; arr. June, at Boston (N. L. June 13–20, 1715). Outward bound for Great Britain (N. L. June 20–27, 1715).

[*Name Not Given.*]   James Hamilton, master, from [not given] ; arr. [not given], at Boston.   Cleared for Ireland (N. L. Nov. 28–Dec. 5. 1715).

1716

TRUTH AND DAYLIGHT, galley, Robert Campbell, master, from Cork; arr. May 21, at Boston (N. L. May 21–28, 1716; Record Com. Rept. 29, p. 232).   Names of passengers given.   Outward bound (N. L. May 28–June 4, 1716).

MARY ANN, ship, Robert Maccarell, master, from Dublin; arr. June 18, at Boston (N. L. June 18–25, 1716; Record Com. Rept. 29, p. 235).   John Gallard and his waiting man.

GLOBE, ship, Nicholas Oursell, master, from Ireland; arr. June 25, at Boston (N. L. June 25–June 2, 1716; Record Com. Rept. 29, p. 236).   Names of passengers given.   "Protestants."

1717

[*Name Not Given.*] —— Montgomery, master, from Waterford; arr. [not given] at Piscataqua (N. L. July 2–9, 1716).

[*Name Not Given.*]   Master not given; from Ireland; arr. at Boston.   Passengers ordered to Spectacle Island in June.   (Province Laws 1716–17, chapter 52).

GLOBE, ship, Alexander Dowglase, master, from Dublin; arr. Aug. at Boston (N. L. Aug. 12–19, 1717).   Sundry servants to serve for four to nine years.   Governor Shute reported fourteen male servants from Dublin.

[*Name Not Given.*] Robert Montgomery, master, from Ireland; arr. Sept. at Boston (N. L. Sept. 2–9, 1717).

[*Name Not Given.*] Archibald MacPheaderies, master, from Ireland; arr. Sept. at Piscataqua (N. L. Sept. 23–30, 1717).

FRIENDS GOODWILL, Edward Gooding, master, from Larne and Dublin; arr. Sept. at Boston (N. L. Sept. 9–16, 1717). Fifty two persons. Great hardships. See in chapter I a reference to Governor Shute's report of nine servants from Belfast.

1718

[*Name Not Given.*] Alexander Miller, master, Robert Homes, mate, from [not given]; arr. [not given] at Boston. Cleared for Ireland (N. L. March 24–31, 1718; Rev. W. Homes in his Diary says sailed April 10th).

[*Name Not Given.*] —— Gibbs, master, from Dublin; arr. May 16, at Marblehead (N. L. May 12–19, 1718). Irish and Scotch servants.

WILLIAM AND MARY, ship, James Montgomery, master, from Ireland; arr. July 25, at Boston (N. L. July 21–28, 1718; also C. Mather). Cleared for Dublin (N. L. Aug. 25–Sept. 1, 1718).

[*Name Not Given.*] John Wilson, master, from Londonderry; arr. July 28 ? at Boston (N. L. July 28–Aug. 4, 1718; also Lechmere). Boys, young women and girls.

ROBERT, brigantine, James Ferguson, master, from Glasgow and Belfast; arr. Aug. 4, at Boston (N. L. Aug.

4–11, 1718; also Lechmere). Cleared (N. L. Aug. 18–25, 1718).

WILLIAM, ship, Archibald Hunter, master, from Coleraine; arr. Aug. 4, at Boston (N. L. Aug. 4–11, 1718; also Lechmere). Outward bound for Ireland (N. L. Sept. 15–22, 1718).

MARY ANNE, ship, Andrew Watt, master, from Dublin; arr. August, at Boston (N. L. Aug. 4–11, 1718). Servants. Cleared for Great Britain (N. L. Aug. 18–25, 1718).

DOLPHIN, pink, John Mackay, master, from Dublin; arr. Sept. 1, at Boston (N. L. Sept. 1–8, 1718; also Lechmere). 20 odd families. Servants, boys, tradesmen, &c.

MACCALLUM, ship, James Law, master, from Londonderry; arr. Sept. 6 ? at Boston (N. L. Sept. 1–8, 1718; also C. Mather). Intended for New London. Went to the Kennebec. Cleared for Londonderry (N. L. Dec. 1–8, 1718).

[*Name Not Given.* MACCALLUM ?] Master not given. From Ireland; arr. Sept. at Casco Bay (N. L. Sept. 22–29, 1718). Passengers and a minister.

BEGINNING, sloop, John Rogers, master, from Waterford; arr. Oct. at Boston (N. L. Oct. 27–Nov. 3, 1718).

RETURN, schooner ?, Joseph Newall, master, from Glasgow; arr. Oct. at Boston (N. L. Nov. 17–24, 1718).

MARY AND ELIZABETH, Alexander Miller, master, Robert Remes [Homes], mate, from Londonderry; arr. Oct. at Boston (N. L. Oct. 20–27, 1718; also Rev. W. Homes's Diary). Full of passengers. Cleared (N. L. Dec. 8–15, 1718).

JOSEPH AND MARY, ship, Eben Allen, master, from [not given]; arr. [not given], at Boston. Outward bound for Ireland (N. L. Dec. 8–15, 1718).

GEORGE, snow, Grashinham Salter, master, from [not given]; arr. [not given], at Boston. Outward bound for Ireland (N. L. Dec. 29, 1718–Jan. 5, 1719).

1719

JANE, ship, John MacMaster, master, from Glasgow and Belfast; arr. June 9, at Boston (N. L. June 8–15, 1719; Record Com. Rept. 13, p. 57). List of passengers warned, p. 57.

[*Name Not Given.* JOSEPH ?] Philip Bass, master, from Londonderry; arr. Aug. 21, at Kennebec River (N. L. Aug. 17–24, 1719). 200 passengers.

GLOBE, ship, John Mackay, master, from Dublin; arr. Aug. at Boston (N. L. Aug. 10–17, 1719). Sundry servants.

JOSEPH, ship, Samuel Harris, master, from Ireland; arr. Sept. ?, at Boston (N. L. Aug. 31–Sept. 7, 1719). Six men and boys and one woman's time.

MARY, schooner, Philip Rawlings, master, from Dublin; arr. Sept., at Boston (N. L. Sept. 21–28, 1719). Six weeks passage.

AMSTERDAM, John Wakefield, master, from Ireland; arr. Oct., at Boston (N. L. Oct. 12–19, 1719).

ELIZABETH, ship, Robert Homes, master, from Ireland; arr. Nov. 3 ?, at Hull and Boston. (Mass. Resolves, 1719, chapter 68.) About 150 passengers, some with smallpox. List of warnings (Record Com. Rept. 13, p. 63).

[*Name Not Given.*] —— Dennis, master, from Ireland;
arr. Nov., at Boston. List of persons warned. (Record Com. Rept. 13, p. 64).

MARY AND ABIGAIL, Eben Allen, master, from [not given];
arr. [not given], at Boston. Outward bound for Ireland (N. L. Nov. 30–Dec. 7, 1719).

GRAY-HOUND, ship, Thomas Arnold, master, from [not given]; arr. [not given], at Boston ? Outward bound for Ireland (N. L. Jan. 5–12, 1719–20).

1720

[*Name Not Given.*] William Jarvis, master, from [not given]; arr. [not given], at Boston. Cleared for Ireland (N. L. April 4–11, 1720).

AMITY, James Goodman, master, from Cork; arr. April, at Boston (N. L. April 25–May 2, 1720). Outward bound (N. L. May 9–16, 1720).

JOSEPH, Philip Bass, master, from [not given, Kennebec River ?]; arr. [not given], at Boston. Outward bound for Ireland (N. L. May 5–9, 1720).

MARGARET, Luke Stafford, master, from Dublin; arr. Aug. 4, at Marblehead (N. L. Aug. 1–8, 1720). Nine weeks voyage.

[*Name Not Given.*] Benjamin ? Marston, master, from Ireland; arr. Aug., at Salem (N. L. Aug. 22–29, 1720). Taken by pirates. Had several passengers.

[*Name Not Given.*] Nathaniel Jarvis, master, from Ireland; arr. between Aug. 29 and Sept. 5, at Boston (N. L. Aug. 29–Sept. 5. 1720). See below.

[*Name Not Given.*]   Robert Homes, from Ireland; arr. Aug. 28, at Boston.   (Rev. W. Homes's Diary.) Homes may have been mate to Jarvis above.

RETURN, Jos. Newell, master, from Dublin; arr. Sept., at Boston (N. L. Sept. 5–12, 1720).

MARY, schooner, Philip Rawlings, master, from Dublin; arr. Sept., at Boston (N. L. Sept. 21–28, 1720).

JOSEPH, Philip Bass, master, from Ireland; arr. Oct., at Boston (N. L. Oct. 17–24, 1720).

ESSEX, brigantine, Robert Peat, master, from Ireland; arr. July ?, at Salem (N. L. Oct. 17–24, 1720).   Held up by Capt. Thomas Roberts, a pirate.

PROSPERITY, Josiah Carver, master, from Ireland; arr. Nov., at Boston (N. L. Nov. 21–28).

EXPERIMENT, George Read, master, from Londonderry; arr. Dec., at Boston (N. L. Dec. 5–12, 1720).   Cleared for Ireland (N. L. Dec. 19–26, 1720).

APPENDIX II

The petition which now hangs in the rooms of the New Hampshire Historical Society at Concord can still be read, with the exception of a few names which have faded out since Mr. Parker, the historian of Londonderry, copied them in 1850. These are now given between brackets. The address occupies the top of the sheet, extending across its face. The words "To His Excellency the Right Honourable Colonel Samuel Suitte, Governour of New England——" do not fill an entire line, but are written large and are centred. The rest of the address reads: "We whose names are underwritten Inhabitants of ye North of Ireland Doe in our own names and in the names of many others our neighbours, Gentlemen, Ministers, Farmers and [End of line] Tradesmen, Commissionate and appoint our trusty and well beloved Friend The Reverend Mr William Boyd of Macasky to repair to His Excellency the Right Honourable [End of line] Collonel Samuel Suitte Governour of New England, and to assure His Excellency of our sincere, and hearty Inclinations to Transport our selves to that very excellent and [End of line] renowned Plantation upon our obtaining from his Excellency suitable incouragement. And further to act, and Doe in our names as his Prudence shall direct. Given under [End of line] our hands this 26th day of March Annoq Dom. 1718."

Below this address are the autograph signatures, arranged in eight columns of equal length. Where Mr. Parker's rendering of a name differs from my own *I have given Parker's form below in italics*. A question mark indicates that although we may agree, the form is still open to question. An asterisk marks names beginning with a small written b. In these cases I read "Black," not "Clark," "Beverelle," not "Ceverelle," and "Blaire," not "Claire." My study of the petition has been aided by holding a negative photographic plate before a strong light. I am indebted for this negative to the kindness of Miss Edith Shepard Freeman, Librarian of the New Hampshire Historical Society.

The names follow:

[FIRST COLUMN AT THE LEFT.]
James Alexander
James Nesmith
David Craig
Neall McNeall
  Weall McNeall
Thomas Orr
William Caldwell
?Jaˢ Moore Jr
?Wm. Slamon
  Sam Gunion. Perfectly distinct. Looks like Siem-1on. Possibly for William Slemmons
Matthew Love
  Lord
Robrt Knox
Alexᵈʳ McGregore
James Trotter
Alexander McNeall
Robert Roe
  Roo

Joseph Watson
Robert Millar
John Smeally
  Much faded.
John Morieson
James Walker
Robert Walker
Robert Walker
    His
Wilam ✕ Calual
    mark
  Calwall. Difficult
William Walker
    His mark
Samuel ✕ Young
Alexander Richey
James Morieson
    His mark
Josheph ✕ Beverlam
    His R mark
Robert Crage
John Thomson
  Thompson. Clear

Hugh Tomson
James Still
James Hoog
Thomas Hanson
John Hanson
Ritchard Etone
James Etone
Thomas Etone
Samuell Hanson
James Cochran
James Hulton
Thomas Hultone
    Haseltone. Or ffultone
John Cochrane
William Cochrane
    His
Samuel ╳ Hunter
    mark
[John Hunter]

[SECOND COLUMN.]

Thomas Hunter
    His
Daniel ╳ McKerrel
    mark
ffergos Kenedey
    Horgos (?)
    His
?John ╳ Setone
    mark
    Suene (?) Well written,
    but elusive.
Adam ╳ Dickey
    His mark
    Ditkoy
Alexander Kid
Thomas Lorie
Thomas Hines
    His
Will ╳ Halkins
    mark

Georg Anton
John Colbreath
*William Baird
    Caird
John Gray
?John Hostowne
    Woodman (?) Last four
    letters very clear.
Andrew Wattson
William Blair
Joseph Blair
    His
Hugh ╳ Blare
    mark
William Blare
Samuel Anton
James Knox
Robert Hendry
John Knox
William Hendry
William Dunkan
David Duncan
John Muree
    Murray?
James Gillmor
Samuel Gillmor
Alexander Chocr^an
Edward M Kene
John Morduck
    His
?Samuel ╳ McMun
    mark
?Molcam Calual
    Henry Calual
Thomas McLaughlen
Robert Hoog
John Millar
Hugh Calwell
William Boyd

John Stirling
Samuel Smith
John Lamond
Robert Lamond
Robert Knox
Wm Wilson
Wm Paterson

[THIRD COLUMN.]

Stephen Murdoch
Robertt Murdoch
John Murdoch
William Jennson
James Rodger
John Buyers
Robert Smith
Adam Dean
Randall Alexander
Thomas Boyd
Hugh Rogers
John Craig
Wm Boyle
Benj Boyle
Ja. Kenedy
M'G. Stirling
    A blot comes between the
    M. and the S.
Samuel Ross
John Ramsay
John McKeen
James Willsone
Robert McKeen
John Boyd
Andrew Dunlap
James Ramsay
William Park
John Blair
James Thompson
Lawrence McLaughlen

Will Campibell
James Bankhead
Andrew Patrick
James McFee
?James Tonson
    Or Temen?
Gorg Anton
James Anton
George Kairy
Thomas Freeland

[FOURTH COLUMN.]

Peter Simpson
Thomas M'Laughlen
Robert Boyd
Andrew Agnew
James King
Thomas Elder
Daniel Johnstone
Robert Walker
David Jonston
James Steuart
John Murray
Thomas Blackwel
Thomas Wilson
John Ross
William Johnston
John King
Andrew Curry
?John Leech
    Parker omits. Looks
    like Jueeh.
?James Brighym
    Parker omits.
Samuel Code
*James Blak
Thomys Gro
Thomys Anton
James Gro

*John Black
  Clark
Thomas Boyd
Andrew McFaden
  Thomas McFaden
David Hanson
Richard Acton
*James Blaire
  Claire
Thomas Elder
*Jeremiah Blaire
  Claire
*Jacob Black
  Clark
Abram Baverly

[FIFTH COLUMN.]

Robert Johnston
Thomas Black
Peter Murray
John Jameson
John Cochran
Samuell Gonston
Thomas Shadey
William Ker
Thomas Moore
Andrew Watson
John Thonson
James McKerrall
Hugh Stockman
Andrew Cochren
*James Barkley
  Carkley
Laurence Tod
  Dod
?Sandrs Mear
John Jackson
James Curry
James Elder

James Acton
?Gorg Gregory
  Parker omits.
Samuel Smith
Andrew Dodg
James Forsaith
Andrew Fleeming
Gorge Thomson
James Brouster
Thomas Kengston
  Parker omits.
James Baverlay

[SIXTH COLUMN.]

James Smith
James Smith
Patrick Smith
*Sameuel Beverelle
  Ceverelle
James Craig
Samuel Wilson, M. A.
Gawen Jirwin
Robert Miller
Thomas Wilson
William Wilson
James Brice
Ninian Pattison
James Thompson
Joⁿ Thompson
Robt Thompson
Adam Thompson
Alexander Pattison
Thomas Dunlop
John Willson
David Willson
John Moor
James McKeen
John Lamont
John Smith

Patrick Orr
?Boniel Orr
William Orr
John Orr
Jeams Lenox
John Leslie
John Lason
?John Colvil
Samuel Wat
James Crafort
James Henderson
Matheu Slarroh
David Widborn
Luk Wat
Robert Hendre
William Walas
Thomas Walas
?Thomas Enoch
  Cewch?
William Boyd
William Christy
John Boyd
William Boyd
Hugh Ker
  The last nineteen are possibly in one handwriting.

[SEVENTH COLUMN.]

Alexr McBride, Phar.
  Bart. There never was a Baronet of this name.
Sam: McGivern
John Murdoch
  Hurdoch
Geo Campbell
James Shorswood
John McLaughlen
Georg McLaughlen
Laurence McLaughlen

?John Hezlet
  Faded.
George McAlester
Thomas Ramadge
James Campbell
David Lindsay
Robt Giveen
James Laidlay
Benjamen Galt
Daniell Todd
Robt Barr
Hugh [Hollmes]
Robt King
John [Black]
Thomas Ramsay
James [Henry]
Francis [Richie]
James Gregg
Robert Boyd
Hugh Tarbel
David Tarbel
        His
John ✕ Robb
       mark
?Peatter Fulltone
  Jeatter Fueltone.
  Possibly John
Robt Wear
[Alex'r Donnaldson]
[Arch'd Duglass]
[Robert Stiven]
Robt [Henry]
[James Pettey]
David Bigger
David [Patteson]
?David Mitchell
  Parker omits.
John Wight

Joseph Wight
Robt Willson
James Ball
?Andrew Cord
  Or Coxe?
James Nesmith
Peter Christy

[EIGHTH COLUMN.]

Jas Teatte, V. D. M.
Thos Cobham, V. D. M.
Robert Neilson, V. D. M.
  Houston
Will: Leech, V. D. M.
Robert Higinbotham, V. D. M.
John Porter, V. D. M.
Hen: Neille, V. D. M.
Tho. Elder, V. D. M.
James Thomson, V. D. M.
William Ker
Will: McClben
  McAlben
Willeam Jeameson
  Or Jennieson?
Wm Agnew

Jeremiah Thompson
Jahon Andrson
George Grege
Andrew Dean
Alexr Dunlop, M. A.
Arch McCook, M. A.
Alex'r Blair
?Boulonget Cochran
  Parker says B. Cochran.
  Fairly clear, but elusive.
William Galt
Peter Thompson
Richart McLaughlen
?John Mccan
  Muar
*John Black
?John Thompson
Samuel Boyd
John Mitchell
James Paterson
Joseph Curry
David Willson
Patrick Anderson
John Gray
James Greg

APPENDIX III

ANDREW McFADDEN'S TRANSPLANTING FROM GARVAGH IN
THE COUNTY OF DERRY TO MERRYMEETING BAY IN 1718

(Copied by Mr. John H. Edmonds from Supreme Court Files, Suffolk
County, Massachusetts, Vol. 895, p. 71)

Jane Macfadden of Georgetown about 82 Years of Age
testifyeth and Saith that She with her late husband Andrew Macfadden lived in the Town of Garvo in the County
of Derry on the ban Water in Ireland belonging to one
Esqr Fullinton being a pleasant place and call'd Summersett and about Forty Six Years ago my Husband and I
removed from Ireland to Boston and from Boston we moved
down to Kennebeck-River and up the River to Merry-
Meeting Bay and set down on a point of Land laying between Cathance River and Abagadussett River and opposite and a litte to the Northward of Brick Island So call'd
and Said point was then call'd by every Body Cathance
point at that day and by no other Name, and As my husband was aclearing away the Trees to Merry-Meeting Bay
he Said it was a very pleasant place and he thought it was
like a place call'd Summersett on the ban Water in Ireland
where they lived and that he would give it the Name of
Summersett after that in Ireland which he did and it hath
gone by the Name of Summersett ever Since, which is now
about Forty five Years ago and at that time there was No
Settlement on Kennebeck-River above Arowswick Island
excepting Our family and two more that she knew of and

there is a large Fish in Kennebeck-River call'd Sturgeon
which Jumps plentifully in the Summer time from the
Mouth of the River Kennebeck where it empty's it Self into
the Sea Near Sequin Island clear up to Teconnett at Fort
Hallifax where I have often been and there is a Number
of Vessells which Yearly come to catch these Sort of Fish
called Sturgeons and the general place where the Vessells
lay is at the head of Arowswick Island about Twelve Miles
from the Sea, and Some Vessells lay at Merry-Meeting Bay
to catch the Said Fish and the general place for catching
Said Sturgeon Fish was in Long Reach and Merry-Meeting Bay there being the greatest plenty as I always un-
derstood and the Vessels that generally come for those
Sturgion fish were Small Schooners and the Deponant
further Saith that the Plymouth or Kennebeck Proprietors
have made large Settlements on Kennebeck river and are
still making them Continually—

Her

JANE X MCFADDEN

mark

Pounalborough June 19:th 1766—

APPENDIX IV

(A) Members of the Charitable Irish Society in Boston

Edward Allen, 1737; Edward Alderchurch, 1737; Joseph Austin, 1739; Robert Auchmuty, Esq., 1740; David Allen, 1740; Adam Boyd, 1737; Thomas Bennett, 1737; Michael Bourns, 1738; Samuel Black, 1738; George Boulton, 1738; Philip Breaden, 1739; John Beath, 1739; James Clark, 1737; John Clark, 1737; Alexander Caldwell, 1738; Andrew Canworthy, 1739; Thomas Cumerford, 1741; Robert Duncan, 1737; William Drummond, 1737; James Downing, 1737; George Draper, 1737; Samuel Douse, 1738; William Dunning, 1739; Peter Dillon, 1739; Henry Dunworth, 1739; Walter Dougherty, 1739; Hugh Dorus, 1739; James Dalton, 1740; William Davis, 1740; Michael Derby, 1740; James Egart, 1737; William Edgar, 1739; William Freeland, 1737; William French, 1739; George Ferguson, 1739; Patrick Fitzgibbon, 1739; Owen Fergus, 1739; John Farrel, 1740; Daniel Gibbs, 1737; George Glen, 1737; James Gardner, 1737; Michael Geoghegan, 1737; John Griffin, 1738; Joseph Gilmore, 1739; John Gradon, 1739; Robert Glen, 1741; William Hall, 1737, President; John Hoog, 1738; John Hutchinson, 1739; Andrew Holmes, 1739; John Harper, 1739; Frederick Hamilton, 1740; James Hughes, 1740; William Holmes, 1740; Andrew Knox, 1737; David Kennedy, 1737; Adam Knox, 1737; John Little, 1737; Joseph Lewis, 1738; Thomas Lawler,

1739; Daniel McFfall, 1737; James Mayes, 1737; Samuel
Moore, 1737; Philip Mortimer, 1737; Patrick Motley, 1737;
Thomas Molony, 1737; David Moore, 1738; John MacMur-
phy, 1738; Adam McNeil, 1738; James McCrillis, 1738;
Thomas McDaniel, 1738; James McFaden, 1738; Lodowic
McGowing, 1739; Michael Malcolm, 1739; John McCleary,
1739; John Moony, 1739; Rev. John Moorehead, 1739, here
in 1727; Hugh McDaniel, 1737; David Miller, 1739; Sam-
uel Miller, 1740; James McHord, 1740; Rev. William
McClennehan, 1741; Archibald McNeil, 1743; William
Moore, 1743; Neill McIntire, 1743, President; John Noble,
1737; Daniel Neal, 1737; James Nelson, 1738; Arthur
Noble, 1740; Isaac Orr, 1737; Peter Pelham, 1737; John
Poyntz, 1737; John Powers, 1739; William Patton, 1739;
John Quig, 1738; Francis Richey, 1737, Vice-President;
Kennedy Ryan, 1739; Joseph St. Lawrence, 1737; Wil-
liam Stewart, 1737; Samuel Sloane, 1738; Robert Sloane,
1738; William Sherrard, 1739; James Stet, 1739; Isaac
Savage, 1739; David Stanley, 1741; Archibald Thomas,
1737; Patrick Tracy, 1737; William Toler, 1738; James
Tabb, 1739; Robert Temple, Esq., 1740; John Thompson,
1740; John Tanner, 1741; Nathaniel Walsh, 1737; Patrick
Walker, 1737; John Whitley, 1738; Peter Williams, 1738.

(B) Names of Fathers on the Presbyterian Baptismal
Records in Boston, 1730–1736

Robert Patton, Andrew Simson, Daniel Camble, Robert
Knox, Samuel Millar, Samuel Sloan, Patrick Camble, John
Little, John McCurdy, William Hogg, James Moor, John
Watts, James Crozier, Robert Rutherford, Robert Morton,

Samuel Smith, John Tom, Robert Kirkland, Alexander
Wilson, John Young, Robert Hodge, William Shirlow,
Elizabeth Hutchinson, William Patterson, Patrick Walker,
Robert Wilson, William Camble, Francis Lee, James Max-
well, William Chessnutt, Jeramiah Smith, James MaClure,
John Harper, David MaClure, James Tatt, James MacQuis-
tion, Robert Speer, Allen Whippie, David MaClare, Roan-
ald Stewart, John Smith, Henry Hodge, Rev. Mr. Moor-
head, George Sinclair, Robert Knox, Thomas Mitchel, Rob-
ert Hodgen, John Gwinn, Andrew Knox, Andrew Nichols,
Robert Dixon, Ephraim Kile, John MacDugall, John Pharr,
Hugh Mickleravie, Robert Ross, Samuel MaClure, Abraham Aul, Charles MaClure, Marnaduck Black, John Quigg,
William Bryant, William Cammeron, John Walker, Wil-
liam Hays, James Hart, William Micklevain, Edward Al-
len, Patrick White, John MaClure, Alexander Orr, James
Mayes, Richard MaClure, William MaClinto, Duncan
MaClane, Patrick Chambers, John Lough, Samuel Smith,
John Fulton, John Karr, John Turk, Benjamin Frizwell,
Robert Montgomery, Ezekiel McNichols, William Mickle-
roy, David Tweed, James Davidson, Henry Hodge, Sam-
uel Karnachan, John Davis, John MacKachan, Daniel
McNeal, John Watts, John Dicky, Robert Hill, William
Lindsay, James Perry, Robert Speer, Robert Cunningham,
John Jonston, Robert Burns, Henry Kelly, Robert Wilie,
James Robinson, James MaCalan, Andrew Menford, Wal-
ter Topham, Alexander Watts, James Willis, David
White, George Sinclair, Gawin Hemphill, James Baird,
Michael Burns, James Tate, Archbald Tomb, James Hart,
John Moor, James Gaudy, William Freeland, John Clerk,
William Williamson, Robert Scott, William Dame, John

Lockhead, John MacKisick, Alexander Cumings, Robert Work, John Kerr, Samuel Gibson, Simon Eliot, Archibald Thomson, Thomas Harkness, William Harmon, William Moor, Thomas Brown, Gilbert Hides, George Hogg, Robert Dunlop, John Britton, James Cowan, Thomas Lawry, Thomas Boggle, James Carlile, Alexander MaClery, Hugh Gregg, John Kennedy, John Alison, Humphrey Caldbreath, James Long, John Bell, Robert Cuthbertson.

APPENDIX V

Birth, marriage and death records in Ulster at the time of the Protestant migration to America are very meagre. Those which relate to members of the Established Church rarely reach back to this period except in the large towns and cities, and facts concerning members of dissenting chapels are still less common. It must be said, however, that many dissenters were married and buried by the Episcopal rector or curate, to satisfy the law. For this reason, and because members of Presbyterian families not infrequently "conformed" in order to hold public office, the following list of vital records will be of service. It is from the Appendix to the 28th report of the Deputy Keeper of the Public Records in Ireland. An asterisk means that the records are in local custody. Italics indicate that the records are in the Public Record Office in Dublin.

Town and County.	Vols.	Baptisms.	Marriages.	Burial.
*Antrim, Antrim.........	4	1700–1755	1700–1756	1700–1754
*Ardkeen, Down.........	2	1746–	1746–	1746–
Ardstraw, Tyrone.........	5	1728–	1743–	....
*Bailieborough or Moybolgue, Cavan....	5	1744–	1744–	....
Ballyphilip, Down.......	5	1745–	1745–	1745–
Belfast:				
*—— St. Anne, Shankill..	26	1745–	1745–	1745–
Cappagh, Tyrone........	6	1758–	1758–	1758–
*Carrickfergus, Antrim...	7	1740–	1740–	1740–
Clondehorky, Donegal.....	6	1756–	....	....
Clonfeacle, Tyrone........	7	1743–	1761–	1736–
Clonleigh, Donegal	6	1759–	1764–	1764–
*Coleraine	7	1769–	1769–	1769–
Comber	5	1683–	1683–	1683–
*Derry Cathedral (Templemore)	19	1642–	1642–	1642–
*Derryaghey, Antrim.....	6	1696–1738	1696–1738	1696–1738
*Donaghendry, Tyrone...	7	1734–1768	....	....
*Down, Down...........	5	1750–	1752–	1752–
*Drumachose, Derry.....	6	1728–	1728–	1728–
*Dunglass, Tyrone.......	7	1600–?	1754–1766	1754–1767
*Drumholm, Donegal.....	3	1691–	1691–	1691–
*Ematris, Monaghan	7	1753–	1753–	1753–
Enniskillen, Fermanagh.	10	1666–	1666–	1666–
*Glenavy, Antrim........	5	1707–	1813–	1707–
*Killeshandra, Cavan.....	5	1735–	1735–	1735–
*Killyman, Tyrone.......	9	1741–	1741–	1741–
Kilmore, Cavan.........	6	1702–	1702–	1702–
*Lisburn, Antrim	12	{ 1639–1646 { 1661–	1661–	1661–
Lissan, Derry...........	4	1753–	1752–	1753–
*Loughgall, Armagh	7	1706–1729	1706–1729	1706–1729
*Magherafelt, Derry......	6	1718–	1718–	1718–
*Magheralin, Down	9	1692–	1692–	1692–
Mullaghbrack, Armagh ...	10	1737–	1737–	1737–
Newtownards, Down....	10	1701–1736	1701–1736	....
*Saintfield, Down	5	1724–1757	1784–1757	....
*Seagoe, Down...........	9	{ 1672–1731 { 1735–	1676–1731 1735–	1691–1731 1735–
*Shankill, Down	7	1681–	1676–	1675–
Tamlaghtard, Derry.....	4	1747–	1747–	1747–

APPENDIX VI

Home Towns of Ulster Families, 1691–1718

Since the ministers of dissenting congregations had little or no legal standing during the earliest years of the emigration to New England their records of births, marriages and death do not appear to have been preserved, except in isolated cases. But the records of presbytery and synod were kept with great care, and the latter have been printed to the year 1820. They give the name of the ruling elder in each congregation for the year of the general synod, and often the names of commissioners sent to the synod to represent local interests. Names of witnesses in cases which came before the synod also help to establish the home towns of Presbyterian families. Names of Ulster towns are usually given here as they are spelled in the records. A complete list of Irish townlands was printed at Dublin in 1861 under the title "Census of Ireland. Index to townlands and Towns, Parishes and Baronies." The meeting houses stood in the towns here given, but some parishioners lived in adjoining towns. The site of the meeting house and the bounds of each church's influence were subjects for contention at the meetings of presbytery and synod.

R. E. means Ruling Elder.

C. stands for Commissioner.

W. stands for Witness and P. means Petitioner.

The Cathedral records of Londonderry have been copied

from the supplement to Mr. Morrison's History of Windham. A few references to families may be found in the Journal of the Association for the Preservation of the Memorials of the Dead in Ireland. Additional information might have been gathered from the Ulster Journal of Archæology.

A

ACHESON, George, R E 1711 — Donegal, Donegal
ACHINVOLE, Samuel, R E 1716 — Ballycarry, Antrim
ADAIR, Alexander, C 1708 — Belfast, Antrim
    Robert, C 1709 — Drogheda, Louth
    Thomas, R E 1711 — Sligo, Sligo
    William, R E 1698 — Ballymena, Antrim
AGNEW, Alexander, R E 1706 — Loughbrickland, Down
    Andrew, R E 1717 — Belfast, Antrim
    James, R E 1707 — Ballymoney, Antrim
    John, R E 1708, 15, 18 — Finvoy, Antrim
    Mr William, C 1714 — Minterburn, Tyrone
AIKEN, William, 1709 — Ballycogly, Derry?
AITKEN, James, R E 1707, 11, 15 — Ballinderry, Antrim
ALLEN, Hector, R E 1706, 10, 12 — Stonebridge, Monaghan
    James, R E 1697 — Randalstown, Antrim
    John, R E 1694, 1704, 11, 12, 15 — Cairncastle, Antrim
    John, R E 1704 — Ballykelly, Derry
    John, R E 1718 — Randalstown, Antrim
    Patrick, C 1691, 1701 — Dunagor (Donegore, Antrim?)
    Robert, C 1718 — Garvachy, Down
    Thomas, R E 1713 — Corboy and Tully, West Meath
    William, R E 1706 — Garvagh, Derry
ALLISON, John, R E 1712 — Donaghmore, Down
    Thomas, bapt. 1663 — Londonderry
ANDERSON, Archibald, R E 1717 — Fannet, Donegal
    Isaac, m. 1727 Margaret Cochran — Londonderry
    James, R E 1710, 15 — Dunean, Antrim
    Samuel, R E 1710 — Ballymena, Antrim

ANDREWS, Robert, C 1708 — Belfast, Antrim
  Mr Robert, R E 1712 — Belfast, Antrim
  Thomas, R E 1705 — Ramelton, Donegal
  William, C 1708, 11 — Glen and Drumbanagher, Armagh

ARBUCKLE, James, R E 1703, 13, 16, C 1708 — Belfast, Antrim
ABESKIN, Robert, R E 1709, 17 — Strabane, Tyrone
ARMOUR, John, R E 1704 — Dromore, Down
  John, R E 1711 — Maghera, Derry
ARMSTRONG, Andrew, R E 1707 — Castledawson, Derry
  George, C 1715 — Monaghan, Monaghan
  John, C 1708 — Belfast, Antrim
  John, R E 1708, 14 — Cavanaleck, Tyrone
  John and Janet, 1681 — Londonderry
  Joseph, bapt. 1711 — Londonderry
  Robert, C 1692 — Maghera, Derry
  Robert, R E 1705 — Castledawson, Derry
  Thomas, R E 1707 — Ballybay, Monaghan
  Thomas, R E 1704 — Clogher, Tyrone
  William, R E 1711 — Connor, Antrim
  William, R E 1717 — Braid, Antrim
ATCHESON, George, R E 1709 — Donegal, Donegal
AUSTIN, James, C 1706 — Coleraine, Derry

B

BAGNOL, Mr Alexander, C 1718 — Dublin
BALLENTINE, James, C 1708 — Newry?, Down
  James, R E 1708, 9, 12, 16, 17 — Newry, Down
BANKHEAD, Hugh, C 1691, 1706, R E 1698 — Coleraine, Derry
BARBER, Adam, R E 1706 — Markethill, Armagh
  David, R E 1706, 9 — Limavady, Derry
  John, R E 1705 — Omagh, Tyrone
BARNET, John, married 1681 Katherine Gilpatrick — Londonderry
  John, 1709 — Ballycogly, Wexford

BARNET, Robert, R E 1697   Carnmoney, Antrim
   William,   married   1665,
     Catherine Vance   Londonderry
BARR, Charles, of Raphoe, mar.
    1684, Janet Ramsey   Londonderry
BATHO, John, of Derry m. 1701
    Ann Patterson   Taughboyne, Donegal
BAYLY, Alexander, R E 1710   Ballee, Down
   ——, Mr., C 1717   Antrim, Antrim
BETY, James, R E 1712, 18   Anahilt, Down
   Richard, R E 1698   Anahilt, Down
   Richard, R E 1694   Hillsborough, Down
   Thomas (Beatie), C 1712, 15 Ballinderry, Antrim
   Thomas, R E 1694   Upper Killead, Antrim
   William, C 1692   Derriloran, Tyrone
   William, R E 1714   Ballynahinch, Down
   William (Beatie), R E 1717   Comber, Down
BEGGS, James, R E 1706, 9, 11, 14 Ballycarry, Antrim
BELL, Alexander, R E 1711   Drum, Armagh
   Francis, R E 1710, 12, 14   Aughnacloy, Tyrone
   Francis, C 1711, 14   Aghaloo, Tyrone
   James, R E 1711   Comber, Down
   Mr James, C 1717   Antrim, Antrim
   John, R E 1694   Downpatrick, Down
   John, R E 1698   Ahoghill, Antrim
   John, C 1708   Belfast, Antrim
   John, C 1708   Ballyroney or Moneymore, Derry
   Thomas and Jean, 1683   Londonderry
   Thomas, 1709   Tirkvillan, Derry?
   William, R E 1694, 1705   Carrickfergus, Antrim
BERRY, Alexander, R E 1715   Saintfield, Down
   Thomas, R E 1704   Galway, Galway
BEST, Thomas, R E 1706   Sligo, Sligo
BIDDELL, John, R E 1703   Monreagh, Donegal
BIGGAR, Joseph, C 1708   Belfast, Antrim
BIGGOM, Hugh, R E 1715   Keady, Armagh
BILLSLAND, John, R E 1711, 18   Clough, Down
BIRNEY, Alexander, R E 1710   Cavanaleck, Tyrone

BLACK, John, C 1708 — Belfast, Antrim
 Mr Samuel, C 1714, 15 — Monaghan
BLACKWOOD, John, R E 1706, 12,
 16 — Bangor, Down
 Robert, R E 1716 — Carrickfergus, Antrim
BLAIR, Bryce, R E 1705, 8, 9, 15,
 C 1708 — Belfast, Antrim
 James, R E 1703 — Donegore, Antrim
BLAKELEY, David, R E 1712 — Holywood, Down
BOLTON, James and Margaret,
 1682 — Londonderry
BONES, John, R E 1712 — Donegore, Antrim
BOY, Francis, R E 1698 — Burt, Donegal
BOYD, Adam and Katreen, 1678 — Londonderry
 Archibald, R E 1698 — Dervock, Antrim
 David, C 1692 — Ballymoney, Antrim
 Hugh, R E 1708, 11 — Dervock, Antrim
 Hugh, C 1708 — Belfast, Antrim
 James, R E 1704 — Dervock, Antrim
 James, R E 1716 — Larne, Antrim
 John, R E 1704, 7, 10, 11,
  13, 14, 15 — Brigh, Tyrone
 John, P 1706 — Macosquin, Derry
 John, R E 1706 — Cookstown, Tyrone
 John, R E 1709 — Omagh, Tyrone
 Robert, R E 1703 — Ballymena, Antrim
 Robert and Joanna, 1688 — Londonderry
 Samuel, R E 1716 — Donaghmore, Down
 Thomas, C 1710 — Ballyhalbert, Down
 Thomas and Jean, 1687 — Londonderry
 William, married 1658
  Agnes Young — Londonderry
BOYLE, Henry, R E 1709 — Monreagh, Donegal
 Thomas, R E 1713 — Islandmagee, Antrim
BRADY, William, R E 1711 — Ballyrashane, Antrim
BRALTON, William, R E 1697 — Burt, Donegal
BRATTON, John, C 1692 — Taughboyne, Donegal
BRENAN, Thomas, R E 1711, 15 — Carrickfergus, Antrim

BRISBIN, James, R E 1703	Cookstown, Tyrone
BRODLY, Mr., R E 1712	Strabane, Tyrone
BROOMFIELD, William, R E 1707	Fintona, Tyron
BROWN, Charles, R E 1713	Braid, Antrim
Francis, R E 1715	Glenarm, Antrim
George, R E 1692	Drumall, Antrim
Hugh and Elizabeth, 1683	Londonderry
Hugh, R E 1713	Downpatrick, Down
Hugh, R E 1717	Bangor, Down
James, R E 1703, 4, 15	Braid, Antrim
James, R E 1709	Ramelton, Donegal
James, R E 1694, 1710	Connor, Antrim
James, R E 1708	Donegal, Donegal
John, C 1692	Carrickfergus, Antrim
John, R E 1704	Cookstown, Tyrone
John, R E 1713	Limavady, Derry
John, R E 1714	Killinchy, Down
Mr John, P 1716	Dungannon, Tyrone
Patrick, R E 1705	Drum, Monaghan
William, R E 1706, 10	Moneymore, Derry
William, R E 1708	Armagh, Armagh
William, R E 1711	Aughnacloy, Tyrone
William, R E 1711	Islandmagee, Antrim
William, R E 1714	Armagh, Armagh
BROWSTER, James, R E 1708	Aghadowey, Derry
BRYCE, Edward, Esq., C 1708, 18	Belfast, Antrim
BRYSON, Archibald, R E 1718	Stonebridge, Monaghan
James, R E 1715	Connor, Antrim
James, R E 1705	Antrim, Antrim
James, R E 1708	Cookstown, Tyrone
John, R E 1703	Moneymore, Derry
John, R E 1712	Coagh, Tyrone
Mr John, C 1717	Antrim, Antrim
Thomas, R E 1704	Randalstown, Antrim
Thomas, R E 1707	Lisburn, Antrim
BURNSIDE, John, R E 1697	Clogher, Tyrone
BUTTLE, David, C 1708	Belfast, Antrim
Mr George, C 1718	Belfast, Antrim
BYERS, John, R E 1717	Clough, Down

C

CADERWOOD, Hugh, R E 1709, 17 — Drum, Monaghan
Mr Hugh, C 1718 — Cootehill, Cavan
CAIRNS, William, C 1691 — Clogher, Tyrone
CALDWELL, David and Jean, 1683 — Londonderry
James, R E 1703 — Larne, Antrim
John, R E 1692, 8 — Cairncastle, Antrim
John, R E 1709 — Ballindreat, Donegal
William, R E 1697 — Ballindreat, Donegal
CALLY, John, R E 1703, 17 — Kilraughts, Antrim
CAMOND, Archibald, C 1711 — Donaghmore, Down
CAMPBELL, Alexander, R E 1694 — Antrim, Antrim
Archibald and Janet, 1683 — Londonderry
Cornelius, R E 1713 — Ballyrashane, Antrim
James, R E 1708 — Ballee, Down
John, R E 1703, 4, 5 — Carnmoney, Antrim
John, R E 1714 — Magherally, Down
John, R E 1697, 1707 — Cairncastle, Antrim
Jos., R E 1718 — Killead, Antrim
Matthew, R E 1697, 1706, 9 — Dervock, Antrim
Patrick, R E 1704, 12 — Dublin
Robert, R E 1714 — Rathfriland, Down
Robert, R E 1715 — Ballyrashane, Antrim
Thomas, R E 1705, 11, 13, 14 — Ballybay, Monaghan
Thomas, R E 1706 — Aughnacloy, Tyrone
William and Ann, 1683 — Londonderry
CANNY, John, R E 1698 — Ballynahinch, Down
CARGILL, David, R E 1694, 1707, 17 — Aghadowey, Derry
CARLILE, William, C 1698 — Blarise, Down? (south of Lisburn)
William, R E 1710 — Newry, Down
CARR, James, R E 1697 — Minterburn, Tyrone
CARSON, Andrew, R E 1704 — Ardstraw, Tyrone
John, R E 1705 — Cairncastle, Antrim
John, R E 1708 — Ballyclare, Antrim

CARSON, Robert, R E 1697 — Strabane, Tyrone
    Samuel, P 1718 — Dublin?
CASE, William, R E 1717 — Boveva, Derry
CHADS, Henry, R E 1692, 8,
    1704, C 1708 — Belfast, Antrim
    Henry, Jr., C 1708 — Belfast, Antrim
CHALMERS, Alexander, R E 1703
    5, 15 — Tullylish, Down
    Alexander, C 1711 — Drumbanagher, Armagh
    David, R E 1697, 1709, 10 — Cookstown, Tyrone
    John, C 1711 — Donaghcloney, Down
    John, R E 1705, 13, 18 — Ballee, Down
    John, R E 1706, 11 — Tullylish, Down
    John, C 1708 — Belfast, Antrim
    Robert, R E 1705, 7, 14, 15 — Dromore, Down
CHANCELLER, Robert, R E 1703 — Drumbo, Down
CHARTERS, John, W 1704 — Lisburn, Antrim
    Robert, R E 1706 — Lisburn, Antrim
CHERRY, John, 1697 — Near Hillsborough, Down
CLANDEVIN, James, buried 1675 — Londonderry
CLANCY, William, R E 1708 — Castlereagh, Down
CLARK, James, R E 1718 — Randalstown, Antrim
    John, R E 1694, 8, 1714, 16 — Lisburn, Antrim
    John, R E 1704, 7, 11, 17 — Ballee, Down
    William, R E 1714 — Glenarm, Antrim
CLUGSTON, James, R E 1697,
    1704, 5 — Clough, Down
    John, R E 1694 — Clough or Drumca, Down
COCHRAN, Captain, C 1714 — Kinnaird, Tyrone
    John, R E 1703 — Garvagh, Derry
    Robert, R E 1710 — [Presbytery of Coleraine]
    Thomas, and Elizabeth,
    1684 — Londonderry
COLEMAN, David, R E 1707 — Donegore, Antrim
COLTHEART, John, R E 1706 — Carlingford, Louth
    Michael, R E 1703, 5 — Ballywalter, Down
COMACK, Mr John, C 1715 — Moira, Down
CONOLLY, James, C 1711 — Drumbanagher, Armagh

CORBET, Hugh, C 1713 — Drummarah (near Dromore, Down)

CRAIG, David, R E 1692 — Ballyclare, Antrim
  Hugh, R E 1715 — Macosquin, Derry
  John, C 1710 — Ballywalter, Down
  John, R E 1717 — Cairncastle, Antrim
  John, R E 1716 — Randalstown, Antrim
CRAFORD, ⎫ Archibald, R E
CRAWFORD, ⎭ 1703, 10 — Ballycarry, Antrim
  John, R E 1710 — Donegore, Antrim
  Malcom, R E 1694, 98, 1704, 13, 18 — Donegore, Antrim
  Oliver, R E 1716 — Donagheady, Tyrone
  Robert, R E 1704, 10, 12 — Carrickfergus, Antrim
  Thomas, merchant, 1701 — Belfast, Antrim
  Thomas, R E 1707 — Belfast, Antrim
  William, C 1694, 1708 — Belfast, Antrim
  William, R E 1704 — Omagh, Tyrone
  William, R E 1709 — Brigh, Tyrone
CROOKS, John, R E 1712 — Dunmurry, Down
CUDBERT, John, R E 1713 — Killinchy, Down
  John, R E 1714 — Dublin
CUDDIE, Alexander, R E 1707, 9, 10 — Dungannon, Tyrone
  James, C 1715 — Moira, Down
CULTON, James, R E 1711 — Minterburn, Tyrone
CULVERSON, James, R E 1714 — Donaghmore, Down
CUMMIN, Alexander, R E 1703 — Monaghan
  James, R E 1703 — Loughbrickland, Down
  John, C 1715 — Kilraughts, Antrim
CUNNINGHAM, Alexander, married 1681 Mary Rankin — Londonderry
  Andrew and Mary, 1682 — Londonderry
  John and Grizell, 1705 — Londonderry
  John and Mary, 1684 — Londonderry
  Capt. Michael, R E 1704 — Glendermot, Derry

CURRY, David, R E 1708 — Letterkenny, Donegal
  Hugh, R E 1714 — Ballymena, Antrim
  John, R E 1707 — Comber, Down

D

DARRAGH, James, R E 1707 — Ardstraw, Tyrone
DAVIDSON, John and Mary, 1705 — Londonderry
  John, R E 1710 — Benburb, Tyrone
  Robert, R E 1706 — Braid, Antrim
  Robert, R E 1713 — Rathfriland, Down
  Thomas, R E 1718 — Urney, Tyrone
DAVIS, Theoplihis, 1650 — Londonderry
DAWSON, William, C 1692 — Carrickfergus, Antrim
DAYBURN, Archibald, R E 1706 — Strabane, Tyrone
DICK, Quintin, C 1715 — Ballymoney, Antrim
  William, R E 1706 — Randalstown, Antrim
DICKSON, Thomas, R E 1703 — Castlereagh, Down
  William, R E 1715 — Downpatrick, Down
DICKEY, Alexander, R E 1704 — Mourne, Down
  John, R E 1694, 8, 1704, C 1701 — Clare, Armagh
DINGMORE, Robert, C 1715 — Ballymoney, Antrim
DINGWELL, John, C 1711 — Congreg'n of Galway
DINNISTON, John, R E 1698 — Ballindreat, Donegal
DIXON, Hugh, R E 1710 — Killinchy, Down
DOBBIN, Hugh, R E 1716 — Bailieborough, Cavan
DONELSON, Thomas, married 1725 Martha Parke — Londonderry
DONNALDSON, John, R E 1704, 8, 16 — Islandmagee, Antrim
DOUGLAS, Henry, C 1692 — Lurgan, Armagh
  William, C 1712 — Narrow-Water, Down
DRAHAME, George, R E 1707 — Newry, Down
DRENAN, Archibald, R E 1716 — Moneymore, Derry
DRENNAN, James, 1701 — Session of Carmony
DUCHALL, Mr James, C 1718 — Antrim, Antrim
DUGAN, James, R E 1712 — Lurgan, Armagh
  William, R E 1718 — Markethill, Armagh

DUNBAR, Andrew and Mar-
      garet, 1695   Londonderry
     William, R E 1697   Ramelton, Donegal
     William, R E 1704   Donaghmore, Donegal
DUNCAN, Mr Anthony, C 1717 Antrim, Antrim
     William, R E 1710   Fintona, Tyrone
DUNLAP, Adam, R E 1718   Keady, Armagh
DUNLOP, Allen, C 1694   Ballymoney, Antrim
     James, R E 1694   Ballywalter, Down
     Moses, R E 1703, 12, 15   Aghadowey, Antrim
     Nathaniel, R E 1707, 8, 10 Keady, Armagh
     Mr Samuel, P 1716   Athlone, Roscommon
     William, R E 1692   Upper Killead, Antrim
     William, R E 1704   Limavady, Derry
     William R E 1712   Keady, Armagh
DUNN, James, 1709   Inniskillen
     Joseph, R E 1710, 13   Randalstown, Antrim
     Jorias, R E 1717   Randalstown, Antrim
     Peter, C 1698   Down, Down
DUNWOODY, John, R E 1713   Drumbo, Down
DYATT, Hugh, C 1708   Belfast, Antrim
DYKE, James, C 1709   Moneymore, Derry

E

ECCLES, Hugh R E 1703, 16   Killead, Antrim
     John, C 1708   Belfast, Antrim
EDGAR, John, R E 1698   Moira, Down
     John, R E 1717   Dunean, Antrim
     John, R E 1716   Dunmurry, Down
EDWARDS, George, R E 1713, 18 Clare, Armagh
     James, R E 1707   Castlereagh, Down
     Thomas, Esq., R E 1717   Castlederg, Tyrone
EGELSHAM, Thomas, R E 1717 Connor, Antrim
ELDAR, Samuel, R E 1708   Burt, Donegal
     Thomas, R E 1716   Ballyrashane, Antrim
EMPILL, James, R E 1697   Aghadowey, Derry
ENNIS, Josias, R E 1715   Donegore, Antrim
ESPY, William, R E 1713   Cookstown, Tyrone
EWART, George, R E 1705, 7, 15 Clare, Armagh

F

Fairise, John, W 1704	Dunmurry, Down
Fee, John, C 1715	Monaghan
Fenton, William, R E 1705	Islandmagee, Antrim
Ferguson, Andrew, 1709	Drummullan, Derry?
Gilbert, C 1715	Moira, Down
Richard, R E 1718	Lurgan, Armagh
Dr Victor, C 1708, R E 1710, 17	Belfast, Antrim
Ferne, Anthony, C 1708	Summer-hill, Fermanagh?
Ferns, Samuel, C 1710	Summer-hill, Fermanagh?
Mr William, C 1714	Kinnaird, Tyrone
William, R E 1716	Glennan, Monaghan
Ferron, William, R E 1704	Minterburn, Tyrone
Ferry, Robert, R E 1706	Islandmagee, Antrim
Samuel, R E 1715	Islandmagee, Antrim
Ferrys, John, R E 1704	Dunmurry, Down
Ferys, John, R E 1707	Enniskillen, Fermanagh
John, R E 1712	Killeshandra, Cavan
William, R E 1715	Ballynahinch, Down
Fettys, William, R E 1706	Downpatick, Down
Finlay, James, R E 1718	Carrickfergus, Antrim
William, R E 1698	Sligo, Sligo
Finnie, Robert, R E 1711	Ballindreat, Donegal
Fisher, James and Janet, 1661	Londonderry
James, R E 1707	Benburb, Tyrone
John, R E 1698	Armagh, Armagh
John, R E 1707, 11, 16, 17, 18	Benburb, Tyrone
Fleck, Hugh, 1709	Achavan, Derry?
Fleming, John, R E 1698	Ballyclare, Antrim
Forbes, James, R E 1716	Ballee, Down
Foster, John, R E 1694, 1704	Ahoghill, Antrim
Francis, John, R E 1718	Bailieborough, Cavan
Fraser, Mr James, R E 1717	Loughbrickland, Down
Frisell, Hugh, R E 1717	Rathfriland, Down
Fulton, Peter, R E 1704	Macosquin, Derry
William, R E 1704, 6, 9	Cardonagh, Donegal

G

GA, George, R E 1704, 12, 17 — Downpatrick, Down
GALBREATH, Capt. Robert, C
   1710 — Summer-hill, Fermanagh?
   Capt. Robert, R E 1706, 9 — Killeshandra, Cavan
GALLAND, Edward, R E 1706,
   7, 13, 16 — Finvoy, Antrim
GALT, John, C 1691, 1709 — Coleraine, Derry
   Mr John, R E 1712 — Coleraine, Derry
GARRAN, James, C 1691 — Maghera, Derry
GARVAH, John, R E 1710 — Ballyrashane, Antrim
GAWDIE, James, R E 1714 — Newtownards, Down
GAWDY, John, R E 1713 — Drumbo, Down
GELSOR, Alexander, R E 1714 — Donaghmore, Down
GEMBLE, John, R E 1718 — Ballykelly, Derry
   Peter, C 1715 — Ballymoney, Antrim
   Robert, R E 1714 — Donegore, Antrim
   Robert, R E 1718 — Londonderry
GIBSON, James, R E 1705 — Clogher, Tyrone
GILLIS, Robert, R E 1718 — Islandmagee, Antrim
GILMORE, Mr John, C 1714, 15 — Monaghan
   John, R E 1703 — Rathfriland, Down
GIVAN, John, C 1715 — Kilraughts, Antrim
   Robert, C 1716 — Kilraughts, Antrim
GLASGOW, George, R E 1713 — Keady, Armagh
   James, R E 1698, 1703 — Randalstown, Antrim
   James, R E 1705 — Dunean, Antrim
GLEN, John, R E 1711 — Burt, Donegal
GORDON, Alexander, R E 1708,
   18 — Ballycarry, Antrim
   John, R E 1706 — Larne, Antrim
   John, R E 1711 — Braid, Antrim
   John, R E 1705, 15 — Maghera, Derry
   Rodger, R E 1698 — Braid, Antrim
   Robert, R E 1705, 6 — Castlereagh, Down
   Robert, R E 1710 — Loughbrickland, Down
   Samuel, R E 1705, 8, 15 — Aughnacloy, Tyrone
GRACY, John, R E 1711 — Enniskillen, Fermanagh

GRAHAM, John, C 1692 — Maghera, Derry
  John, R E 1703 — Clough, Antrim
  Richard, R E 1698, 1704, 7 — Monaghan
GRANGER, Gawin, R E 1716 — Cushendall, Antrim
  Thomas, R E 1706 — Dunmurry, Down
GRAY, Alexander, of Taugh-
    boyne, married 1685,
    Alice Jamison — Londonderry
  Archibald, R E 1697 — Ahoghill, Antrim
  Gilbert, R E 1710, 13 — Magherally, Down
  John, C 1717 — Antrim, Antrim
GREDDIN, Alexander, R E 1698,
    1709 — Corboy, West Meath
GREG, John, C 1708 — Belfast, Antrim
  Robert, R E 1705 — Enniskillen, Fermanagh
  Thomas, R E 1711 — Cavanaleck, Tyrone
GRIER, Hugh, C 1702 — Brechy and Kells, Monaghan
  John, R E 1709, 14, 16 — Markethill, Armagh
  Timothy, C 1691 — Kinnaird, Tyrone
GRERSON, Robert, C 1718 — Kinnaird, Tyrone
GRIFFITH, John, ·R E 1697, 8 — Comber, Down
GUTRY, William, R E 1710 — Ballykelly, Derry

H

HALIDAY, Samuel, R E 1716 — Anahilt, Down
  William, R E 1697, 8 — Glenarm, Antrim
HALL, Gilbert, R E 1704, 7 — Ballycarry, Antrim
  Mr Robert, C 1715 — Ballinderry, Antrim
HAMILL, Neil, R E 1704, C 1715 — Kilraughts, Antrim
HAMILTON, Andrew, R E 1708 — Ramelton, Donegal
  Archibald, C 1699 — Killmakevet, Antrim
    (north of Glenavy)
  Capt. Gawin, C 1691 — Tanoch-Neeve, Down
  Henry, R E 1709 — Ray, Donegal
  Hugh, W 1704 — Lisburn?, Antrim
  James, R E 1703 — Dundonald, Down
  James, R E 1714, C 1715 — Holywood, Down

HAMILTON, John, C 1691 Tanoch-Neeve, Down
 John, R E 1710 Limavady, Derry
 Mr John, C 1715 Holywood, Down
 Robert, R E 1694 Kirkdonnell (Same as Dundonald, Down)
 Robert, R E 1708 Monaghan
 Capt. Robert, C 1718 Drum, Monaghan
 William, 1709 Ballydally (Ballydawley, Derry?)
 William, C 1710 Killyleagh, Down
HANDCOCK, Major Thomas, C 1704 Athlone, Roscommon
 Major ——, R E 1708, 11 Letterkenny, Donegal
HANNA, Alexander, R E 1705 Loughbrickland, Down
HANNAH, John, R E 1703, 11 Dungannon, Tyrone
HANYNG, John, R E 1718 Newry, Down
HARESHAW, James, R E 1718 Donaghmore, Down
 John, R E 1711, 14 Loughbrickland, Down
HARPER, John, C 1709 Coleraine, Derry
 Robert, R E 1713, 17 Ahoghill, Antrim
HARVEY, John, C 1710 Londonderry
HASLETON, George, R E 1706, 15 Ballymena, Antrim
HASTIE, John, R E 1715 Ballycarry, Antrim
HEMPHILL, James, R E 1713 Macosquin, Derry
HENDERSON, Archibald, R E 1715 Convoy, Donegal
 James, C 1715 Twenty-Quarter Lands (Near Ballymoney)

HENRY, Alexander, R E 1703 Newtownards, Down
 Daniel, C 1691 Maghera, Derry
 Hugh, R E 1706 Aghadowey, Derry
 Hugh, R E 1709 Bangor, Down
 James, R E 1706, 17 Ballymoney, Antrim
 James, R E 1712 Castledawson, Tyrone
 Mr James, C 1715 Ballymoney, Antrim
 John, R E 1704 Dungannon, Tyrone
 Samuel, C 1717 Sea Patrick, Down
HERE, Nicholas, C 1715 Moira, Down
HERRON, Henry, C 1718 Sea Patrick, Down

HEBRON, Hugh, R E 1706 — Magherally, Down
    James, R E 1711 — Newry, Down
    James, R E 1710 — Vinecash, Armagh
    Samuel, W 1704, R E 1708 — Lisburn, Antrim
    Samuel, R E 1706 — Ballee, Down
    Samuel, P 1716, C 1718 — Sea Patrick, Down
    William, R E 1710 — Minterburn, Tyrone
HEYLYN, Dominick, W 1707, 10 — Macosquin, Derry
HILL, John, R E 1706 — Dunean, Antrim
    John, R E 1705 — Braid, Antrim
    Joseph, R E 1718 — Dunean, Antrim
    William, C 1694 — Near Aghadowey, Derry
HINES, William, married 1649
    Jane Morrison — Londonderry
HOG, James, R E 1716, 18 — Coagh, Tyrone
    James, C 1708 — Coagh, Tyrone
    James, 1709 — Ballygurch, Derry?
    John, C 1691 — Derriloran, Tyrone
HOLLAND, John, R E 1704, 8, 15 — Killyleagh, Down
    Stephen and Mary, 1703 — Londonderry
HOLMES, James, R E 1711 — Clough, Antrim
    Robert, R E 1707, 12, 17 — Islandmagee, Antrim
HOOD, or HUD, David, R E 1697,
    8, 1706, 8 — Carrickfergus, Antrim
HOOK, John, R E 1703, 6, 8, 10 — Dromore, Down
HOPES, John, R E 1698, 1707, 8 — Ballywalter, Down
HOPKIN, Robert, R E 1707, 12 — Limavady, Derry
HOPKINS, Samuel and Eliza-
    beth, 1696 — Londonderry
HORNER, John, married 1683
    Jean Morison — Londonderry
HORSBRUGH, John, R E 1712 — Ballycarry, Antrim
    John, R E 1712 — Omagh, Tyrone
HOUSTON, James, R E 1707, 10 — Maghera, Derry
    Thomas, R E 1714 — Ballyeaston, Antrim
    William, R E 1697 — Clough, Antrim
    William, C 1712 — Ballymagra[an ?] Monaghan?
        (Part of Aghaloo)

How, James, R E 1709   Monaghan
Howat, William, R E 1694   Killinchy, Down
   William, R E 1703   Comber, Down
Hudson, James, R E 1694   Ballyclare, Antrim
Hume, John, R E 1706   Ballyeaston, Antrim
Hunter, Andrew, C 1706, 9   Coleraine, Derry
   Andrew, R E 1703   Ardstraw, Tyrone
   John and Elizabeth, 1683   Londonderry
   John, R E 1706, 8   Ballinderry, Antrim
   Thomas, R E 1703   Minterburn, Tyrone
   Thomas, R E 1703, 5   Ballinderry, Antrim
   Thomas, R E 1717   Killead, Antrim
Hutchen, Hugh, R E 1710   Ervey, Meath
Hutcheson, James, R E 1718   Carnmoney, Antrim
Huy, Robert, R E 1709   Kilrea, Derry

I

Innis, Josias, R E 1706   Donegore, Antrim
Irwin, James, R E 1707   Killeshandra, Cavan
   Thomas, R E 1710   Killyleagh, Down
   William, C 1701   Ballynadrento (near Glenavy, Antrim)

J

Ja, George, R E 1716   Downpatrick, Down
Jack, Andrew and Eleanor, 1713   Londonderry
Jackson, Gilbert, R E 1711, 18   Newtownards, Down
   James, R E 1717   Larne, Antrim
   Peter, C 1699   Antrim, Antrim
   Mr Thomas, C 1717   Antrim, Antrim
Jameson, John, R E 1709, 16   Donegore, Antrim
   Marmaduke, R E 1692   Braid, Antrim
   Thomas, R E 1715   Anahilt, Down
Jamison, John, R E 1697   Anahilt, Down
   Thomas, R E 1710   Anahilt, Down
Johnson, Duncan, C 1708   Coagh, Tyrone

JOHNSTON, James, 1709   Drummullen, Derry?
     James, R E 1703, 11, 12, 16   Armagh
     James, C 1708   Rathfriland, Down
     James, R E 1716   Ballyroney, Down
     John, R E 1697, 1704   Rathfriland, Down
     John, R E 1710   Strabane, Tyrone
     John, R E 1716   Drumbo, Down
     John, W 1708   Belfast, Antrim
     Mr Thomas, C 1714   Trewgh, Monaghan
     Thomas, C 1715   Ballinderry, Antrim
     William, R E 1692   Broadisland, Antrim
     William, R E 1707   Clough, Down
     Capt. William, C 1717   Antrim, Antrim
JONES, Richard, R E 1713   Glendermot, Derry

K

KELL, James, R E 1718   Vinecash, Armagh
KELSO, Henry, W 1706   Raphoe, Donegal
     John, R E 1717   Templepatrick, Antrim
KENKIN, Richard, C 1708   Coagh, Tyrone
KENNEDY, Alexander, R E 1709   Londonderry
     Arthur, Esq., C 1715   Holywood, Down
     Arthur, R E 1713 16   Holywood, Down
     David, R E 1698   Clough, Down
     David, R E 1703   Killyleagh, Down
     David, R E 1712   Cushendall, Antrim
     Horace, C 1710   Londonderry
     Hugh, R E 1711   Kilrea, Derry
     James, C 1691   Clogher, Tyrone
     James, R E 1703, 6, 8, 12   Donaghadee, Down
     James, R E 1706   Dublin
     James, R E 1709   Clogher, Tyrone
     James, R E 1718   Rathfriland, Down
     Mr Jon., C 1715   Holywood, Down
     Joseph, R E 1718   Ballyroney, Down
     Thomas, R E 1717   Ballynahinch, Down
     William, R E 1705   Belfast, Antrim
     William, R E 1709, 10   Castledawson, Tyrone

KENNEDY, Mr William, C 1717 — Antrim, Antrim
KEYS, Roger, R E 1713 — Ballindreat, Donegal
KER, Hugh, R E 1705 — Clogher, Tyrone
    James, R E 1705 — Minterburn, Tyrone
    James, R E 1709 — Donagheady, Tyrone
    John, married 1683 Mary
      McCalam — Londonderry
    Moses, C 1698 — Donaghcloney, Down
    Robert, R E 1708, 10, 16 — Larne, Antrim
    William, R E 1712 — Tullylish, Down
KILGOUR, James, R E 1707 — Donagheady, Tyrone
KINEAR, Mr John, C 1717 — Antrim, Antrim
KING, James, R E 1711 — Dunmurry, Down
    Robert, R E 1698 — Ballyeaston, Antrim
    Robert, R E 1705 — Randalstown, Antrim
    William, R E 1718 — Fintona, Tyrone
KINKEAD, James and Mary,
    1705 — Londonderry
KINLY, Daniel, W 1704, R E
    1710 — Lisburn, Antrim
KNIVEN, William, R E 1697 — Glendermot, Derry
KNOX, Alexander, R E 1705, 7, 12, — Cookstown, Tyrone
KYLE, Jon., 1714 — Belfast, Antrim
    Robert, C 1691 — Tanoch-Neeve, Down
    William, married 1684
      Mary Gee — Londonderry

L

LADLEY, Joseph, R E 1718 — Brigh, Tyrone
LAMOND, Andrew, R E 1711 — Donaghadee, Down
    John, C 1715 — Ballymoney, Antrim
    (See also Camond)
LAPSLEY, John, R E 1709 — Glenarm, Antrim
LAWRENCE, James, R E 1716 — Maghera, Derry
LAWRIE, Andrew, R E 1714 — Ballee, Down
LAWRY, John, R E 1708 — Donagheady, Tyrone

LUKE, John, R E 1705 — Bangor, Down
LYLE, James, R E 1712, 15 — Larne, Antrim
    Thomas, C 1708 — Belfast, Antrim
LYN, John, R E 1708 — Ballykelly, Derry
LYND, Adam, R E 1713 — Cookstown, Tyrone

M

McALEXANDER, Mr Daniel, C
    1718 — Cootehill, Cavan
McALLISTER, Alexander and
    Ann, 1725 — Londonderry
McALPIN, James, C 1710 — Killyleagh, Down
McBRIDE, Andrew, R E 1694 — Rathfriland, Down
McCALA, John, R E 1703 — Finvoy, Antrim
    Mr, R E 1714 — Billy, Antrim
McCALL, James, R E 1716 — Keady, Armagh
    John, R E 1706 C 1706 — Lurgan, Armagh
McCANE, Alexander, C 1709,
    R E 1715 — Moneymore, Derry
    Robert, R E 1716 — Dervock, Antrim
McCARTNEY, Alexander, R E
    1717 — Killinchy, Down
    George, C 1708 — Belfast, Antrim
    Isaac, C 1708, 18, R E
    1709, 16 — Belfast, Antrim
McCLANE, John, R E 1718 — Castlereagh, Down
McCLATCHY, James, R E 1711 — Markethill, Armagh
    James, C 1717 — Magherally, Down
McCLELLAN, James, R E 1708 — Loughbrickland, Down
    James, C 1718 (June) — Magherally, Down
    John, R E 1706 — Maghera, Derry
    John, R E 1710 — Killeshandra, Cavan
McCLINSKY, William, R E 1708,
    16 — Ballynahinch, Down
McCLURE, James, R E 1705, 12 — Markethill, Armagh
    James, R E 1710 — Ballinderry Antrim
    James, C 1712 — Glenavy, Antrim

McComb, Alexander, R E 1707 Portaferry, Down
McCome, Hugh, R E 1716 Portaferry, Down
 James, R E 1713 Minterburn, Tyrone
McComphy, Edward, R E 1692 Lisburn, Antrim
McConchy, George, R E 1717 Moneymore, Derry
 James, C 1715 Monaghan
 Robert, C 1694 Armagh, Armagh
 William, R E 1705 Ballyeaston Antrim
 William, R E 1708 Ballymena, Antrim
 Mr William, C 1717 Antrim, Antrim
McConnell, James, R E 1715,
 18 Comber, Down
McCord, James, 1709 "In the Moor"
 Thomas, 1709 Edruna, Derry?
McCormick, Andrew, R E 1708 Carnmoney, Antrim
 Hugh, R E 1703 Portaferry, Down
 John, R E 1703, 7 Ballyclare, Antrim
 William, R E 1708 Clough, Down
McCracken, William, P 1711 Letterkenny, Donegal
McCrea, James, R E 1703 Ray, Donegal
McCreigh, David, R E 1708 Moneymore, Derry
 John, R E 1703 Ballybay, Monaghan
 John, 1709 Drumady, Derry?
McCrery, William, R E 1718 Bangor, Down
McCullogh, David, R E 1714 Carrickfergus, Antrim
 Fergus, R E 1709 Minterburn, Tyrone
 Henry, 1708 Belfast, Antrim
 James, R E 1706 Ballynahinch, Down
 John, R E 1692 Broadisland, Antrim
 John, R E 1705 Ballycarry, Antrim
 John, R E 1708, 10 Ballybay, Monaghan
 John, R E 1718 Larne, Antrim
 Robert, R E 1708 Carlingford?, Louth
 Robert, R E 1703 Vinecash, Armagh
 William, R E 1712 Rathfriland, Down
McCully, Thomas, R E 1692 Ballyeaston Antrim
McCutchen, James, R E 1711,
 15 Portaferry, Down

McCutchen, William, R E 1706 Corboy, West Meath
McDonnell, Robert, R E 1717,
18 Portaferry, Down
McDowell, Daniel, R E 1717 Markethill, Armagh
John, R E 1713 Newry, Down
McDug, Robert, R E 1713 Castledawson, Tyrone
McElwayne, John, R E 1710,
12, 18 Braid, Antrim
William, R E 1697 Moneymore, Derry
McEntyr, Robert, R E 1705 Donagheady, Tyrone
McFarlin, John, R E 1716 Badoney, Tyrone
McFedrick, Gilbert, R E 1710 Ballymoney, Antrim
McFerran, Patrick, C 1714, 18 Breaky, Monaghan?
McFrudin, Gib., R E 1697 Ballymoney, Antrim
McGahy, Samuel, R E 1718 Killinchy, Down
McGarroch, John, R E 1716 Comber, Down
McGau, Richard, 1709 Ballynarga, Tyrone
McGee, John, R E 1710, 16 Clough, Down
McGennis, Glassny, P 1712 Newry, Down
McGie, Hugh, R E 1717 Donaghmore, Down
McGill, Hugh, C 1710 Ballywalter, Down
James, C 1718 Girvachy, Down?
Mr John, C 1713, R E 1712,
13, 16 Dromore, Down
John, Esq., 1708 Rathfriland, Down
John, R E 1710 Ballyeaston, Antrim
McGlahry, Andrew, R E 1718 Glennan, Monaghan
McGown, Cornet Alexander,
C 1715 Ballymoney, Antrim
Hugh, R E 1704, 13, 14, 16 Donaghadee, Down
McGuffock, Fergus, C 1714 Minterburn, Tyrone
McGusty, David, R E 1709 Enniskillen, Fermanagh
McIlwain, Andrew and Kath-
erine, 1726 Londonderry
McKa, John, R E 1717, 18 Glenarm, Antrim
MacKee, David, married 1665
Margaret Patterson Londonderry
James, R E 1707 Drumbo, Down

MacKee, James, R E 1709 — Ballydally, Derry?
John, R E 1694 — Moneymore, Derry
John, R E 1694 — Maghera, Derry
John, 1709 — Ballygurch (Ballygurk, Derry?)
William, R E 1711 — Ballywalter, Down
McKelly, Daniel, C 1694 — Near Aghadowey, Derry
McKenry, William, R E 1703 — Carrickfergus, Antrim
McKewn, Alexander, R E 1709 — Moneymore, Derry
Mackey, John, R E 1703 — Ramoan, Antrim
Macky, Alderman, C 1716 — Londonderry
McKibbin, Hugh, R E 1713 — Newry, Down
James, R E 1707, 12 — Loughbrickland, Down
McKinly, Patrick, R E 1705 — Ballyclare, Antrim
McKitrick, John, C 1704 — Kirkdonnell, Down
John, R E 1710 — Cushendall, Antrim
McKnaight, James, C 1698 — Down
James, R E 1703 — Downpatrick, Down
John, W 1704 — Lisburn, Antrim
William, R E 1703 — Moira, Down
McKneely, John, R E 1715 — Bailieborough, Cavan
McMaighan, William, R E
1711, C 1712, 15 — Moira, Down
McMaster, Mr George, C 1717 — Antrim, Antrim
John, R E 1692, C 1717 — Antrim, Antrim
John, R E 1705 — Donegore, Antrim
McMullen, John, 1708 — Rathfriland, Down
Mr Robert, R E 1712, 14, 15, — Ballyroney, Down
William, 1709 — Millinaho, Derry?
McMurdy, Hans, C 1718 — Sea Patrick, Down
McMurran, Mr William, C 1716 — Monaghan
McMurray, John, R E 1710 — Comber, Down
John, R E 1712 — Ballee, Down
Robert, R E 1711 — Ballyroney, Down
McNedny, Robert, R E 1715 — Castledawson, Tyrone
McNeil, C 1718 — Belfast, Antrim
Capt., C 1713, R E 1716 — Dundalk, Louth
John, C 1708 — Coagh, Tyrone
McQuistin, David, R E 1710 — Enniskillen, Fermanagh

McRobert, Andrew, R E 1717 — Kilmore, Down
McTyre, Andrew, R E 1707 — Cardonagh, Donegal
Magee, James, R E 1708 — Dunmurry, Down
Maglaghlin, Robert, R E 1704 — Clough, Antrim
Mahaffy, Hugh, R E 1709 — Ballybay, Monaghan
Mains, John, R E 1712 — Saintfield, Down
    John, R E 1714 — Clough, Down
Mairs, David, C 1715 — Ballinderry, Antrim
Maithland, Alexander, R E 1704, 16 — Enniskillen, Fermanagh
Man, John, R E 1714 — Islandmagee, Antrim
Marshall, Mr Hugh, R E 1712 — Clough, Down
    James, C 1691 — Taughboyne, Donegal
    Walter, R E 1713 — Londonderry
Martin, Alexander, R E 1710 — Omagh, Tyrone
    Colin, R E 1709 — Killinchy, Down
    Daniel, R E 1710 — Markethill, Armagh
    David, R E 1710 — Ballynahinch, Down
    James, R E 1711, 12, 13 — Carnmoney, Antrim
    James, R E 1715, 17 — Castlereagh, Down
    John, R E 1705 — Lisburn, Antrim
    John, 1705 — Drumbo, Down
    William, R E 1706 — Belfast, Antrim
Maskimine, John, R E 1708 — Downpatrick, Down
Mathew, John, R E 1705 — Dunmurry, Down
Mathy, William, R E 1694 — Glenarm, Antrim
Matire, Maurice, R E 1706 — Cavanaleck, Tyrone
Maxwell, Andrew, R E 1704 — Ballynahinch, Down
    Andrew, C 1708, R E 1711 — Belfast, Antrim
    Arthur, R E 1706, 8, 10, 11, 12 — Drumbo, Down
    Arthur, C 1712 — Ballinderry, Antrim
    William, R E 1705 — Strabane, Tyrone
Menzies, Adam, R E 1708 — Stonebridge, Monaghan
Mercer, John, R E 1697 — Killead, Antrim
    John, R E 1703 — Dunmurry, Down
    Thomas, R E 1697 — Enniskillen, Fermanagh
Metcalf, Mr George, R E 1709, 12 — Dublin

METCH, Mr, R E 1712　Cavanaleck, Tyrone
MILES, William, R E 1703　Anahilt, Down
MILLAR, David, R E 1704, 16　Aghadowey, Derry
　John, R E 1712, 14　Ballyclare, Antrim
　Mr John, C 1717　Antrim, Antrim
　Robert, R E 1709　Fintona, Tyrone
　Robert, R E 1717　Ballykelly, Derry
MILLIKEN, Robert, C 1708　Belfast, Antrim
　Thomas, R E 1707, 18　Ballynahinch, Down
MILLING, Archibald, R E 1715　Donaghadee, Down
MILLS, Daniel, R E 1703, 5, 10　Dublin
　John, R E 1703　Macosquin, Derry
MITCHELL, Alexander, 1709　Liscasy, Tyrone
　David, C 1691　Donaghmore, Tyrone
　James and Jane, 1686　Londonderry
　John, R E 1692, 1710, 13,
　　C 1705　Glenarm, Antrim
　John and Esther, 1686　Londonderry
　William, R E 1718　Belfast, Antrim
MONTGOMERY, Francis, C 1711　Cong'n of Galway
　John and Joanna, 1682　Londonderry
　John, R E 1717　Donegore, Antrim
　Nathaniel, R E 1704, 7, 13,
　　17　Tullylish, Down
MONYPENNY, Robert, C 1708　Dundalk, Louth
MOODIE, John, R E 1714, 16　Clare, Armagh
MOORE, Adam, R E 1717　Ballyeaston, Antrim
　Alexander, C 1708　Belfast, Antrim
　David, R E 1708　Cairncastle, Antrim
　Francis, R E 1710, 17　Ballyroney, Down
　Mr Francis, C 1718　Magherally, Down
　Hugh, R E 1707　Omagh, Tyrone
　John, C 1694　Aghadowey, Derry
　John, R E 1703　Aughnacloy, Tyrone
　John, R E 1705　Macosquin, Derry
　John, 1706 (brother-in-law
　of John Whitehead; Bar-
　bary captive)　Coleraine, Derry

MOORE, John, C 1711   Aghaloo, Tyrone
   John, R E 1712   Newtownards, Down
   John, R E 1713   Ballycarry, Antrim
   John and Ann, 1699   Londonderry
   John, married Elizabeth
     Morrison, 1701   Londonderry
   Patrick, R E 1708   Fintona, Tyrone
   Robert, R E 1697, 8   Killyleagh, Down
   Robert, R E 1704, 8   Monreagh, Derry
   Mr Robert, C 1714   Ballymagraan?
   Mr Robert, C 1718   Drum, Monaghan
   Samuel, R E 1708   Maghera, Derry
   Thomas, R E 1707   Ramelton, Donegal
   Thomas, R E 1709   Urney, Tyrone
   William, R E 1709   Ray, Donegal
   William, C 1706, 12, R E
     1710, 12, 17   Moira, Down
   William, R E 1710, 12, C
     1715   Clough, Antrim
   William, C 1712   Ballymagraan?
MOORHEAD, Thomas, R E 1716 Ballywalter, Down
   William, C 1694   Killinchy, Down
MOREHEAD, William, R E 1709 Ardstraw, Tyrone
MORRISON, James, R E 1714 Macosquin, Derry
   James and Mary, 1701 Londonderry
   Mr Joseph, C 1712, 16 Londonderry
   Robert and Ann, 1683 Londonderry
   Robert, R E 1709   Ballykelly, Derry
MORSON, James, R E 1698   Donaghmore, Donega'
MUNDALE, William, R E 1698 Dunean, Antrim
MURDOGH, James, R E 1704 Ballymena, Antrim
   James, R E 1712   Maghera, Derry
MURPHY, Daniel, C 1708   Dundalk, Louth
MURRAY, Horas, R E 1706   Minterburn, Tyrone
   James, R E 1707   Newtownards, Down
   James, R E 1713   Comber, Down
   William, R E 1711   Larne, Antrim

N

NEIL, Daniel, R E 1715 — Bangor, Down
    Robert, R. E 1717 — Cushendall, Antrim
NEILSON, Alexander, R E 1707 — Dunean, Antrim
    Robert, R E 1694, 1707 — Larne, Antrim
    Robert, R E 1697, 8 — Antrim, Antrim
    William, R E 1704 — Antrim, Antrim
NESBIT, John, R E 1703, 5, 6 — Ervey, Meath
    Nathan, C 1718 — Ban Breaky,. Monaghan?
    Richard, R E 1713 — Donagheady, Tyrone
NESMITH, James, married Jane
    Bennumas, 1659 — Londonderry
NEVIN, Andrew, R E 1697, 1706 — Ballyclare, Antrim
    William, C 1691 — Glendermot, Derry
NORTON, Mr. Richard, C 1718 — Dublin
NUTT, Robert, R E 1698, 1709 — Glendermot, Derry

O

O'CAHAN, John, R E 1704, 13 — Maghera, Derry
O'NEILL, John, Esq., P. 1717 — Shane's Castle, Antrim
ORR, Abel, R E 1711 — Dublin
    David and Isabel, 1683 — Londonderry
    James, R E 1710 — Mourne, Down
    James, R E 1712 — Comber, Down
    John, R E 1708 — Boveva, Derry
    John, R E 1714 — Drumbo, Down
    Mr Patrick, C 1715 — Clough, Antrim
OUGHTERSON, John, C 1711 — Drumbanagher, Armagh
OUSTEAN, James, C 1691 — Coleraine, Derry
OWENS, Hugh, R E 1709 14, 16, 18 Connor, Antrim

P

PAGE, John, R E 1716 — Armagh?
PARK, Andrew and Jane, 1704 — Londonderry
    John, R E 1713, 15 — Ballyclare, Antrim
    Robert and Mary, 1697 — Londonderry,

PARKER, John, R E 1716 — Dunean, Antrim
    Samuel, R E 1712 — Connor, Antrim
PATERSON, Arthur, R E 1704 — Ray, Donegal
    Arthur, R E 1709 — Burt, Donegal
    David, R E 1711 — Monreagh, Donegal
    Garvin, R E 1707, 11, 13, 14, — Killyleagh, Down
    John, R E 1694 — Newry, Down
    John, R E 1697 — Dunpatrick, Down
    John, R E 1707 — Carrickfergus, Antrim
    John, R E 1708, 18 — Dungannon, Tyrone
    John, C 1708 — Elden-derry, Armagh?
    John, R E 1708, 14 — Tullylish, Down
    John, R E 1711, 15 — Lurgan, Armagh
    John, married Margaret
      King, 1681 — Londonderry
    John and Anne, 1695 — Londonderry
    Peter, R E 1706 — Kilraughts, Antrim
    Robert, R E 1715 — Billy, Antrim
    Samuel, R E 1703 — Ballywillan, Antrim
    Walter, C 1691 — Taughboyne, Donegal
    Walter, R E 1707 — Monreagh, Donegal
PATON, John, R E 1715 — Ballykelly, Derry
    Joseph parish Donagh,
      married 1699, Mary Mc-
      Gillharan — Londonderry
    Thomas, R E 1707 — Urney, Tyrone
PATRICK, Robert, R E 1697 — Ardstraw, Tyrone
PAXTON, James, R E 1713 — Ballyroney, Down
    Thomas, C 1713 — Monaghan
PEACOCK, Doctor, C 1708, 9, R E
    1710 — Belfast, Antrim
PIKAN, Andrew, R E 1704 — Donagheady, Tyrone
PINKERTON, John, married Eliza-
    beth Graham, 1684 — Londonderry
PIPER, Hugh, R E 1718 — Winterburn, Tyrone
POLLOCK, Charles, R E 1706 — Donagheady, Tyrone
    William, R E 1717 — Dunmurry, Down
PORTER, Alexander, R E 1704 — Comber, Down

PORTER, Andrew, R E 1711 — Ballyclare, Antrim
James, R E 1703 — Burt, Donegal
James, R E 1705 — Magherally, Down
James, R E 1709 — Loughbrickland, Down
James, R E 1716 — Ballindreat, Donegal
John, R E 1716 — Dromara, Down
Mr William, C 1715 — Monaghan
POTTS, Mr David, C 1716 — Monaghan
John, R E 1717 — Letterkenny, Donegal
Thomas, R E 1715 — Cushendall, Antrim
PRINGLE, Alexander, C 1714 — Kinnaird, Tyrone
Hugh, R E 1710 — Drum, Monaghan
PURLY, Thomas, R E 1708 — Magherally, Down

Q

QUIGLEY, John and Mary, 1618 — Londonderry

R

RAINEY, Hugh, R E 1698, 1704 — Castledawson, Tyrone
James, R E 1694, 7 — Dunean, Antrim
John, C 1708 — Belfast, Antrim
John, R E 1714 — Castledawson, Tyrone
Robert, R E 1706, 9, 11 — Antrim, Antrim
Mr Robert, Sr., C 1717 — Antrim, Antrim
Mr Robert, Jr., C 1717 — Antrim, Antrim
William, R E 1697, 1711 — Belfast, Antrim
William, Sr., C 1708 — Belfast, Antrim
William, Jr., C 1708 — Belfast, Antrim
RAMAGE, John, R E 1711 — Glendermot, Derry
RAMSEY, James, married Martha
Henderson, 1685 — Londonderry
RANDLE, John, R E 1705 — Monaghan
RANKIN, James, married Con-
stance McCormen, 1699 — Londonderry
John, married Martha Kin-
kead, 1703 — Londonderry
Richard, 1709 — Tirkvillan, Derry?
Tomlin and Eleanor, 1683 — Londonderry

RAWLSTON, Robert, R E 1707 — Aughnacloy, Tyrone
REA, James, C 1692 — Moneymore, Derry
READ, George, parish Dunboe,
    married Janet Skewin,
    1684 — Londonderry
    Samuel, R E 1703 — Kilrea, Derry
REDMAN, ———, 1697 — Near Hillsborough, Down
    Moses, 1709 — Edruna, Derry?
REID, Henry, R E 1718 — Donaghadee, Down
    Hugh, R E 1704 — Ballywillan, Antrim
    Hugh, R E 1705 — Cavanaleck, Tyrone
    James, C 1694, R E 1707 — Armagh
    John, R E 1694, 1714 — Braid, Antrim
    John, R E 1705 — Portaferry, Down
    John, R E 1709 — Carlingford, South
    John, R E 1716 — Loughbrickland, Down
    Samuel, R E 1707 — Kilrea, Derry
    Thomas, R E 1715, 18 — Ballywillan, Antrim
    Thomas, C 1715 — Ballymoney, Antrim
    William, R E 1704, 10, 13 — Portaferry, Down
RELY, Myles, R E 1707 — Lurgan, Armagh
RIDDEL, Robert, R E 1698 — Urney, Tyrone
RITCHIE, Daniel, R E 1715 — Templepatrick, Antrim
RITCHY, James, R E 1707 — Randalstown, Antrim
ROBB, Alexander, R E 1710, 13 — Saintfield, Down
ROBERTSON, John, R E 1698 — Dunmurry, Down
ROBINSON, George, R E 1709 — Newtownards?, Down
    Robert, R E 1708 — Glendermot, Derry
    Thomas, R E 1708 — Benburb, Tyrone
    Hugh, R E 1710 — Glendermot, Derry
RODGER, James, R E 1703 — Omagh, Tyrone
ROGERS, Robert and Abigail, 1703 — Londonderry
    William, C 1708 — Belfast, Antrim
ROLAN, Claud, 1709 — Ballynahone, Derry?
Ross, Alexander, R E 1704 — Bangor, Down
    James, R E 1710 — Finvoy, Antrim
    James, P 1712 — Derry
    John, R E 1716, 17 — Ballymena, Antrim
    Robert, C 1691 — Tanoch-Neeve, Down

ROSSBOTHOM, Matthew, R E 1697 Lisburn, Antrim
RUSSEL, George, R E 1706   Carnmoney, Antrim
     James, R E 1698   Dundonald, Down
     James, C 1715   Holywood, Down
     John, R E 1707   Boveva, Derry
     John, R E 1709   Castlereagh, Down
     William, R E 1711   Letterkenny, Donegal
RUTHERFORD, Elias, R E 1716   Ballybay, Monaghan

S

SCOT, George, R E 1716   Rathfriland, Down
     Hugh, R E 1711   Donegore, Antrim
     James, R E 1717   Bailieborough, Cavan
     Matthew, R E 1705, 7, 10   Donaghadee, Down
     Patrick, R E 1717   Drumbo, Down
     Thomas, R E 1718   Ballywalter, Down
     William, R E 1703   Ramelton, Donegal
     William, R E 1711   Rathfriland, Down
SEAWRIGHT, Gilbert, R E 1715   Magherally, Down
SELKIRK, William, R E 1694   Lagan Presbytery
SHARP, Nicholas, C 1708   Coagh or Ballinderry, Antrim
SHARPES, William, C 1708   Belfast, Antrim
SHAW, George, R E, 1717   Lurgan, Armagh
     Capt. John, R E 1708, C
       1717, 18   Antrim, Antrim
     Mr John, C 1712, 18   Antrim, Antrim
     Mr Patrick, C 1712   Antrim, Antrim
     William, C 1691   Donegore, Antrim
     William, C 1699   Antrim, Antrim
     William, R E 1705   Comber, Down
     Capt. William, R E 1715   Antrim, Antrim
     Col. William, C 1717, 18   Antrim, Antrim
     William, Esq., R E 1707, 12,
       C 1712   Antrim, Antrim
SHENNAN, James, R E 1698   Tyrone?
     John, P 1704   Tandro-gee, Armagh?
     John, R E 1708   Limavady, Derry
SHIELDS, George, R E 1703, 16   Killinchy, Down

SIM, William, R E 1714	Comber, Down
SIMPSON, Thomas and Elizabeth, 1680	Londonderry
William and Janet, 1684	Londonderry
SIMSON, James and Ann, 1681	Londonderry
John, R E 1711	Keady, Armagh
SINCLAIR, William, R E 1717, 18	Dublin
SIRRILAW, John, R E 1709	Aghadowey, Derry
SKELTON, John, R E 1705	Ballynahinch, Down
SLOAN, Jo:, R E 1694	Broadisland, Antrim
John, R E 1705 13	Moneymore, Derry
John, R E 1712, 18	Ballybay, Monaghan
SMART, John, R E 1697	Vinecash, Amargh
SMELY, Robert, R E 1708	Ardstraw, Tyrone
SMILY, Samuel, R E 1704	Larne, Antrim
SMITH, David, C 1694	Belfast, Antrim
George, R E 1718	Kilmore, Down
James, C 1691; 1701	Donegore, Antrim
James, C 1694	Macosquin, Derry
James, R E 1713	Cushendall, Antrim
John, R E 1703, 9	Lisburn, Antrim
John, R E 1712	Magherally, Down
John, R E 1707, 10, 15	Carnmoney, Antrim
John, R E 1715, 18	Carlingford?, South
John, R E 1715	Belfast, Antrim
Lancelot, R E 1718	Dunmurry, Down
Robert and Mary, 1686	Londonderry
Robert, R E 1698	Kilrea, Derry
Robert, R E 1712	Ballymena, Antrim
Samuel and Katherine, 1692	Londonderry
Samuel, R E 1713	Belfast, Antrim
Samuel, Jr., 1714	Belfast, Antrim
William, C 1691	Newry, Down
SMYTH, William, C 1711	Moy-water, Mayo
SPEIR, Robert, C 1691, 1709	Ballyclug, Antrim
SPENS, James, R E 1694	Drumbo, Down
STARRAT, James, R E 1706	Ahoghill, Antrim
STEEL, Andrew, R E 1715	Ballindreat, Donegal
Francis and Martha, 1696	Londonderry

STEEL, Gawin, C 1715, R E 1718   Clough, Antrim
     John, R E 1707, 10, 13   Bangor, Down
     John, R E 1718   Dunpatrick, Down
     Thomas, R E 1708   Vinecash, Armagh
STEPHENSON, James, R E 1712   Brigh, Tyrone
     Robert, R E 1716   Vinecash, Armagh
     William, R E 1712   Ballindreat, Donegal
STEUART, Alexander and Sara
     (McLaughlin), 1694   Londonderry
     Archibald, R E 1706   Comber, Down
     James, R E 1708   Dunean, Antrim
     John, R E 1698   Killinchy, Down
     John, R E 1708   Bangor, Down
     Robert, C 1700   Lisburn, Antrim
     William and Mary, 1697   Londonderry
     William, R E 1704, 6, 8   Killinchy, Down
STEVENSON, James, R E 1703, 5   Brigh, Tyrone
     James, C 1709   Ballyclug, Antrim
     James, R E 1709   Boveva, Derry
     John, R E 1708   Brigh, Tyrone
     Robert, 1707   Molena
         (near Londonderry)

STEWARD, William, parish of
     Lifford, married Margaret
     Wallis of Lifford, 1700   Donegal
STEWART, Andrew and Kath-
     erine, 1693   Londonderry
     George and Charity, 1683   Londonderry
     James, R E 1703   Dunean Antrim
     John, R E 1698   Dungannon, Tyrone
     William, R E 1711   Killinchy, Down
STIRLING, Archibald, R E 1704,
     9, 12   Finvoy, Antrim
     John, R E 1692, 4   Templepatrick, Antrim
     John, R E 1715   Benburb, Tryone
STITT, Thomas, R E 1717   Mourne, Down
STONES, Edmund, R E 1710   Armagh, Armagh
STRAIGHT, James, R E 1713   Loughbrickland, Dowr

STRAITON, George, C 1692 — Lurgan, Amargh
STRAWBRIDGE, James, R E 1706 — Burt, Donegal
STREAN, Adam, R E 1692 — Ahoghill, Antrim
 John, R E 1711 — Stonebridge, Monaghan
STUART, Archibald, C 1715 — Kilraughts, Antrim
 Hugh, R E 1692 — Ballyclug, Antrim
 John, C 1694 — Killinchy, Down
 John, R E 1718 — Kilraughts, Antrim
 Thomas, R E 1714 — Dunmurry, Down
 William, R E 1716 — Killyleagh, Down
 Mr William, C 1717 — Antrim, Antrim
SUTLER, James, R E 1704 — Garvagh, Derry
SWAN, John, R E 1692 — Under Killead
 William, C 1691 — Donaghmore, Tyrone
SWARNBECK, George, R E 1717 — Dunmurry, Down
SYMINTON, John, R E 1713 — Donaghmore, Down

T

TAGGARD, Thomas, R E 1705 — Ardstraw, Tyrone
TAGGART, Francis, R E 1717 — Ballyclare, Antrim
TATE, William, C 1691 — Armagh
TAYLOR, Alexander, R E 1718 — Lisburn, Antrim
 David, R E 1710, 15 — Donaghmore, Down
 James, R E 1714 — Saintfield, Down
 John, C 1708 — Belfast, Antrim
 Thomas, R E 1694 — Killyleagh, Down
TAYT, David, R E 1711 — Cushendall, Antrim
TEAT, Thomas, C 1698 — Blarise?, Down
TEMPLETON, Adam — Ballywillan, Antrim
 Alan, C 1715 — Ballymoney, Antrim
 John, R E 1707, 11 — Magherally, Down
 Matthew, R E 1707, 9 — Braid, Antrim
THOMB, Hugh, R E 1708 — Braid, Antrim
THOMPSON, David, R E 1698,
 1704, 7 — Moneymore, Derry
 David, R E 1714, 15, 17 — Coagh, Tyrone
 George, R E 1709 — Ballymena, Antrim

THOMPSON, James and Katherine, 1695	Londonderry
John, R E 1697, C 1709	Coleraine, Derry
John, R E 1713, 18	Ballymena, Antrim
John, R E 1710, 17	Newtownards, Down
Robert, R E 1706	Ballykelly, Derry
Robert, R E 1706	Glendermot, Derry
Robert, R E 1717	Cavanaleck, Tyrone
Thomas, R E 1713	Cavanaleck, Tyrone
William, R E 1708	Randalstown, Antrim
THOMSON, Alexander, R E 1711	Maghera, Derry
Andrew, C 1698	Loughbrickland, Down
Michael, R E 1697, 1718	Moira, Down
Samuel, R E 1710	Antrim, Antrim
TODD, Andrew, R E 1711, 16, 17	Saintfield, Down
George, R E 1708	Ballyeaston, Antrim
James, R E 1717	Vinecash, Armagh
John, C 1708, 9, 11, R E 1708, 9, 11	Donaghmore, Down
John, C 1714	Kinnaird, Tyrone
John, R E 1714	Minterburn, Tyrone
TOM, Robert and Mary, 1684	Londonderry
TOPLIS, Joseph, R E 1707, 10	Dublin
TOULAN, John, R E 1692	Carrickfergus, Antrim
TRAIL, Mr. James, R E 1717	Killyleagh, Down
TRYMBLE, Robert, R E 1709	Clough, Down
TURK, John, C 1715	Twenty Quarter Lands (near Ballymoney, Antrim
TWEED, David, R E 1708	Cong'n of Galway
TYLER, Evan, C 1711, R E 1718	Kilraughts, Antrim

U

UPTON, Clotworthy, R E 1711, 12, 16	Templepatrick, Antrim
URY, William, C 1691	Clogher, Tyrone

V

VANS, Mr Archibald, C 1718 — Drum, Monaghan
  John, parish Moville, married Elizabeth Quinne, 1683 — Londonderry
  Patrick, R E 1699, 1703, 4 — Magherally Down
  Patrick, R E 1717 — Ballywalter, Down
  William, 1709 — Achavan, Derry?
VERNOR, John, R E 1697 — Castledawson, Tyrone
  Jon., C 1691 — Maghera, Derry
  Robert, R E 1067, 7 — Connor, Antrim
  William, R E 1706, 8 — Castledawson, Tyrone

W

WACHOP, Samuel, R E 1713 — Fintona, Tyrone
WALBUR, John, married Janet Hog, 1684 — Londonderry
WALKER, Andrew, C 1713 — Drummarah, Down
  John, R E 1698 — Limavady, Derry
  John, R E 1705 — Burt, Donegal
  John, R E 1718 — Ballyrashane, Antrim
WALLACE, David, R E 1709 — Fannet, Donegal
  Hugh, R E 1707 — Ballymena, Antrim
  Hugh, R E 1718 — Saintfield, Down
  Hugh, R E 1707, 12 — Killinchy, Down
  Hugh, R E 1706, 10, 14 — Ballywalter, Down
  Hugh, R E 1711 — Ravara, Down
  James, R E 1708 — Portaferry, Down
  James, R E 1715 — Loughbrickland, Down
  John, R E 1692 — Donegore, Antrim
  Robert, R E 1718 — Loughbrickland, Down
  William, married Margaret Morrison, 1663 — Londonderry
WARD, Thomas, R E 1705 — Dunfanaghy, Donegal
WARRINGTON, Thomas, R E 1708 — Dublin
WATERSON, William, C 1708, 9 — Glen and Drumbanagher, Armagh

WATSON, Gilbert, R E 1704 — Aughnacloy, Tyrone
James, C 1711 — Aghaloo, Tyrone
John, R E 1716 — Castlereagh, Down
Robert, R E 1712 — Urney, Tyrone
William, R E 1697 — Dungannon, Tyrone
William, R E 1712 — Killyleagh, Down
WATT, Hugh, R E 1703, 4, 7 — Markethill, Amargh
WEIR, Mr Robert, C 1717 — Antrim, Antrim
William, R E 1712, 14 — Moneymore, Derry
WHITE, James, R E 1697 — Ballywalter, Down
John, R E 1717 — Billy, Antrim
WHITELAW, Alexander, R E 1714, 15 — Vinecash, Armagh
WHITESIDE, Mr Arthur, C 1717 — Antrim, Antrim
Peter, R E 1705 — Killead, Antrim
WHYTE, James, R E 1715 — Larne, Antrim
WIGTON, William, R E 1717 — Clogher, Tyrone
WILLIAMS, George, R E 1713 — Ballyeaston, Antrim
WILLIAMSON, John, R E 1711 — Anahilt, Down
Thomas, R E 1713 — Ballywalter, Down
WILSON, Alexander, R E 1710 — Tullylish, Down
Alexander, R E 1717 — Ballybay, Monaghan
Alexander, R E 1715 — Kilrea, Derry
Andrew, R E 1707 — Ballyeaston, Antrim
Edward, C 1708 — Belfast, Antrim
Capt. Francis, R E 1704, 5, 11 — Corboy, West Meath
Hugh, R E 1711 — Ballykelly, Derry
James and Elizabeth, 1683 — Londonderry
James, R E 1692 — Islandmagee, Antrim
James, R E 1705 — Ballymena, Antrim
James, R E 1711 — Fintona, Tyrone
John, R E 1698 — Ardstraw, Tyrone
John, C 1699, 1716 — Killmakevett, Antrim (north of Glenavy)
John, R E 1714, 16 — Ballinderry, Antrim
John, R E 1706 — Brigh, Tyrone
John, R E 1708 — Donegore, Antrim
John, R E 1710 — Dunmurry, Down

WILSON, John, R E 1711	Bangor, Down
John, R E 1714	Portaferry, Down
John, R E 1717	Keady, Armagh
Robert, R E 1698	Rathfriland, Down
Robert, R E 1709, 16	Ballyeaston, Armagh
Robert, R E 1706, 10	Clogher, Tyrone
Robert, C 1708, 14	Belfast, Antrim
Samuel, R E 1713	Newtownards, Down
Thomas, R E 1711	Ballyeaston, Antrim
Mr Thomas, C 1717	Antrim, Antrim
William, R E 1694	Islandmagee, Antrim
William, R E 1707, 13	Ballykelly, Derry
William, R E 1712, 15	Ballyeaston, Antrim
William, R E 1717	Anahilt, Down
WINDRON, John, R E 1710	Templepatrick, Antrim
WIRLING, James, R E 1708	Newtownards, Down
WOODBURN, George, R E 1710	Kilrea, Derry
WOODS, James, R E 1707	Dunmurry, Down
James, R E 1710, 14	Lurgan, Armagh
James, C 1714	Belfast, Antrim
John, R E 1716, 18	Tullylish, Down
WOODSIDE, Robert, R E 1718	Ballyclare, Antrim
WOOL, John, R E 1703	Ballee, Down
WORKMAN, John, P 1706	Macosquin, Antrim
WRIGHT, John, R E 1718	Ballymoney, Antrim
WYLIE ⎱ James, R E 1698 WYLY ⎰	Carnmoney, Antrim
John, R E 1703, 11, 12, 14, 16, 18	Ahoghill, Antrim
William, R E 1705	Finvoy, Antrim
William, R E 1707, 10, 13	Dervock, Antrim

Y

YOUNG, John, merchant, 1701, 15 Belfast, Antrim

INDEX

A

Abbeville, 294
Abbott, C. H., quoted, 200, 202
Abercrombie, James, 285
    Rev. Robert, 115
Abernathy, 294
Abernethy, Rev. John, 75
Ability, 308, 309
Acheson, Matthew, 231, 233
Acton, James, 328
    Richard, 328
Adair, 292
Adams, 294
    William, 262
Adrian, 292
Aghadowey, 106, 107, 156, 188; on map, 39; session book of Presbyterian church, 119; site of meeting house, 120; poor in, 122; letter from church at, 259; view of Parish church, 297
Agnew, Andrew, 227
    William, 330
Agriculture, 283
Aiken, Edward, 262
    James, 262
    William, 262
Alderchurch, Edward, 333
Alexander, 231 233
    David, 228, 233
    James, 184, 262, 325
    John, 183, 184
    Randall, 102, 262, 327; noticed, 255
    William, 228, 233
Alison. 282
    John, 336
    Robert, 125
Allan, David, 288, 333
Allen, Eben, 320, 322
    Edward, 170, 333, 335
    John, 82, 285
    Joshua, 82
    Peter, 271
    Sylvanus, 82
    William, 278
Allen township, 278
Allison, 281, 292
    Richard, 271
    Samuel, noticed, 255, 262
American Antiquarian Society, 197
"Amity," ship, 322

"Amity," snow, 317
"Amsterdam," ship, 321
Anderson, 275, 294
    Allen, noticed, 255, 262
    James, 262
    noticed, 255
    Rev. James, 277
    John, 262, 330
    Patrick, 330
    William, 125
Andover, on map, 178; Scotch Irish at, 200-202
Andrews, Rev. Jedediah, 28, 36, 280
Annapolis, N. S., 155
Anne, Queen, Presbyterians under, 15; Ulster under, 63-64
Anton, George, 326
    James, 327
    Samuel, 326
    Thomas, 327
Antrim, town, view of, 73
Archibald, John, 262
    Robert 121, 125
Ardreagh, 123, 128
Ardstraw, 100, 187, 191, 223
Armenius, 75
Armstrong, James, 213, 288
    John, 209, 213
    John, in Boston, 146, 149; and the "Robert," 205; petition of, 249
    Robert, 262
    Simeon, 209, 213
Armstrong family, 209
Arnold, Thomas, 322
Arrowsic, 331, 372; on map. 204
Art, Scotch Irish in, 301, 303, 309
Ashe, Bishop, 67
Aston, 281
Atlantic, crossing, 151
Auburn, 185
Auchmuty, Robert, 166, 262, 333
Aul, Abraham, 170, 335
    James, 155
Austin, Joseph, 333
Ayrshire, 1

B

Bacon, Edwin M., 153
    Jacob, 114
Baird. James, 335
    Thomas, 183, 188
    William, 326

Murdock, John, 326, 327, 329
  Robert, 327
  Stephen, 327
Murray, 281
  John, 192, 326, 327
  Rev. John, 117
Musgrove, 281
Music, 193
Myers, on the Irish Quakers, 28

N

Nazareth Church, 294
Neal, 294
  Daniel, 334
Nealson, James, 156
Needham, 155, 239
Neely, 293
Neill, Rev. Henry, 100, 102
Neilson, Rev. Robert, 101, 330
Nelson, 288
  James, 334
  John, 231, 236
Nepmug country, 12
Nesbitt, 294
Neshaminy Creek, 58, 278
Neshaminy, Penn., 266
Nesmith, James, 252, 264, 325, 330 ;
  noticed, 255
Nessley, 281
Nevin, Alfred, quoted, 30
Newall, Joseph, 320
Newberry, 294
Newcastle, 35, 36, 117
Newcastle, Delaware, 267
Newel, John, 230, 236
Newell, Joseph, 323
New England emigrants to Ireland,
  11 ; Scotch Irish, 266
New Hampshire, 308
New London, 113, 142
Newton, Marmaduke, 31
  Richard, 31
Newtown Limavady, 42
New York, Scotch Irish in, 268, 269
Nicols, 294
Nichols, Alexander, 261, 264
  Andrew, 335
  James, 261, 264
  John, 155
Nickel, Thomas, 122, 125
Noble, Arthur, 334
  John, 334
Non-subscribers in Antrim, 75-76
North, Mrs. Mary M., quoted, 21
North Carolina, 308
Nutfield, settled, 242

O

O'Cahan, Grany, 122
  Nealy, 125
Octorara Creek, 58
Oliver, Daniel, 305

Omagh, houses at, 3
Orr, Alexander, 335
  Boniel, 329
  Isaac, 334
  John, 329
  Patrick, 329
  Thomas, 325
  William, 329
Oursell, Nicholas, 318
Owen, 281
  Rev. John, 113
  Philip, 12

P

Page, Charles D., 261
Paine, James, 285
Painter, 281
Pakachoag Hill, 177, 180
Palmer, 115, 173, 281 ; settlers, 182
Park, 282, 327
  Lawrence, 178
Parke, John, 114
  Patrick, 114
  Robert, 114 ; letter on emigra-
  tion, 282-284
Parker, 278
  Rev. E. L., 241, 252 ; and Shute
  petition, 324 ; quoted, 131,
  199, 200, 203
Paterson, James, 271, 330
  William, 327
Patterson, Abraham, 184
  David, 329
  John, 192
  Peter, 264
  Vincent, 114
  William, 192, 335
Pattison, Alexander, 328
  Ninian, 328
Paton, 294
Patrick, Andrew, 327
  John, 183
  Robert, 192
Patten, Robert, 175
Patton, Robert, 169, 334
  William, 334
Patuxent, 27, 33
Paxtang, 278
Peables, John, 183, 192
  Patrick, 183, 184
  Robert, 182, 183, 184, 191
Pearson, 294
Peat, Robert, 323
Peck, Noah, 213
Pedan, 275
Peg of Limavaddy, 99
Pejepscot, 218, 225
Pelham, 115
  Charles, 172
  Peter, 172, 334
Pelham, Mass., settlement, 184
Pendale, 281
Pennock, 281